T0314240

The independent advisory industry is on the cusp of a monumental change, and Philip Palaveev lays out in this book the essential elements to ensure that your firm is one of the survivors in the new era coming to the RIA landscape. Whether you are a firm founder or a rising leader, *G2: Building the Next Generation* lays out the path to create a transformational firm that empowers both generations.

Tim Chase, CEO, WMS Partners LLC

With this book, Philip Palaveev provides a roadmap for advisory firms to address the most challenging issue in our business today: attracting, developing, engaging and retaining the next generation of leaders. *G2* is a thorough analysis of all the issues we encounter in developing the next generation of leaders, but what makes it so valuable are the stories and practical strategies that can be applied in our business today to help meet that challenge. Philip's previous book, *The Ensemble Practice*, provided a detailed look at the team based approach to building a successful advisory business. *G2* is a natural extension of that effort and a must read for anyone with an interest in the future of the advisory industry.

Stephen Stelljes, President of Client Services and G2 Leader,
The Colony Group LLC

G2: Building the Next Generation completely captures the experience of G2 advisory firm owners. From the challenges we face emerging from the shadows of the founding partners to the opportunities that abound to grow the firm and add our mark to its footprint, this book covers the gamut. As a G2 firm owner myself, Philip clearly demonstrates his understanding of a firm's development at this stage, providing perspective and tangible action steps for G2 leaders to rise to the occasion and add real value to the firm's long-term growth. It's a must read for both founding partners and G2 professionals alike as firms take the next step of growing past their founders to achieve a lasting level of success.

Susan Mitcheltree, Principle & Equity Partner and a G2 Leader,
Berman McAleer

G2

Building the Next Generation

Philip Palaveev

WILEY

Library of Congress Cataloging-in-Publication Data is available:

ISBN 9781119370062 (Hardcover)
ISBN 9781119370093 (ePDF)
ISBN 9781119370079 (ePub)

Cover Design: Wiley
Cover Image: © simon2579/Getty Images

10 9 8 7 6 5 4 3 2 1

Contents

Preface

I have always striven to work with the largest and most successful firms in the advisory industry. I have always wanted to be the consultant who knows the most, works with the top people in the top firms, and has answers to the most difficult questions. You could say I have more than a little ambition. After I wrote my first book, *The Ensemble Practice*, I thought that my next book would be called *Super-Ensembles*, a book about the biggest, largest, fastest-growing, and smartest firms.

Working with professionals in the leadership development program we run at The Ensemble Practice made me realize that I have been focused on the wrong phenomenon. What the industry needs most is not a description of how to be bigger and more complex, or how to work with bigger clients. Rather, firms need to know how to develop professionals who are capable of making bigger and better enterprises. You can't build a big, successful firm without a strong, well-functioning team of colleagues and partners. Indeed, achieving success with my own firm and career depends on our ability to develop the next generation.

I was not a founder at my first two firms. I was part of G2, or the second generation of professionals who joined later. For 12 years I looked up to the founders, but at times I also questioned their leadership. I felt that they should be doing more to help professionals like me who were growing in their careers. Now that I am a founder, it is time for me to develop and grow the careers of those behind me. If I fail at that task, I will have achieved nothing at my own firm.

Nothing can be achieved at a professional service firm without having talented, well-prepared people who are dedicated to the firm and want to make it better. Those people don't magically appear on the doorstep begging to join. They come when they are younger, inexperienced, unsure, searching, and needing guidance. It is the most critical function of the firm to help them become those experienced and productive professionals we all want. At Moss Adams, we spent seven years looking to hire someone with five years of experience. This book offers a better approach.

As an industry, we have become very good at taking care of clients. We need to get better at taking care of each other. The greatest challenge—and opportunity—facing our industry today is the development of the next generation of professionals. So here it is: These pages are a record of everything I have seen and learned about developing professional careers. There remain many questions to answer, mountains to climb, and rivers to cross on the career path for G2 advisors. Still, I hope this book makes the hike easier and perhaps more fun!

Philip Palaveev
May 2017

Acknowledgments

I would like to thank all the amazing professionals who are part of the *G2 Leadership Institute*. This begins with the G2 participants whose experience and thoughts helped shape much of this book. I have also learned so much from my colleagues at the program—Sam Allred, Tim Kochis, and Susan Dickson.

I am grateful to every client I have ever worked with. It is the nature of consulting that you bring knowledge to every engagement, but you also learn from every professional you talk to. I have been fortunate to work with some of the best firms and best leaders in the industry.

Finally, I want to say what joy it has been to practice together with my team at The Ensemble Practice. I am excited to work together toward building the premier firm in the financial services industry.

CHAPTER 1

Who Are G2s?

There were about 30 people in the room. They were gathered for a study-group meeting and half of them were founders who years ago had started some of the largest and most successful advisory firms in the country. The other half were younger. They had joined the firms in the last 10 years as employees and had over time risen to become owners and leaders in their respective organizations. This collection of firms was called the younger group *G2*, short for second generation, to signify that they were not founders but rather the *next* generation.

A founder by the name of Richie Lee stood up. He spoke slowly and his words were rather poetic. "If a business is like a painting," Richee said, "I want my business to be a beautiful painting that people can see even after I am gone. I want it to be a painting that lasts and endures."

Becky Krieger, one of the G2 participants, got up to respond and what she said, to this day, best illustrates for me the dynamic between the generations of leaders inside advisory firms. "Richee," she said, "You have to remember we are artists, too. We are not here just to preserve your painting. We are here because we want to create our own works as well. We want to add to your painting and we want to paint our own!"

Rebecca represents the G2s whom this book is about. They are talented, ambitious, and driven. They are experienced and accomplished in their profession. They are young but not youngsters; they have one or two decades of achievements behind them. They are looking to continue the work of the founders and eager to build and create their own. They are the future of the advisory industry and they are ready to take over.

G2 has already begun to take over, in fact. Many G2 members are owners (partners) in their respective firms. Some are COOs and CIOs. G2 professionals are managing client relationships, leading teams of people, and striving to be leaders.

Every firm needs a G2 if it is to have a chance of lasting beyond the involvement of the founders. Firms that lack a G2 or those where G2 is under-developed will likely dissipate or be merged and sold into bigger entities over the next 10 years. Firms that have developed their next generation, in contrast, will be magnets for other practices who want to merge with them. They will not run out of energy or people as the founders approach retirement.

G2 may be the future of the advisory industry, but it cannot take over yet—not without some help from firms and the industry at large. Having spent most of my early professional career as G2, I can easily relate to the challenges facing the next generation. Some are challenges that G2 members created themselves, and others are deficiencies in the environment where they grew their careers. Now that I am founder of my own firm and working with G2 partners, I can also relate to the feelings of the founders. It is difficult to trust a generation that is so eager but still unproven.

I have written this book as a bridge between founders and G2 because, ultimately, the truth is this: *G2 is the future of the industry, and successful firms need to hire and embrace these younger professionals.* Firms that fail to do so will have short remaining lifespans. To flourish, G2 members need to learn not only how to be good professionals (i.e., how to attract and service clients) but also how to be good owners, managers, and leaders of their firms. They need to learn how to make good decisions, put the best interests of the business first, and inspire others. Good firms will find a way to cultivate their management skills, educate them about being owners, and give them the opportunity to become leaders.

I hope you will follow me in this exploration of why G2s are the future of the advisory industry.

Defining G2

The term *G2* includes the cadre of professionals inside advisory firms who:

- Are not founders and did not join the firm in the first 10 years of business—in other words, they were not part of the start-up phase of evolution.
- Have at least five years of experience in their field—they are experienced and not just starting out.
- Occupy key positions in their firms—they are lead advisors or team leaders in operations.
- Are considered future owners or are already owners in their firms, meaning they are invested in the future success of the firm in career, emotional, and financial terms.

- Are seen as successors to the founders, not necessarily individually but as a group.
- Most of all, self-identify as future leaders of the firm who both preserve the legacy of the founders and look to take the firm further and make it better.

Thousands of G2 professionals are already rising to prominence inside the advisory industry. More importantly, thousands are missing entirely. According to the *2016 Financial Performance Study* of financial advisory firms produced by The Ensemble Practice LLC, the typical advisory firm started in 1997.[1] Today, those firms generally have more than 20 years of history and have grown to be sizeable and successful organizations. As these firms have matured, their need to hire more people has increased. Unfortunately, not many firms have.

A well-publicized report by research firm Cerulli Associates indicates that 43 percent of advisors are over the age of 55 and intend to retire in the next 10 years (although intention is not the same as action).[2] The same report claims that only 11 percent of advisors in the industry are younger than 35. These numbers cause research firms to predict that we will be missing as many as 280,000 advisors in the next 10 years, after accounting for continued growth and retirement.

The 46 percent of advisors who fall between these two age brackets— younger than 55 but older than 35—are the subject of this book. However, age is not a factor that defines G2. The focus is on professionals who are experienced and accomplished but have not yet had their turn at driving the business.

Developing the Next Generation Is Critical

Too often the development of G2 is equated with succession. While the logic here is solid—develop G2 successors or you will have to sell the firm in order to retire—it is also incomplete. Firms need G2 for growth! The typical advisory firm doubled in size every four to five years in the period between 2003 and 2014.[3] While growth has slowed down in the past three years, firms continue to need more people, more professional capacity, and, most of all, more leaders.

---

[1] InvestmentNews Research, "2016 Financial Performance Study" (InvestmentNews, 2016).
[2] Cerulli Associates, "Advisor Metrics 2013: Understanding and Addressing a More Sophisticated Population."
[3] See note 1.

G2s as Agents of Growth

G2 professionals are not just successors. They are agents of growth who bring skills and talents firms otherwise would not have. As a firm adds more client relationships, it needs professionals who can manage those relationships. In my experience and depending on the business model, a lead advisor can manage only 40 (for multifamily-office and ultrahigh-net-worth firms) to 150 (for general financial advisory firms) client relationships. If client rosters exceed those numbers, the firm must find a new advisor.

The hope of every firm is that its advisors will be just as talented and dedicated as the founders when working with clients. What is more, it is not just the hope but very much a requirement of firms that advisors do not defect to a competing firm that is trying to take away clients. Advisors are asked to remain with the firm—ideally for the duration of their careers—since clients do not look forward to changing professionals. These dual expectations of excellence and longevity are unique to professional service firms and even more pronounced in financial advisory firms. While attorneys and CPAs can and do change employers, advisory firms expect to hold onto their professionals and clients for many, many years.

It seems to me that for every 100 or so additional clients, a firm needs to hire at least one professional who brings both an extraordinary skillset and a dedication to the firm. The new hire must be experienced and credible enough to lead clients, be loyal to the firm, and be integrated into its culture to stay for a long time. Before these professionals become the successors, they will be the leaders of growth. This is why every firm needs its own G2 advisors and cannot have enough of them.

Many firms have tried to bypass the need to hire and develop G2 advisors by leveraging the founders more. I have worked with clients where single founders or small groups of founders have surrounded themselves with capable service people. These service people tackle much of the work, but they cannot lead client relationships. This means of leverage, combined with careful client selection, can certainly take a firm to a billion or more in assets under management (AUM). But even with leverage, the day will come when capacity is exhausted. Moreover, a firm with extreme leverage can be very fragile.

Beyond increasing a firm's capacity, G2 professionals bring a skillset that perhaps the founders never had. Many hold MBA degrees and have experience in management and operations. Often the proponents of structure and process, they become the first COOs of many firms. They help clarify organizational structures, define positions, and establish career tracks. Their growth puts pressure on firms to create governance and ownership structures that can allow for many to participate, and they encourage founders to remember the long view.

G2s as the Gateway to the Next Generation of Clients

As advisors age, so do their clients. My experience has been that clients brought in by the founders are typically no more than five years older than their advisor's age and usually no younger than 10 or 15 years. As clients age, their assets shift into distribution mode, their rate of new referrals declines, and their exit from the firm nears. Many firms intellectually understand the need to attract younger clients but struggle to do so.

G2 advisors are the gateway to younger clients. Just as the founders brought in their peers—business owners, executives, and professionals who shared their social network and stage of life—G2 professionals can do the same. A 65-year-old founder is not likely to find a 35-year-old doctor to bring in as a client, but a G2 professional is. That young doctor has her entire career ahead of her and will soon be the kind of client that every firm wants. The same is true for the emerging entrepreneurs and executives, and perhaps even the second generation of wealthy families. The G2 generation of advisors will bring the next generation of clients.

G2s as Managers, Leaders, and Successors

G2 professionals are not just the advisors of the future. They are the managers of the future, as well. As the number of clients grows, so will the number of people in the firm. What used to be a small firm with 10 to 15 people on staff will quickly become a true organization with 50 to 80 employees. Every employee needs direction, management, encouragement, explanation, training, mentoring, and, above all, attention. As the organization grows, the ability of the founders to remain in control and, more importantly, to manage their ever-growing team diminishes.

There are many theories about how many direct reports a manager can have, but few sources will argue that one or two founders can control and manage an organization with 50 people on staff. According to a *Harvard Business Review* article, the typical CEO has between 5 and 10 direct reports.[4]

---

[4]Gary L. Neilson and Julie Wulf, "How Many Direct Reports?" *Harvard Business Review* (April 2012).

Another author argues that managers should ideally spend around six hours a week with their direct reports.[5] Again, this implies a number of direct reports no larger than seven. It is not my intention to debate the best number of direct reports. Rather, the point is that as a firm grows, founders need to delegate management to their G2 colleagues. Retaining full control over all management responsibilities is unfeasible.

G2 professionals may also be able to relate much better to new employees in the firm. Since G2 advisors are typically in their thirties and forties, they are in a better position to communicate and manage the Millennials joining the firm. I know from personal experience as a subordinate, that the best person to be your manager is someone who has been in your shoes in the not-so-distant past and understands the challenges and characteristics of your position.

As G2 professionals become better managers, many will also develop into leaders of the firm. A leader is someone who makes difficult decisions and leads others by example to implement those decisions. Most firms need more leaders. As the scope of operations grows, as the number of people increases, and as firms enter into new markets and new locations, they need more leaders who can propagate the culture of the firm and guide its ever-growing team. That is the role of G2 professionals. They are leaders who will help the firm grow.

Of course, they are (potentially) successors, too. Every founder will need to eventually exit the business, one way or another. When that day comes, firms that have a strong cadre of G2 professionals will have many options. They can keep the ownership of the firm within the team and focus on internal succession. Alternatively, they can merge with another team and become part of a bigger regional or national firm. Finally, they can be acquired, and chances are that a motivated group of younger professionals will increase the number of potential buyers and the price they are willing to pay. Some of those options, of course, are available to firms who don't have G2s but in those cases, when internal succession is not possible, the terms of a merger or a sale will never be as good. Firms with G2 professionals hold all the cards.

Just Hiring Them Is Not Enough (But Start There)

At Moss Adams, we always looked to hire consultants with five years of experience. Unfortunately, those are hard to find. One day it dawned on us that

---

[5]Laura Vanderkam, "Why Managers Should Spend Exactly Six Hours a Week with Each Employee," *Fast Company* (July 14, 2014).

for a seven-year period we had been looking for professionals with five years of experience. If you want to have experienced professionals on your team, you need to be willing to grow them within your organization.

Limitations of the Free Agent Market

Relying on the free agent market alone is rarely a good strategy. First, the free agent market in the advisory industry is not very active. The *2015 Adviser Compensation & Staffing Study* produced by The Ensemble Practice LLC estimates that for professional positions, the turnover in the industry is less than 5 percent. This means that the supply of experienced talent is not very abundant. What is more, integrating experienced professionals in the processes, structures, and culture of a firm is a difficult and slow process.

Every firm dreams of hiring a professional who has years of experience and can manage 100 client relationships while developing new business and helping to grow and manage the firm. Furthermore, most firms hope to find a professional who is collaborative and open to integrating into the culture of the firm. Of course, this unicorn profile is in high demand. Fulfilling it practically pays for itself and generates an immediate addition to profits. While every firm seeks this dream professional, such a person is rarely available for hire. Chances are that people like this are highly valuable members of a team where they are well compensated. Very likely they are part of the ownership of their firm.

Developing Professionals Who Fit the Dream Profile

There is another profile that is quite available for hire, but firms don't seem willing to give it attention. These are the many young professionals with finance degrees, often even MBAs and CFP certifications, who are looking to begin their careers in the industry and struggling to find firms that will hire them at the entry level. The recognition of the financial advisory industry and the increase in the number of schools teaching personal financial advice is helping create a supply of inexperienced professionals. They can certainly fit the dream profile, but they need firms that will invest in 10 years of training and developing to help them grow into it.

The importance for firms to hire and grow professionals cannot be emphasized enough. This includes not only professionals they need now or next year, but also professionals they will need in the next 5 or 10 years. A mature professional needs 10 to 15 years of training and development. This means that firms that want to have highly productive G2 advisors who are ready to contribute next year should have hired those professionals 10 years ago. While this may seem like a very long-term perspective, it is the only reliable way of creating an ample supply of future professionals.

What G2 Professionals Need

For G2 professionals to become the future of a firm, they will need experience, training, and opportunities to apply their training. While firms have become quite adept at imparting professional knowledge and training on client service processes, that alone is not enough to turn G2 professionals into true future drivers of a firm. For that to happen, firms need to train on additional types of skills and provide experiences that G2 professionals don't currently receive.

G2s Need a Chance to Drive the Car

I grew up in Eastern Europe, where young people very rarely had a car or ready access to one. We grew up riding buses and trains. That said, we all went to driving school and got licenses. So when I bought my first car at the age of 25, I had had a license for seven years but had no idea how to drive. Just as you can't learn how to drive a car by watching your dad, G2 professionals are not going to learn how to be leaders by watching the founders. They need opportunities to "drive the car" on their own.

If leadership consists of difficult decisions, then G2 professionals need to be in positions where they can make such decisions and be responsible for the results without being overseen or "saved" by the founders. They must have the opportunity to take on the challenges inherent to leadership:

- Leading a client service team, including staffing, managing. and training that team
- Managing employees, delivering performance evaluations, and being responsible for employee contributions and overall development
- Leading a committee and being responsible for the execution of all plans made by that committee, ideally in the context of a firm-wide business plan
- Championing a new market and paving the way for the firm to grow and expand into that market, including responsibility for the results of that initiative (or lack thereof)
- Implementing a new service or new process, including training others on using that process

- Researching and championing a new technology that can be used across the firm
- Driving a marketing initiative and becoming responsible for its results

There are many other examples possible, and they all share a common characteristic: They offer G2 professionals the opportunity to take ownership of an initiative that is important to the firm. Side projects with little at stake for the firm don't create real opportunities to learn or contribute. Real opportunities come when there is real responsibility.

Another characteristic inherent in these opportunities is the ability to involve others. Projects that can be accomplished by one person are important, but they teach little in terms of motivating and organizing a team. In fact, they often teach professionals to be too self-reliant, since they suggest that individuals can be successful on their own. This notion can be damaging to professionals later in their careers, when they will likely come to the realization that doing everything on your own is very limiting.

Finally, and very importantly, G2 professionals need to be responsible for the results of these leadership opportunities. They need to be recognized for successes, but also held responsible for failures.

G2s Need the Opportunity to Fail

You will never learn to box by punching the heavy bag. You need someone who can punch back. Similarly, you will never learn to lead without being responsible for the lack of success. Projects that fail are very important: They tell us what not to do. They help us learn about ourselves and our reactions, motivations, and ability to persevere. They tell us about our ability to lead others. It is very easy hosting a party if you don't have to pay the bar tab. The cost of failures is what keeps leaders honest and what makes leaders accepted. We learn whom we can trust when things go wrong.

Founders often struggle with letting their best people fail. Parents are very familiar with this feeling. It is like watching your child learn how to ride a bike. Training wheels can't stay on forever. At some point, you must run along with your child, holding the bike and catching her when she falls. But you can't do that forever. Eventually you have to let go of the bike and watch your child wobble around, milliseconds away from disaster. In fact, you know your child will sooner or later show up crying with a bloody knee or elbow. Unfortunately, there is no other way to learn to ride a bike.

For a firm to truly give G2 professionals a chance to lead, it has to be willing to let them fail. Yes, this could mean losing some clients and perhaps upsetting people (founders included), but the learning process is not complete until we know what it feels like to fail.

G2s Need to Take Over Client Relationships

Everything in professional services, and particularly in personal financial advice, begins with being able to impress clients and earn their trust. That trusted relationship is the building block of a professional career. Trust translates into growth through referrals. Trust allows a professional to build and maintain a team. Trust facilitates the ability of a professional to establish himself as a manager and leader internally. If G2 professionals can't earn the trust of their clients, they can't progress past the second-tier position in their firms.

As obvious as this sequence may be, many professional careers stop at the second chair because firms are not giving young advisors enough opportunities to step forward and earn the trust and respect of clients. Firms heavily prioritize client retention and are unwilling to risk changing the lead advisor on a relationship. This stunts the development of younger advisors, who seem to always be supporting but never leading.

At some point, a firm must realize that the career of a talented professional is much more important to the future of the firm than the relationship with any single client. A good professional will typically manage $1 million or more in revenue, lead a team, and contribute to growth. Very few clients can have the same impact. This is not to suggest that firms should sacrifice client service or experiment on clients. It simply means that firms should systematically give their best G2 people the chance to shine in front of clients. It also means that firms should prepare clients for these coming changes so that they are supportive and encouraging of the process.

G2s Need to Become Better Business Developers

Business development (i.e., sales) is the Achilles' heel of independent advisory firms. Built on a foundation of client service and retention, firms are often concerned that a sales focus will undermine the culture of the firm and focus professionals on the wrong agenda. Giving in to these fears results in a firm that is overdependent on the founders or a few select rainmakers. Younger professionals in these firms never receive training in business development and are often quickly labeled as "not entrepreneurial." In the *2016 Financial Performance Study*, only 25 percent of firms report that they provide any business development training to their professionals.

As with most of the challenges faced by G2s, often all that is needed to overcome the obstacle is some training, some encouragement, and some patience. Behind the success story of every good business developer is usually a patient mentor who helped frame sales in the right way: meeting needs and creating solutions rather than pushing unnecessary and unwanted products. Mentors serve as an example and explicitly or implicitly provide young professionals with a process for identifying needs and communicating solutions.

G2 professionals are usually the victims of this cultural dysfunction: They are trained to focus only on service and stay away from sales, and then they are blamed for not contributing to growth. Every professional can learn to be a competent business developer. Firms simply need to incorporate growth into their values, provide the training, and coach patiently.

G2s Need to Learn to Manage People

There was a dark saying in my first firm that "for every new manager we promote, we lose one analyst" (i.e., an entry-level employee supervised by the new manager). Unfortunately, there was a lot of truth to that. The same phenomenon occurs in advisory firms. As young professionals advance in the early stages of their careers, they usually do so on the strength of their knowledge and professional experience. Then, suddenly, the moment arrives when they begin to manage other people and become responsible for the performance of others. This first experience can be uncomfortable and shocking. For many, it ends in disappointment and the determination to never manage again. Some professionals also get labeled as difficult to work with, when all they needed was more experience and guidance on how to manage.

Lee Iacocca, the former CEO of Chrysler, put it best: "A major reason capable people fail to advance is that they don't work well with their colleagues."[6] Managing people effectively requires a change of mentality and a skillset that is rarely included in professional programs. Even if someone has the theoretical knowledge of management, the practical reality is something else entirely. Behavior is often unpredictable, and theory can be limited in its application to the many situations that occur in real life. Managers need training and experience on how to handle the people on their teams. This experience can only come with time and exposure to situations and people.

Given opportunity and time, most G2 professionals can become competent managers. However, one of the biggest mistakes firms make is to panic at

---

[6]Lee Iacocca, *An Autobiography* (New York: Bantam Books, 1984).

the first sign of trouble and pull their professionals away from management. In fact, while most professional service firms manage service teams from within (i.e., professionals manage other professionals), advisory firms continue to search for some kind of elusive HR department that will deal with management and shelter advisors from having to train and supervise their junior colleagues. This notion is not only naïve (it does not work), but it also damages the careers of all involved. Early management struggles are normal, and G2 professionals need training, guidance, and mentoring on how to be good managers of people.

G2s Need an Ownership and Governance Structure

Advisory firms have very high expectations of their professionals. They expect them to achieve the highest levels of professional expertise, excel at building client relationships, and dedicate the rest of their professional careers to their firms. For this commitment to be mutual, professionals traditionally receive the opportunity to become owners. This financial investment is material but also symbolic. It signifies that the firm highly values the professional, and that the professional agrees that her career and capital will rise and fall with the firm.

Ownership is a necessary part of the strong mutual commitment between a professional and the firm, and firms should not seek to replace it with compensation mechanisms and synthetic technicalities. For ownership in the firm to have meaning and significance, however, firms need to create an ownership structure and governance process that allows G2 professionals to thrive.

The key to a thriving firm is stability. Stability allows the next generation to form expectations and to invest in the long-term future of their careers and the firm. Governance should be built around a careful balance between executive function in the hands of dedicated managers and the broad representation of the partner group. Clear criteria for professional advancement, including criteria for who becomes an owner, will bring the values of the firm to bear. There is no better way to put values into action than to tie them to the criteria for who is successful in a firm and who benefits financially and career-wise from the success of the firm.

A firm that combines the training of future managers and business developers with a balanced governance and ownership model will always have a bright future. No matter how much the industry consolidates or how the business models change, the experience of every other professional services industry clearly shows that there is always room for the success and growth of a firm with a dedicated, motivated, and talented team of professionals. That rule especially applies to a firm with a depth of next-generation talent.

G2s Are the Future

As the Dalai Lama says, "There are only two days in the year when nothing can be done. One is called yesterday, and the other is called tomorrow." G2 professionals are the future of the advisory industry, and that future depends on the decisions you make and the steps you take today. It is never too soon or too late to begin developing the next generation.

If you are a founder and have made it past this first chapter, chances are that somewhere in your firm there are one or more professionals for whom you have high hopes. Perhaps this text will help you develop them into the colleagues and partners that you want them to be.

If you are a G2 professional and have made it past this first chapter, perhaps you are wondering where your career will take you and what your firm will do in the future. We hope that this book gives you a path to follow and some practical advice to make that path easier.

Think of G2s as "going to...." Where would you like to go? Whether you are a founder or a G2 member, experienced or just starting out, this is an exciting time to be in this industry. Your career can give you all the professional challenges and personal satisfaction that you seek. Invest in yourself, invest in your people, invest in your team, and invest in your firm, and chances are good that you will see a return on your investments.

CHAPTER 2

The Career Track

The most critical factor for the success of an advisory firm is its ability to attract and retain talented people. As business management expert David Maister writes in one of his books: "Given both the scarcity and the power of good coaching, it is entirely possible that a firm's competitive success can be built on a superior ability to get the best out of its people."[1] In other words, a firm's ability to train and develop professionals may very well be one of its most sustainable competitive advantages. Technology, efficiency, and investment process play a role, but at the end of the day, firms that can find the best people are the ones that will be the fastest growing and most profitable.

A career track is a vital tool in the development of people and is key to long-term success. This applies not only to G2, but also to all present and future generations of employees. Without a career track, professional development becomes an arbitrary combination of experience, informal mentoring, personal relationships, and exposure to opportunities. This unstructured approach will likely waste the talents of many professionals who would have become valuable contributors to the firm in the presence of more structured and training. Many talented people may never develop because they are never taught a vital skill. Deserving professionals may never be promoted if they are not noticed by the right people. Some may quit because without a view of the finish line they become exhausted or demotivated. It may be very difficult to ask professionals for patience as they gain the necessary experience to advance. Establishing a path for advancement and support can help professionals fulfill their potential. A career track gives people reasonable expectations for their success in a firm and lets them know how they will benefit financially, intellectually, and socially at every step.

---

[1] David Maister, *Managing the Professional Service Firm* (New York: Free Press Paperbacks, 1997).

Career tracks are present in every profession, and they date all the way back to medieval guilds. Young aspiring craftsmen went through regimented training to first become apprentices and then journeymen. Journeymen could demonstrate their skills to earn admission into the guild and become master craftsmen. The system provided a way for the guild to regulate competition, but it also ensured that those who presented themselves as craftsmen actually had the skill to perform. This is how Michelangelo trained and this is how accountants, lawyers, engineers, and consultants continue to be trained.

A career track helps a firm recruit talent, particularly talent that is in the very early stages of development. The presence of a structured process with clear milestones encourages those who are beginning their professional journey and serves the same purpose as mile markers in a marathon. If you think about running 26.2 miles at the start of the race, the distance can be overwhelming. But if you focus on running the next mile, the task becomes practical and achievable. Similarly, when starting in a firm as an entry-level professional, the goal of reaching the top of the profession, the finish line, may seem daunting or too distant. A career track encourages young professionals to think of the practical next step rather than the faraway destination.

A career track also benefits the firm. It achieves three very important objectives:

1. **Creates reasonable expectations:** Employees always want to know what will happen next and they will likely ask questions such as: Why should I invest my efforts and talents in *your* firm? Will I be successful if I do? How do I know I can trust *you* to lead me to success? Even when such questions are not explicitly asked, they always linger beneath the surface. A career track is not a guarantee for success, but it does help employees feel less anxious about the future.

2. **Promotes the idea of progress:** Progress helps motivate. Without visible progress it may be difficult to continue putting in effort. A career track enables employees to develop goals that can be structured around the needs of the firm and its values. The achievement of goals can be rewarded with advancement, which can bring desired financial rewards and prestige.

3. **Brings a sense of fairness to the firm:** In an environment where highly ambitious people are brought together in the pursuit of professional success, many times it will be necessary to explain why one person is advancing while another is not. Without a career track, changes in compensation and other perks become very difficult to explain. In the absence of a system, the firm can be suspected of being run by the "likes me, likes me not" rule.

A career track is vital for the success of a professional services firm. Let's examine what a career track looks like in the advisory industry.

The Advisory Career Track

The idea of what makes a career track in the advisory world is constantly being refined. After all, this is a young industry that is still discovering its best practices. Furthermore, a career track will not and should not look the same in every firm. That being said, there are similarities between firms—particularly large organizations that tend to have a career track similar to the one outlined ahead.

Associate

The associate is the entry-level position. Associates are also called paraplanners, support advisors, analysts, or junior advisors. Associate responsibilities include gathering financial data; researching funds, products, or stocks at a basic level; drafting financial plans; creating financial models; and managing client data. Associates are often present in meetings but typically do not meet with clients alone. Associates may also have some administrative responsibilities such as completing paperwork, working with clients to make sure documents are signed and delivered, or taking notes and recording them in a CRM (customer relationship management) system. The position reports to a more senior member of the service team, usually a service advisor or lead advisor.

The associate position is defined by the accumulation of technical knowledge. Associates should focus on learning the systems and service methods of the firm (e.g., planning, trading, etc.), acquiring certifications, and completing education programs. Many associates (27 percent, according to the *2015 InvestmentNews* survey[2]) hold a Certified Financial Planner (CFP) designation.

The expectations of the position are defined by the achievement of competency-based goals. Compensation in independent firms is based on a salary with incentives tied to the performance management system of the firm. The *2015 InvestmentNews* survey shows that associates earn a

---

[2]InvestmentNews Research, *Adviser Compensation & Staffing Study* (InvestmentNews, 2015), p. 102.

salary between $45,000 and $65,000 and incentive compensation (bonuses) between $4,000 and $10,000.[3]

Advancement to the next position is based on the associate's ability to demonstrate technical expertise and a good understanding of the service process used by the team. Advancement also signals the ability to work as a member of the service team and a willingness to embrace the efforts and policies of the firm.

Service Advisor

The service advisor is responsible for client service and performs many of the steps in the client process. Responsibilities include preparation of financial plans, analysis of portfolios, and subsequent trading and rebalancing (which may also be done by a separate department). Service advisors answer many client questions pertaining to planning or wealth management, and they are expected to have significant expertise. They work extensively with clients, handling meetings either on their own or together with lead advisors. A service advisor is often called the *second chair*, to borrow a term from the legal profession. As second chair, they may substitute for the *first chair* and are generally expected to have a relationship with the client.

The service advisor position is defined by service, meaning the ability to accomplish what the client needs. Through experience, service advisors combine the technical expertise of associates with the ability to communicate with the client. They often supervise their associate colleagues, thus learning how to manage people. It is not unusual to see service advisors handle some relationships as lead advisors. This combination of first and second chair is desirable to see in more experienced service advisors before they are promoted.

This is also the position where training in marketing and business development begins. A service advisor's activities in terms of growth should focus on assisting with the firm's marketing plan. They may also establish themselves in organizations and niches that will later become the center of their new business activities.

The expectations of the position are defined by productivity and the quality of work. Service advisors are often measured on how many relationships they handle and the feedback they receive from clients.

Compensation for service advisors is salary-based and ranges between $55,000 and $88,000.[4] The position receives incentive compensation

---

[3] Ibid.
[4] Ibid., p. 89.

between $7,000 and $16,000. The wide range of salaries reflects a similarly large range of responsibilities. Professionals at the top of the scale are highly capable of working independently and may have more than a few client relationships where they serve as lead advisor.

Promotion to the next position is driven by the service advisor's proven ability to earn the trust and respect of clients and lead client relationships.

Lead Advisor

The lead advisor is responsible for independently managing client relationships and guiding clients through their wealth management, financial planning, and investment decisions. Lead advisors can also be referred to as senior advisors, wealth managers, or senior planners. These are the professionals to whom clients look for guidance. They may get support from other staff, but lead advisors are the ones who have to answer difficult questions.

Additional job responsibilities include training and developing the service team and cultivating new business. According to the *2016 InvestmentNews Survey*, lead advisors are typically asked to add $67,000 or more in new client revenue,[5] although, admittedly, only 27 percent of firms set such business development goals. Still, even if the goal is not always quantified, the expectation is there.

The lead advisor position is defined by the word *relationships*. The ability to communicate and empathize with clients is a critical skill. Success is measured by the number of clients served and the associated revenue. The number of clients lead advisors are expected to serve ranges considerably, depending on the type and size of the firm. My experience has been that in multifamily office firms the number of client relationships per lead advisor may be as low as 15 to 20, whereas in a firm more focused on investment advice the norm can be as high as 120 to 150. Client retention is paramount to the success of the position.

Compensation for lead advisors ranges from $120,000 to $200,000.[6] There are also considerable incentives ranging between $14,000 and $43,000 that reflect productivity, individual success, and the achievement of firm results. In addition, it is not uncommon for the firm to pay a separate bonus for business development.

In a few firms, the position may bifurcate into two types of lead advisor: (1) service-oriented advisors with higher productivity goals and lower business

---

[5] Ibid., p. 69.
[6] Ibid., p. 86.

development expectations, and (2) advisors who focus on business development, with higher sales goals and a lower service load. Compensation usually reflects this difference in responsibilities through higher bonuses and lower base salaries for business developers.

Partner

A partner is an owner, but that title does not necessarily describe the associated responsibilities. Very often, the position could be correctly described as a *lead advisor*; the title *partner* simply signifies a higher level of success and experience. Not all partners work in client service. Some may work in operations or management. Still, making partner has traditionally been the measuring stick of a career in professional services, and we continue to see it as part of the career progression.

The criteria for making partner include proven productivity, success in business development, commitment to the firm and its values, and personal character. In many firms, business development is what makes the difference between owner and non-owner advisors. That said, such a decision should be subject to significant discussion. (For more on necessary qualities for partners, see Chapter 11.)

Partners are usually asked to manage and lead. At the least, they should have a strong ability to manage the team they work with and perhaps contribute to the overall development of talent in the firm. Partners should also lead by example, exhibiting the values of the firm to the rest of the professionals. This includes the full range of values that the firm espouses, from expertise and passion for client service to how they treat employees and each other. For example, in a firm that truly believes in a balance between professional ambition and personal life, the partners should be the ones setting an example of how to balance both. Finally, partners often sit on committees and participate in the governance structures in the firm.

Partners in many firms have a compensation structure that takes a dramatic departure from the rest of the employees. It is not uncommon to see silos (i.e., where individuals are paid based primarily on a percentage of the revenue they personally generate). However, independent registered investment advisors (RIAs) are more frequently using a salary-based method, with salaries ranging from $131,000 to $231,000 according to the *2015 InvestmentNews* survey.[7] The incentive compensation to partners ranges from

---

[7] Ibid.

$30,000 to $100,000. In addition, partners receive a percentage of the profits of the firm (dividend) corresponding to their ownership of the firm.

Variations and Tenure

The four positions outlined earlier describe the advisory career track in many but not all firms. In general, a career track should reflect the nature and structure of the ideal client service team, and many differences exist between firms. For example, some firms use the descriptor *senior* at every step to create two levels within the same position. For example, a firm may have "senior associate" and "senior advisor" as steps in the career track. Other firms do not recognize "partner" as a step on the ladder, instead looking at that title as an investment option available to many employees. This is a valid approach. My tendency to put partner as the top step is likely personal bias, having come up in a large public accounting firm.

The lead advisor position is also treated differently across firms. Some firms think of lead advisors as business developers and leave client relationships to service advisors. Other firms give sales responsibilities only to partners. All of these approaches are perfectly valid, but they need to be consistent with the values of the firm. An established career track can ensure the path is fully described and well communicated to professionals at all levels.

Please note that we have not discussed a recommended tenure for these positions. A defined number of years in each position should not be part of a career track. Some people travel up the career ladder quickly while others take more time. Just because someone has survived behind a desk for 15 years does not mean that person should become a partner. Nor should someone who has been in the industry for 20 years automatically become a lead advisor. These decisions should be based on a professional's competency, experience, and track record. Returning to our marathon analogy, slow runners do not get to ride in a car through the last leg of the course so they can finish the race. It might sound brutal, but if everyone makes it to partner, the career track becomes meaningless.

Non-Client-Facing Career Tracks

Every firm struggles with the issue of providing a career track to non-client-facing staff. Opportunities for advancement may be fewer, and levels of responsibility may be less clear. That said, many large firms share a similar framework to define the steps in non-advisory career tracks:

- **Operations or admin specialist (entry level):** Professionals in this position support advisory teams or serve as members of client service teams. This position is entry level for new hires in operations or administration. Specific responsibilities can include client service administration, administrative support, executive support, performance reporting, and new accounts.
- **Senior specialist:** This is the higher level of the operations or admin specialist position (e.g., senior client service administrator). The *senior* label indicates a greater experience and the added responsibility of training other staff.
- **Team leader or director:** This position leads a team of operations and administrative specialists. Common professional titles include office manager, trading manager, director of client service administration, and human resources manager, among others. The emphasis shifts from performing individual responsibilities to managing people.
- **Department leader:** This is the highest level of responsibility, with oversight of multiple teams and a significant portion of the operations or administrative functions of the firm. Professional titles include chief administrative officer, chief technology officer, and, most frequently, chief operations officer. Department leaders are frequently considered for ownership.

The key to tackling the operations career track is to look not only at the progression of skills and experience, but also at the progression of responsibilities. In most firms, the first step up is based on expertise (the senior specialist) while the next step is based on the ability to manage and lead other team members (the team leader or director). Finally, the ability to contribute at the highest level in the firm defines the top of the career track (the department leader).

I will spend more time discussing the criteria for partnership for operations and administrative staff in Chapter 11, Adding Owners, but here I will mention that operations and administrative employees should have the ability to become partners. Their contributions may differ from those made by professionals on the advisory career track but they are still of vital importance to the firm.

Progressing through the Career Track

A firm's career track encourages clarity, helps define expectations, and ties performance to advancement and rewards. While firm owners should be up front, specific, and fully transparent about how a professional can progress through a career track, the advancement process cannot be reduced to a mathematical formula and should not be calculated in a spreadsheet, no matter how sophisticated.

Formulas versus Human Judgment

The formula approach might seem like a good idea, as it removes human judgment from decisions and prevents some of the "likes me, likes me not" games that occur in every firm. However, most of the characteristics and qualities professionals need to advance in their careers are hard to measure and, therefore, hard to formulate.

How would you measure somebody's ability to earn a client's trust, for instance? How would you gauge the ability to exercise good judgment in difficult situations? How would you measure the ability to train other advisors? You might try, but your measurements would be incomplete and flawed. The collective opinion of firm leaders may seem subjective, but it will likely be much closer to the truth.

The desire to use formulas often disguises a reluctance to have difficult conversations. It is easier to tell team members to plug their parameters into a spreadsheet than talk to them about their lack of progress. As difficult as these critical conversations may be, they are much more effective for both sides. The need for one such difficult conversation arises when someone's career plateaus.

Stagnation versus Progression

Some firms like McKinsey & Company are famous for their up-or-out policies. Every two years, associates are either promoted or let go. This approach is an extreme example of encouraging progress through the career track. Every spot on the team is considered a valuable asset that bestows training and opportunities on the holder. The firm requires a return on that investment. NFL teams, which are limited to 53 roster spots, tend to function in the same way: You either show progress or you're out.

Career stagnation is a difficult issue to manage. The best response depends on the nature of the firm and the overall environment. If someone is not progressing but continues to perform well in his or her current job, the key question becomes whether that person is "clogging the pipe." Ask yourself: "Is she stopping others from progressing?" If the answer is no, then she can continue to be a valuable and productive member of the team. If, however, she is preventing others from advancing, there is a problem. The solution may need to be unpleasantly drastic.

In firms with a cross-team structure, where there are no permanent teams and professionals work with multiple departments, one person being stuck is not an issue. This is most likely to occur at the service advisor position. The service advisor fulfills the job's responsibilities and is well liked in that role, but cannot move into leading client relationships. If career stagnation is not preventing another analyst from advancing, then keeping the service advisor in her current position is fine. However, if teams are permanent and the same three professionals (e.g., lead advisor, service advisor, and analyst) always work together, then a service advisor who is stuck can stifle the advancement of an analyst. This may be one of the reasons for using a cross-team structure.

Suppose Alex was hired seven years ago but is stuck at the service advisor position. Pat, who was hired five years ago, is already on the way to becoming a lead advisor. Should Pat be promoted ahead of Alex? This would probably upset Alex, who is a good service advisor but not prepared for a lead role. These kinds of difficult decisions arise when professionals in career stagnation are passed by newer hires.

Tenure versus Performance

Tenure should never be a guideline for career progress. Many firms disagree and prefer to reward loyalty. The danger of rewarding tenure is that under-achieving employees can block the progress of more motivated and competent colleagues. Either way, someone is going to be upset, whether it's an employee who is not progressing and feels passed by, or a very talented employee who is ready for promotion but cannot get ahead.

Some years ago, I was coaching my son's recreational soccer team. On recreational teams, coaches cannot discriminate in terms of positions or playing time based on the skills of a kid. Coaches are not even allowed to break kids into skill-level groups for drills and practice. The goal is to encourage kids to play soccer without feeling marginalized or uncomfortable because of their skill level. Given the mission of the league, the policy absolutely makes sense. The problem is that every year my team lost several players. Guess who those players were? They were always our best players. A firm is not a recreational team. It is driven by very different goals, ambitions, and values and therefore it needs to focus on results, not just participation.

Deciding which behaviors should be rewarded depends heavily on an organization's culture. Some firms focus on *taking care* of their people, much like how a family operates. Once you are in the family, the group takes care of you no matter what. In such an environment, it makes sense to reward tenure, loyalty, and similar values. It is easier to focus on these softer values in a prosperous and growing industry than it is in a very competitive, slow-growing one.

For most firms, however, performance is the behavior that matters most. The firm will best succeed in pursuing its vision when more employees achieve their individual goals and perform better as they meet the firm's overarching goals. Without strong individual performance, a firm's success becomes tenuous, and it is unable to advance any employees' careers.

A particularly difficult area of performance is business development, the ability to bring new clients to the firm. Some firms view career progress as the increasing ability to sell, which is often measured by a professional's success at bringing in new clients. Again, this is a cultural decision that depends on the values of the firm. I believe that it is a very good practice to train and teach business development from the early stages of a career, but it is unreasonable to expect consistent results until a professional reaches the lead advisor role.

Being Flat

We have so far made the assumption that every firm wants to use a career track as its system of advancement, with professionals moving up the ladder. That is not always the case. Many firms actually strive to be *flat*, without hierarchy. Should advisories have hierarchy at all? Perhaps this top-down structure feels too much like working in a bank and is a concept that Millennials will reject.

Founders of advisory firms who desire to build flat organizations are driven by the desire to be democratic, treat people equally, and differentiate themselves from the cultures of banks and brokerage firms. Unfortunately, while the intentions are good, the lack of differentiation in careers, compensation, and opportunities can, ironically, create questions about fairness and foster dissatisfaction among the ranks.

Not everything is equal in a company nor should it be. Entrepreneurs sometimes treat employees like children. They feel a sense of responsibility for them and desire to treat everyone equally. However, parity among all employees in an organization is not a virtue. In fact, it is often a company's worst problem. When there are no differences in position, compensation, recognition, opportunity, or ownership, a firm can suffer from dissatisfaction, low morale, high turnover, and a poor atmosphere.

I once visited a firm with a policy of open seating. No one had an office and there were no private spaces. The idea was primarily to encourage collaboration and also to eliminate the hierarchical signs of power. The sentiment is inspiring, but it does not translate well to the reality of a workplace. For instance, can you guess where the desks of the CEO and the more senior people were located? In the corners next to the windows. A hierarchy and its signs always emerge one way or another. You may be better off controlling how those signs emerge and are displayed rather than accepting the inevitable and often unpredictable results.

When discussing advisory structure, *hierarchy* is not even the right word. A better word is *status*. Everyone has status in his or her organization, whether it's documented or not. The organization tells you who is the boss of whom, controls how people gain status, and steers them toward the right types of behavior. Without an effective hierarchy, status is earned in ways that can be counterproductive or plain wrong. Status may come down to who has been around the longest, who works with the largest client, who talks to the CEO, and so on. Ideally, status is earned through performance, as is compensation.

There is a reason cars have one wheel and one driver. If every seat had a wheel and pedals, the car would never reach its desired destination. This is often what flat organizations are like. When groups and committees have no leadership, they can find it hard to progress—at both individual and organizational levels. Hierarchy, even if it's just at the temporary project level, helps get things done. Projects are completed faster and often better. Differentials can take many forms: actual hierarchical differences, diverse forms of compensation, special employee recognition, or pieces of ownership offered. Each of these differentials has its own advantages, but they tend to work better together.

Treating people differently is not just about hierarchy. One of the reasons it's important to treat people differently is that it, perhaps unexpectedly, fosters a stronger sense of fairness. If all people in an organization are treated exactly the same, a time will come when those who perform the best will feel that the system is not fair. Those who contribute the most do not receive adequate rewards, which can squash motivation. Great performance not only comes from a person's talent, but is also a result of his effort and passion. Those who apply themselves the most expect to be recognized and rewarded. If they aren't, they feel they are being treated unfairly.

Without any differential in treatment, staff can't tell whether they are making progress in their careers. There are no milestones to indicate if they are any closer to their professional goals. In fact, they can't even tell what the goals are. Such an environment tends to discourage rather than encourage. What's worse, people start developing their own goals and milestones, which often fail to coincide with the firm's vision. People can become focused on trivialities, such as whom the CEO talks to the most or who was invited to what meeting. These things become unreasonably important.

The flat organizational chart is often a virtue only to the founders of advisory firms. For everyone else, promotions are a goal, a measure of progress that gives employees a sense of achievement. When there are only two professional positions in a firm, associate and partner, associates will feel like marathon runners without mile markers and become disheartened. Whether they are at mile 10 or mile 15, they have a very long distance to go. They might not even know they are on the right track or what they are supposed to do next. Those questions can become overwhelming. Meanwhile the partners, junior or senior, will not be much happier.

Top Performers

Careers and career progression are the dream that fuels the forward momentum of the firm. The desire to achieve and progress is powerful, and therefore opportunities are invaluable. While theoretically a successful firm may offer an unlimited number of successful careers, in practice at any given point in time in most firms the number of opportunities is scarce and therefore very valuable. This brings us to a critical question: Should a firm recognize its top performers and treat them differently, or should a firm treat everyone the same?

The first mistake organizations make is not clarifying what constitutes a *top performer* and who those people are. Firms are often reluctant to acknowledge the top employees for fear of upsetting the others. The result is counterproductive. The employees at the top are frustrated and those who aren't performing well are not more inspired to improve. Ignoring this problem is naïve. It is very clear to everyone that some professionals work with more clients, generate more revenue, and train people better. People already know who the better performers are. When the leaders of the firm don't acknowledge it, they destroy the sense of fairness and miss an opportunity to define what matters.

That missed opportunity is significant because there may not be a better way to motivate change than through public recognition and praise. If we were to compare a firm that publicly praises top-performing professionals for their business development contributions to a firm in which partners are paid for business development but individual results are kept secret, it is my belief that the first firm is likely to see better performance. Praise is a very powerful motivator. Compensation, especially if the results are kept private, will only reward what is already happening. As any teenager can tell you, peer pressure is a powerful force of change. Now, if both praise and compensation are combined, the results will likely be outstanding.

When you define and measure top performance, you also create an opportunity to tie it to rewards and promotions, while also emphasizing fairness. But even those companies that want to compensate performance have a hard time doing so when there is no history of it. A new rating system can seem scary, and it can be unclear which metrics to use. If professionals have never been scored or evaluated, a new compensation structure could produce surprising—even shocking—results or seem arbitrary and unfair. If a firm wants to change behavior, it should start by measuring and reporting individual results. Once staff understands those measures, it will be easier and more acceptable for them to tie performance to pay.

Employees are not children, and they do not want to be treated as such. What they need is not equal treatment but an equal start and access to opportunities. If they have clarity in the rules and goals, they will be able to take care of their own results. They are very capable of managing their own careers. In fact, many of them want to have more control. *Flat* is a relative term: The Appalachian Mountains are flat next to the Himalayas. *Flatter* may be good, but *too flat* will drive those away who want the challenge—and the reward—of climbing to the top.

A strong firm culture will have a well-thought-out way of recognizing and celebrating top achievers. Once that is in place, a firm may build additional levels of differential by awarding promotions and pay. Recognizing the best will ultimately help everyone.

Reaching the End of the Track

Career tracks foster structure and a sense of progress, but they are not meant to be the same for everyone. Some professionals travel their path faster, and others take more time. Some stop along the way and others pause but ultimately resume their progress. Insisting that everyone arrive at the destination together is a fine principle for a family trip, but not for a successful firm. And the endpoint will differ from individual to individual. Partnership is not necessarily the final destination for everyone.

When I was eagerly working toward a partnership at Moss Adams, I tended to see it as the finish line of a marathon—that glorious moment of triumph that makes the hard work worthwhile. Partnership was going to make me happy, successful, and rich—or so I thought. Let's just say it did not work that way.

It did not make me rich, and I have had my happy and unhappy days. But partnership did introduce me to the next step. Being a partner means evolving from a practitioner into a business owner. As partner, you gain a new set of responsibilities and challenges to conquer. When you climb a mountain, the view is indeed spectacular, but you also, perhaps for the first time, see other mountains worth climbing.

CHAPTER 3

Recruiting G2

Building the next generation of advisors begins by recruiting them. This statement may appear obvious, but in reality, many firms wait too long to hire. Some search for unrealistic levels of experience and talent, holding out for that perfect hire. Others abstractly *look to hire* but never make that public or take concrete action. A firm's hiring practices should be a top priority for both founder and G2 professionals. So vital to long-term success, recruitment strategy should become part of an organization's day-to-day activities and intrinsic culture. In order for a firm to build a deep cadre of professionals who can someday contribute to growth, client service, and management, it has to start by recruiting a class of talented—if perhaps inexperienced—individuals.

Not every firm must hire at entry level, nor must every employee join at the same level of experience. A successful firm combines experienced hires with entry-level positions. More importantly, a successful firm is always hiring. According to Dale Yahnke, CEO and co-founder of Dowling & Yahnke, a large and successful independent RIA in San Diego, "Adding talented people should be just as important and approached in much the same way as adding clients."

Large accounting firms discovered this phenomenon long ago. They understand that for every 10 hires, more than two-thirds will eventually leave the firm[1] for a number of reasons: change of careers, change of firms, desire for different work–life balance, relocation, random events, and so on. Of the

---

[1]Susan C. Borkowski and Mary Jeanne Welsh, "Survey Says! Why People Leave Public Accounting," PICPA.org, December 1, 2015. Accessed April 16, 2017, from https://www.picpa.org/articles/picpa-news/2015/12/01/survey-says!-why-people-leave-public-accounting. The article reports that only 24 percent of women and 37 percent of men were still employed with their Big-4 accounting firm.

remaining hires, not all will progress through the career track, and some will find themselves stuck at different levels of experience and performance. So in order to find a talented partner, someone who can develop new business and manage and build a team, firms need to hire around 10 inexperienced individuals. The problem is that you never know which new hire will become the future partner.

Much has been written on the subject of hiring, and when it comes to selecting a hiring methodology, there are many good ones from which to choose. While it is not my specific area of expertise, I want to share a process that has worked well for me and that we frequently recommend to our clients. The process relies on thorough vetting in stages and involves the entire team with whom the person will be working. The combined perspective resulting from multiple professionals conducting multiple rounds of interviews and vetting should result in hires that meet expectations. It is also the process we use in my firm.

Beginning with the End in Mind

Napoleon famously pronounced that there is a general's baton in every soldier's backpack. The same principle applies to new hires at a firm. While I was at Moss Adams, we would say that we never wanted to hire anyone who we didn't believe would be a partner someday.

Many firms make the mistake of hiring people with limited potential just because they fit a position and can perform the required tasks well. However, these employees lack the talent or ambition to progress. For example, it is an easy temptation to hire people who are going to be very good service advisors (i.e., second-chair advisors) but show little desire or ability to take over client relationships. The result is a team made of Robins with very few Batmen.

This imbalance is not a sustainable situation. What is worse, firms will frequently promote the Robins to Batman positions to avoid having to discuss their lack of career progress. Superhero metaphors aside, the point is that sometimes firms promote professionals to lead positions but never give them responsibilities inherent to the role, since they are not capable of handling them.

In contrast, successful firms begin with the end in mind. The argument here is that firms should only hire professionals who have the education and theoretical training to be lead advisors. New hires should bring a well-rounded set of talents and experience that will allow them to progress through the entire career track. If they have not yet completed their CFP designation, perhaps they have a window to do that, but not an indefinite one. Firms should also focus on hiring professionals who have the social skills to become relationship managers.

Beginning with the end in mind also means hiring people who are not the easiest to work with, but who have the potential to excel. Talented people are not always easy to get along with. They are very curious and ask a lot of questions. They tend to be impatient, as they have achieved many things in their lives faster than those around them. They may think they know better than someone with 10 years of experience, even if they just started yesterday. Yet, these annoying know-it-alls will someday be your best business developers, your ideal partners, and, perhaps, your future CEOs.

The temptation is very strong to look at the middle. As a case in point, some time ago my colleagues at Fusion (my previous firm) and I were looking at the results of a popular personality test. It was an assessment tool that measures a variety of personality characteristics (e.g., independence, desire to socialize, collaborative nature, etc.) on a scale from 1 to 10. Someone had defined the suggested range of values for each characteristic, and the recommendations were solidly down the middle for practically all traits. It seemed to say: "Hire between 4 and 7!"

The problem was that when we looked at the test scores of our best advisors—or even our own scores, the scores of the firm's leaders—they were full of 1s and 10s. These extreme values made someone an entrepreneur, a business development engine, or a creative genius. Talent is not found between 4 and 7. That's where safety lives.

This little speech is not intended to steer you away from hiring to fit a position's description. However, it should encourage you to look past the specific skills of the position and toward the next levels. The best hires are those who will not only excel at the analyst or service advisor position, but also someday comfortably progress to the lead advisor position and beyond.

Hiring Levels

"Free agents," experienced hires who come into the organization at a high level, play an important role in the strategy of a firm. They can add instant capacity. They can bring a skill that was lacking. They can import experience that was missing. They can start a department or a function. They can show the way to the next stage of evolution. These are all good uses of high-level hires. However, the staffing strategy of a successful firm cannot rely on continuously finding free agents. Ultimately, firms have to figure out how to grow talent organically, from the bottom up.

High-level hires come with some challenges, the first of which is compensation. They are high-priced and can often disrupt the existing compensation parity in the firm. It is not uncommon for a firm to recruit a new lead advisor and find out that the person commands a market price of say $180,000. If internally grown advisors have salaries below this level, this presents the firm with a conundrum: Do we pay the new hire $180,000 and hope that the others don't find out? Do we let the person go and not fill the position we need? Do we make the hire and upgrade everyone's compensation at a great cost?

Experienced hires can also challenge the culture of the firm: They come with their own way of doing things. They bring their own sets of values and expectations. They tend to be less flexible or receptive to changing the way they approach clients or operations. Integrating them is not easy and requires more energy and caution.

Finally, experienced hires are simply not very available. Advisory positions in the industry have a very low turnover rate. Finding lead advisors in most markets is very difficult and not a very reliable way to fill capacity needs.

In contrast, inexperienced but well-educated and eager hires are quite available. My experience has been that entry-level positions in successful firms usually receive a tremendous amount of interest. There seem to be many highly talented individuals who are interested in careers in financial advice and looking for a place to get started. They are well prepared theoretically and have a good understanding of what a career in advice and wealth management entails. Of course, the larger and more successful a firm is, the more likely it is to receive interest from potential candidates.

Large firms fully take advantage of that availability. Some of the leading firms in the industry are already very well known as recruiters at the premier universities and colleges in their hometowns. In fact, this may be the most underappreciated advantage of being a large firm: the ability to recruit top talent and take risks with people.

Becoming the Employer of Choice

Large consulting and accounting firms have long recognized the ability to attract top talent as a competitive advantage. Just as building a brand is very important for attracting clients, there is also such a thing as building an employer brand. Employers of choice have a reputation for providing opportunities and successful careers to talented individuals.

Creating a brand as an employer is similar to creating a brand as a service organization. It requires a track record of success, as well as the endorsement of existing employees (just as enthusiastic clients help you attract new clients). An employer brand feeds off efforts to communicate the organization and its unique value proposition to the marketplace (i.e., the pool of prospective employees). Doing this effectively requires associating the brand with more than just the things the firm does, but also what the firm stands for, its mission and values. Combined, a strong message as an employer and a strong communication plan can establish the firm as a premier place to work.

Accredited Investors in Minneapolis is a prominent independent firm with about $1.4 billion in AUM (as of February 2017).[2] The firm has a team of 34 employees and is recognized as one of the "Best Places to Work" by the *Minneapolis/St. Paul Business Journal.*[3] Becky Krieger, who leads recruiting for the firm, believes that this recognition has helped the firm find the talent it needs. Since receiving the award, the firm has had an ample supply of résumés and interested candidates, which has allowed Becky to cherrypick talent from the best local programs.[4]

Similarly, Captrust—one of the largest advisory organizations in the country, with 17 offices nationwide—is doing a lot to position itself as a great organization for both clients and employees. Captrust also assists local offices to achieve recognition and obtain access to top talent. The recruiting efforts of the firm are led by the director of HR, who focuses on attracting talent.

Many CEOs in the industry are coming to the realization that recruiting is one of their top priorities—just as important as mergers and acquisitions.

---

[2] InvestmentNews, Adviser Center RIA Database, 2016. Accessed April 16, 2017, from http://careers.investmentnews.com/adviser-center/profile/243.
[3] Kim Johnson, "Business Journal Names 2016 Best Places to Work Honorees," *Minneapolis/St. Paul Business Journal* (June 27, 2016).
[4] Becky Krieger, interview (February 2016).

Bob Bunting, a former CEO of Moss Adams, told the audience during a presentation in February 2016 that he spent almost all of his time in his last year at the firm recruiting talent.[5] In fact, the last thing he did as CEO was to call 100 professionals across the country who he thought would make great additions to the Moss Adams team.

Advertising

The single most obvious way to recruit is to advertise an open position and attract as many candidates as possible. However, many advisory firms do not do this; if they advertise at all, they post openings only within their referral network. The logic is that while open advertising attracts a very high number of résumés, the quality of candidates is low and someone on staff has to spend hours sifting through the pile to find the good applicants. While that is a real and perhaps unpleasant consequence of advertising, the reward for going through the pile is the ability to invite many qualified candidates to interview.

The biggest problem with not advertising a position is that it limits the applicant pool to a very small selection. When the number is so limited, you don't have a good basis for comparison. In chess, there is a maxim that says, "When you find a good move, look for a better one!" The same should be true for recruiting. When you find a good candidate, look for a better one! Time and again, I see advisory firms hiring people they have met only once because they like them. What the firms are missing out on is all the other candidates who could have been even better, if only the firms had collected more résumés. Sifting through résumés and interviewing candidates is a top-priority task, not an administrative chore.

Good advertising has the following components:

- **Detailed description of the position:** Describe the position as well as you can and use industry-standard terminology that is easy to understand. If you have arcane position descriptions, translate them into familiar industry descriptions that are clearer to people outside your organization.
- **Enthusiastic language:** Get candidates excited about your firm. Describe the firm in a compelling way that drives interest.

---

[5]Bob Bunting (principal, RL Bunting Consulting, and former CEO of Moss Adams LLP), interview (February 2016).

- **Focus on careers:** Advertise a career, not just a job. The job being advertised should be clear, but the opportunity to grow beyond the position is what will attract the best candidates.
- **Open-ended compensation:** Avoid getting bogged down in compensation detail. A good job ad should not explicitly list compensation, but rather refer to compensation as *competitive* or *in line with the industry.* Actual dollar numbers shift the focus to the wrong discussion. You want to preserve the ability to offer higher compensation to exceptional candidates and a lower level of compensation to hires with less experience.

There are dozens of good places to advertise a position. At The Ensemble Practice, we prefer to use LinkedIn's job-posting capabilities, but we have also seen good results from numerous other recruiting sites. Some obvious choices that should not be missed are:

- The local premier college or MBA school
- The job-posting sites of the FPA and the CFA Institute
- Social networking sites such as Facebook and LinkedIn

A good rule of thumb is to advertise until you collect at least 10 résumés from people whom you are very excited to talk to at a first-round interview.

Recruiting in Small Markets

Some firms in smaller markets get quite discouraged by the size of their recruiting pool. If you have a good company that offers solid potential for career growth, you should not be shy about recruiting out of market and helping your future employees move. Younger people are mobile. Without stereotyping them, one of the best characteristics of young professionals is their ability to adapt. Many talented candidates would be willing to move in order to work for a high-quality firm.

Moving assistance does not have to be too extensive. Covering moving expenses and/or providing a recruiting bonus to offset the cost of rental deposits can be quite effective. The most difficult part for firms is not the cost but rather the commitment: Can you offer this person enough opportunity to justify the move? Is the person likely to have a good career at your firm? This is why a good process is essential.

There may be a large commitment inherent in moving a professional from say, Chicago to Portland, to pursue a job, but successful firms are taking on that responsibility. When you look at staff at some of the most successful firms in many cities, you will find many advisors relocated specifically to work for that firm. Young people seek opportunity and they are willing to pursue it.

Screening

The way I personally deal with résumés is to sift them into three piles: *yes*, *no*, and *maybe*. I do not hesitate long before adding a résumé to the *no* pile if the candidate lacks the qualifications, relevant experience, or desired educational background. I rarely look back at the *no* pile. If a résumé catches my interest and clearly meets all criteria, it goes into the *yes* pile. *Yes* in this context simply means that we should interview the candidate.

The *maybe* pile is reserved for résumés that have something very interesting about them but are also somehow flawed. For example, the candidate went to a great college but does not have a CFP certification. Perhaps someone is academically accomplished, but not in the field of finance and personal finance. Notice that people do not automatically get a yes because they graduated from an esteemed university. Similarly, they do not get an automatic no for lacking a CFP certification. The *maybe* pile is the place to search for diamonds in the rough.

I return to the *maybe* pile only if I do not collect enough résumés in the *yes* pile. That said, you should make sure that every yes is a *career yes*, not just a *position yes*. The difference is the potential to grow. When you come across candidates who can do the job but have no growth potential, they do not belong in the *yes* pile. At best, they are maybes. Remember: Every recruit could be a future partner.

Interviewing

There are many books and articles that go into depth on how to interview candidates and those are well worth perusing. The following section will focus on the basics. Firms often jump into sophisticated interview techniques without having a good understanding of a few fundamental principles and strategies that could help them. These are highlighted here.

First Interview

1. **Prepare your core list of questions in advance of the first interview:** Having a list of prepared interview questions not only keeps you organized, but also allows you to be consistent from one interview to another. It is unfair to ask one candidate one set of questions, another candidate a completely different set, and then compare the two. This does not mean you should mechanically go from one question to another. There is nothing wrong with going with the flow of conversation. However, at the end of the hour or allotted time, you should have exhausted your core questions.

2. **Budget enough time to meet with candidates:** This helps avoid awkward moments when candidates meet each other in the lobby, or when they are made to wait together as if they are at the dentist. You want to see the candidates' best performance—not nervous, stressed-out versions of themselves. Give them a chance to interview in as relaxed a manner as possible. Consider scheduling breaks between interviews. You will need those yourself.

3. **Score the interviews:** After each interview, write down your notes and score the candidate in five or six categories that are important for the job. These numeric scores should be combined with qualitative notes that allow you to recall the conversation and explain the reasoning behind the grades.

4. **Use multiple interviewers:** Especially in the first round, it is a good idea for more than one interviewer to meet each candidate. Do this by interviewing a candidate with a colleague as a team, splitting the interview, or simply doubling up. There is nothing wrong with multiple people asking the same question. Using multiple interviewers will give you a good perspective on the person and avoid the effect of personality trumping other important characteristics, such as knowledge or analytical skill.

5. **Encourage candidates to ask questions:** Questions reveal a lot about candidates' preparation and knowledge. The questions applicants ask reveal whether they studied the firm before the interview, understand the job well, and have good knowledge of the industry. Questions also reveal priorities. Certain questions will quickly spark my interest in a candidate. For example, these indicate a person is on the right track: How does your firm grow? What makes you better than other firms? Who are your typical clients? What is the career path in your firm? Where do you see the firm in 10 years? Other questions turn me off: What is the compensation for this position? Do you offer parking? What is the vacation policy? That is not to say that those questions are not allowed. What matters is which questions come first.

6. **Listen:** An interview is a time to listen—really listen. Time and again, I catch myself and others assuming we know the answer before even asking the question. Other times it is easy to stop listening past the first two sentences. Making assumptions is a recipe for mistakes. For example, if a candidate has had several jobs over the last five years, it might not indicate a tendency to jump ship. A better strategy is to find the right questions to explore why that was the case. Dig in. Continue to pursue an answer if the first response is unclear.

These six strategies can help you select the best candidates for a second round of interviews. It is a big mistake to only interview candidates once. One interview does not always give you enough time to learn about the person. You are also missing out on the opportunity to reflect on what you have learned in the first round and incorporate it in the second round. Finally, in a second round, you have the chance to discuss an entirely different set of details about the job, now that you have already exchanged quite a bit of information. Before the second interview takes place, there is also the opportunity for some testing.

Testing

Testing is not cheap, and it is also time consuming. Testing candidates between the first and second rounds is a good way to limit the number of tests to only the candidates in whom you truly have an interest. It is also a good way to formulate questions for the second interview. You can also pair test data with interview impressions for a more complete picture. There are two types of tests that you can deploy: skill testing and personality testing. Both make good sense.

Skill testing involves giving candidates a case study and asking them for a response. This technique is extensively used by big consulting firms such as McKinsey and Boston Consulting Group. Case studies reveal a candidate's knowledge, ability to apply knowledge, and thinking style. You can develop your own case studies—in fact, you should. Create case studies around typical problems that professionals will face in their work, and focus on fundamental concepts rather than esoteric details. Make the available information sufficient to answer the questions, but avoid making the answers too obvious.

A good case study solution should be a page or two, combined with any necessary analysis (an Excel spreadsheet, for example). There is nothing wrong with asking candidates to complete the case on their own, away from your office. If they rely on someone else's help, that will quickly become obvious in a second interview.

Personality testing is also used regularly in recruiting, and many firms swear by it. I have some reservations about it. If you conduct personality testing, be very careful to use a test that is compliant with all laws and regulations and not discriminatory. To get the most reliable results, you should consistently use the same test with both candidates and existing employees. The best understanding comes when you can compare the results of a candidate to the results of individuals on the team with whom the candidate will work. This compare-and-contrast approach can perhaps tell you about how this person will communicate with the team and what some challenges will be.

Too often I have seen quality candidates rejected because a personality test seemed to reveal a fatal flaw. First, I am skeptical of the science behind the tests. More importantly, we often misunderstand or misinterpret the results of these tests. I frequently project my own test results (with my name removed) on the screen during a presentation and ask the audience if they think this person is suited to a professional career, and whether this person would make a good business developer. The vast majority of my audiences immediately reject my profile as being very unsuited for a professional career and a certain disaster as a business developer. The reason for this conclusion is that I am an introvert. The very word *introvert* immediately triggers stereotypes about someone who is shy and will have trouble communicating. This is not only a misunderstanding of what an introvert is (being introverted does not mean I am shy or can't talk to people), but also a good example of an overreaction to a single trait.

Second Interview

The second interview is not mandatory. It should be reserved only for candidates who impressed so much in the first interview that you would consider making them an offer. If you don't have at least one good candidate for an offer, you should not invite back the two who were the least bad for a second interview. Instead, go back to advertising and interviewing. Settling for subpar candidates is a horrible option.

The second interview is a chance to follow up on questions and reflect on information obtained from tests. Test results can also inspire many new questions and help you highlight areas you need to explore more deeply (especially if they reveal some warning signs). For example, if I am concerned about someone's ability to work independently given the results in a test, I might formulate the following questions: What is an example of a project you have completed on your own? How much were you supervised in your last position and to what degree did you make decisions on your own? Suppose you are facing this client situation; would you come to me to seek direction or do you feel you have enough information to act on your own?

The second interview is also the right time to discuss all of the job details, including compensation. Since you have more knowledge of the candidate and the candidate has more knowledge of your firm, it is now appropriate to answer questions regarding your policies, compensation philosophy, and so on.

Finally, the second interview is a chance to invite some additional interviewers in to validate your choices. Additional interviewers could include partners or managers from other teams or other departments. After briefly getting to know the top candidates, they can indicate who they believe would be your best choice.

Job Offer

Once you have selected the top candidate, it is time to make the job offer. So many times, the offer is made over the phone with no written follow-up. A written job offer provides many benefits: It documents compensation and all the terms and policies that apply. It avoids any confusion and will not allow for the misunderstandings that can frequently occur with verbal offers. Most importantly, a written offer will allow you to list and get explicit signatures on all the legal covenants that are part of the job contract, including noncompete (if allowable and applicable), nonsolicitation, nondisclosure, and other legal agreements. Those should be written out and frequently reviewed by your attorneys to ensure compliance, as well as to reflect changes in how the industry uses and enforces such agreements.

Opportunistic Hiring

While I am a proponent of advertising positions and following a structured interview process, I also recognize that some of the best hires join a firm through an introduction, without the position necessarily being open and advertised. Another way to express this phenomenon is to say that some of the best firms are always hiring for all professional positions. Elite firms such as WMS Partners in Baltimore, Balasa Dinverno Foltz in Chicago, and Dowling & Yahnke in San Diego are in constant recruiting mode. They are always interested in meeting new professionals and they always welcome qualified candidates.

Imagine you are the CEO of a firm. You come across an individual who has had a good career in public accounting and is interested in becoming a wealth manager. She has a CPA license and extensive tax expertise. Do you wait for a position to open for such an interesting candidate, or do you simply open one for her? Fast-growing, confident, and successful firms gravitate in the direction of opening a new position when they come across the talent they seek.

Elite talent is hard to find and when you come across an extremely talented individual it is unreasonable to make that person wait for a position to open. The advantage of such opportunistic hiring is that talented, motivated people usually have no trouble finding ways to help a successful firm. On the other hand, the problem with this approach is that sometimes you end up with a lot of talented people who don't have enough to do. I once had a client who had accumulated an amazing team of talented partners. They all had Big Four accounting firm backgrounds and they were all very highly regarded. However, there were eight of them, and the firm was only big enough for three or four. They were simply not busy enough. The resulting situation caused frustration, friction between the partners, compensation fights, and, ultimately, no profitability.

Opportunistic hiring works very well when it is paired with growth. Growth creates opportunity for everyone and allows for the quick integration of new hires. When there is growth, professionals who are hired without a position will easily find ways to contribute to projects and functions. The right position will open quickly or emerge as a result of their efforts. In the absence of growth, opportunistic hiring can become a problem. It can lead to frustration for both new hires and existing members of the team, who now have to divide among themselves the few opportunities that exist.

Experienced Hires

Recruiting experienced hires requires a different approach from recruiting for entry-level and more junior positions. In most cases, experienced hires already have a job and a career at another firm. Attracting them is more difficult than just posting an ad. Here are some strategies for recruiting these experienced professionals to your firm.

1. **Recruit the best talent away from other firms:** Recruiting talent away from the competition is just fine. Advisory firms can be almost shockingly collegial, politely declining the chance to hire someone away from a local competitor. The mentality in other industries is very different: Recruiting is seen as an accepted form of competing.

   At Moss Adams, we had a policy that prohibited individual bios and contact information from being published on the website, since that would allow recruiters to quickly identify and contact our best people. Surprisingly, I can almost always go to the website of any advisory firm and find out who their lead advisors are, where they went to school, and how you can give them a call to see if they are interested in another job.

   There is nothing unethical or poorly mannered in recruiting talent away from competing firms. Like the market for clients, the market for talent should not be restricted. It is healthy for firms to compete. While there are certainly lines to be drawn in how talent is recruited, keeping an eye on the top talent of other local firms should be part of the job of a CEO or president.

2. **Create a list of talented people you want to recruit:** Begin with a catalog of people in other firms whom you would love to have on your team. Remember the story about Bob Bunting making 100 phone calls to people he wanted to recruit to Moss Adams? He created that list by going around the firm and asking all the professionals questions: Whom have we lost business to in the last year? Whom do we wish we had on our team?

3. **Develop your message:** Why should talented, experienced professionals join your firm? What sets your firm apart? What makes your firm unique and better than the competition? Why should professionals choose your firm over others? We frequently ask these questions from the client perspective, but the same questions apply when recruiting experienced professionals.

   Experienced hires are likely already successful at their current firms and happy with their careers. To recruit them, you need to offer a significant difference. The opportunity to lead, focus on a particular area of practice, build a better team, or partner with other leading professionals are just several examples of incentives you could offer to attract experienced talent.

4. **Be gentle but persistent:** My former partner and CEO of Fusion, Stuart Silverman, made it a habit to check in with me annually to see if I was interested in leaving Moss Adams to join him at Fusion. The first time he mentioned it, I confidently declined: "No way!" The second time, I wavered: "Perhaps, but not now." The third time, I began to seriously consider it: "I guess we should talk." Persistence is vital in recruiting. Inquire periodically with people you want on your team. The best recruiters I have known are not professional recruiters. They are CEOs who make it a habit to identify the people they want on their team, stay connected with them, and wait for the right combination of opportunity and circumstance to bring them on board.

5. **Use your equity wisely:** Equity is a very powerful recruiting tool, but it can also be very expensive. You don't want to promise partnership to someone who turns out to not be the right fit for your partnership group or culture. Some firms don't allow their top professionals to buy into the firm, or they limit the type of equity available. While offering equity may be a good way to recruit some of their professionals, it should not compromise the other criteria for partnership in your firm.

6. **Offer the chance to lead:** The opportunity to lead is the currency of high-level recruiting. I watched a very high-ranking professional in a publicly traded organization depart and become the CEO of a much smaller firm. He was one of the top people at his previous firm, where he enjoyed a position of power and visibility. The firm's publicly traded status also meant that he was often in the news. In contrast, his new firm was neither public nor well-known. I asked him why he left. His answer was simple: "I wanted to be a CEO!"

   The desire to lead—to create, to inspire, to be in charge—is very strong for those with leadership ambitions. Even as a small firm, you may be able to pry away top people from your larger competitors with the proposition of giving them a chance to lead a department, team, office, or function.

7. **Don't recruit on compensation:** There is a tendency for the winner in a competitive bidding auction to overpay for the prize. Economists call it the winner's curse. This same phenomenon applies to recruiting based on higher compensation. It can lead to overpaying for talent and potentially disrupt the rest of the firm. Trying to keep a very high compensation package secret is a recipe for eventual disaster. If you overpay for one person, you may have to bring the compensation of everyone in the firm up to that level.

Recruiting talented people to the firm should be a high priority initiative at the top of the organization. Adding talent should be seen and treated in a similar way as adding new clients. A good firm will combine disciplined and systematic recruiting at the entry levels of the professional career track with strategic and active recruiting at the more experienced levels. The result is a firm with depth of talent and a premier brand as an employer.

CHAPTER 4

Taking Over Client Relationships

The lead advisor role is the basic building block of the financial advisory industry and a critical achievement in the development of a G2 professional. Before G2 professionals can become owners, managers, or leaders—before they can develop new business or contemplate the succession of the founders—they have to achieve a simple but quintessential milestone: becoming a *trusted advisor* to a client. They need to take over a client relationship. Managing and directing clients, uncovering their needs, and designing a process to meet those needs are the skills that form the foundation of the profession. Being the lead in a client relationship is a vital precursor to achieving any of the other professional milestones. If someone has never led a client, it is premature to contemplate how he or she can lead a firm.

Being the lead proves to be very difficult for many professionals. My experience has been that as many as two-thirds of professionals in the industry fail to cross the chasm that separates the lead advisor role from that of a support or service advisor. As a result, there is a shortage of lead advisors throughout the industry while service and support professionals, in my experience, are in ample supply. I have worked with many firms who have turned away prospective clients because they did not have the capacity to absorb new clients. At the same time, many of those firms had an ample cadre of service advisors who were frustrated in their lack of career progress.

We need look no further than compensation for evidence of how wide this chasm is. According to the *2015 InvestmentNews Adviser Compensation & Staffing Study*, lead advisors earned a median total compensation of $143,000. Service advisors, who are one position below lead advisors, earned

$83,000, just over half of the lead advisor total compensation.[1] This distance is reminiscent of the relationship between doctors and nurses: Both positions are invaluable and rely on each other, but you can't have nurses without doctors, and doctors are compensated significantly higher.

What Is a Lead Advisor?

In many firms, professionals who carry the title of lead advisor—or even partner—do not control any client relationships and have never really had to manage clients. Instead, the professionals still serve a second-chair function for a founder who truly controls the relationship. These firms usually have severe capacity issues, unclear succession prospects, and tension between professionals. This practice, which may be driven by the desire to show progress and please professionals, results in dangerous long-term dynamics. It is a bit like a driving test: You don't want to give a passing grade to all students just to please them. The result would be dangerous to all involved. So, what comprises a passing grade for a lead advisor?

Passing the Lead Advisor Test

The lead advisor is the professional whom the client perceives as his or her *trusted advisor* and who has the influence to change the course of the client relationship. When the client works with a team, it can be difficult to identify the lead advisor in the relationship. A lead advisor will pass the following six-step test:

1. **Has ultimate responsibility for client relationship:** The lead advisor is responsible for identifying client needs and communicating proposed solutions. He or she is tasked by the firm to make final decisions on financial plan design, portfolio management, and wealth management strategies. This does not mean that the lead advisor makes all these decisions alone. Specialists or an investment department could be involved, but the lead is ultimately responsible for final recommendation to the client.
2. **Manages the team:** The lead advisor has the authority to manage the internal delivery team. Most likely, the lead is responsible for managing service advisors, analysts, client service administrators, and others who engage in the delivery of client services.

---

[1] InvestmentNews Research, *Adviser Compensation & Staffing Study* (2015), pp. 86–89.

3. **Effects and communicates changes to engagement:** The lead advisor can change the engagement and will communicate these changes to the client. For example, the lead can increase client fees and is responsible for explaining these changes to the client.

4. **Is accepted as an authority by the client:** The lead advisor's recommendations are accepted without the client seeking further validation from other team members. I once had a colleague who was working with me on several relationships. I could hear his phone ring in his office, and I could hear him say, "Hello, Dan!" to the client. He had a 30-minute conversation with the client, and I could hear him hang up (we have a small office). Then, immediately upon his hanging up, my own phone rang. It was Dan. He was second-guessing the recommendations received and needed validation.

5. **Enjoys the confidence of the client:** Clients confide in their lead advisor and share all relevant information: fears they have, stories they are reluctant to tell, situations that are difficult but important to resolve. If a client is more likely to confide in someone other than his or her *assigned* advisor—whether it concerns a professional change or a major life event— then that trusted advisor is the lead.

6. **Acquires additional opportunities:** The lead advisor is also the professional who receives client referrals when they happen. This last criterion is perhaps optional, as it is not uncommon for clients to reach out to the founders with their referrals even if they follow a different lead advisor in every other way.

Ideally, a lead advisor can easily check off the six items listed above. Notice that the first three criteria on the test are up to the firm or team while the last three are up to the client. The firm has the ability to determine who is responsible for recommending solutions, managing the team, and communicating changes to the engagement. However, the client has to be convinced that the assigned lead advisor is the right person to follow and trust. Let's take a look at how clients choose whom to trust.

How Clients Choose the Lead Advisor

As much as the advisory industry is fond of surveying itself, we have relatively little information about the client decision-making process, particularly when it comes to how clients choose their advisors. The best research so far in that direction was conducted by The Wharton School at the University of Pennsylvania and sponsored by State Street Global Advisors. The 2006 online survey asked 500 clients of private banks, wealth management firms, financial planners, and broker-dealers to answer questions about the process of selecting and working with an advisor. The resulting special report, *Bridging the Trust Divide: The Financial Advisor–Client Relationship*, found that when clients are choosing an advisor they overwhelmingly look for someone they can trust.

Sixty-nine percent of respondents chose trustworthiness as the most important factor they look for in a financial advisor. At a distant second, the ability to understand client needs and goals earned 20 percent of the votes. Good communication came in third with 16 percent.[2] Clearly, trust is an overwhelming factor in the client decision-making process. The question then becomes: How do clients know whom to trust?

Trust can be difficult to establish at the beginning of a client relationship, as it is something that is built up slowly over time. To find out whether an advisor is trustworthy, a client will most likely rely on reputation—particularly one they can validate. This is why so much new business in the industry is developed through referrals. By seeking a referral, clients utilize the transitive property of trust: I trust my friend, and my friend trusts her advisor, so perhaps I can trust that advisor, too.

The importance of referrals puts G2 professionals at a distinct disadvantage when getting started. Referrals usually focus on the individual advisor who led the referring relationship rather than on the firm overall. When a client works with the founder of a firm and makes a referral, a *trust credit* is deposited with the founder. If the prospective client then finds an advisor other than the founder in their first meeting, he or she will have a harder time accepting that relationship.

Following this logic, G2 professionals will be at a disadvantage when trying to initiate a relationship with a client who was referred to the founders. If they instead try to take over the client relationship once it has already been established with the firm, that may turn out to be a very difficult task as well.

Qualities of a Trusted Advisor

Earning the trust of the client is a critical but arduous task. We know from the Wharton survey that clients want a lead advisor who is knowledgeable, ethical,

---

[2]State Street Global Advisors and Knowledge@Wharton, *Bridging the Trust Divide: The Financial Advisor–Client Relationship* (2006), p. 11.

and empathetic, and who has the maturity they expect. Simply put, they want an advisor they can trust. So what are the qualities that G2 professionals need to have in order to become trusted advisors?

Knowledge

A common mistake throughout the industry is to overemphasize the social connection with the client and to neglect how important it is to impress with professional expertise. Since founders made stellar professional impressions long ago, their relationships with clients can seem very social and not particularly business-like. G2 professionals, however, have to take a different route. After you convince the client of your technical expertise, the social connection will naturally follow. This is more of an opinion than a theory or a statistic, but I believe that a client will very willingly work with an expert he never sees socially but will struggle working with a good friend who is not highly competent.

The Wharton survey shows how many advisors underestimate the importance of expertise to clients. Knowledge represents one of the biggest gaps between the values of advisors and clients. Forty-seven percent of clients responded that being knowledgeable is the first criterion for good service, while only 26 percent of advisors thought this was important to clients. Clients clearly consider knowledge to be the number-one factor for meeting their needs (47%), followed by responsiveness (15%). Advisors, on the other hand, emphasize personal rapport (38%) and responsiveness (25%) rather than knowledge.[3]

The advisory business is built on relationships, but firms often misunderstand how G2 advisors can create such a connection. Over many years of working together, advisors and clients become personally connected—their relationship becomes more like a friendship with a shift in focus from business to personal matters. This type of relationship can seem inaccessible to G2 professionals, who often feel discouraged by their inability to become the trusted advisor. After all, G2 advisors are frequently much younger than their clients and often don't move in the same social circles or share the same interests. Attempts to socialize with clients can be awkward and even counterproductive for both sides.

One of my mentors once told me, "You don't have to remember the names of your clients' kids and dogs; you just have to remember everything there is

---

[3]Ibid., 12.

to know about their business." This advice is critical for G2 professionals to understand. You don't start a relationship by trying to golf with your clients. Start it by being an absolute expert in what matters to them. Golfing will come to you later.

Professional Expertise

Expertise comprises more than education or adequate knowledge. Having professional expertise means that you have enough experience and intelligence to apply your knowledge to practice. You have to be able to impress clients beyond just making them feel safe. Many G2 advisors mistake the client's feeling safe for the client's willingness to work with them. Returning to the doctor–nurse metaphor, most patients are quite okay with a nurse providing care, but that is only because they know that the doctor is in the office. Similarly, many clients are perfectly fine meeting with G2 professionals, but they still expect that somewhere, somehow, the founder is supervising the work.

I experienced this phenomenon myself at Moss Adams. Clients were more than willing to be on a call with me, or even in a meeting, but from time to time they would ask, "How is Mark doing?" Mark was Mark Tibergien, my mentor and managing partner of our group. They also continued to copy Mark on e-mails and, even though I replied to all of the messages, they would continue to seek reassurance that Mark was still part of the engagement. As we discussed earlier in our lead advisor test, this is not what being the lead is about.

In response, I would always attempt to lead the client to at least one *aha!* moment during every conversation. In every meeting or call, I would seek to ask an important question the client had never considered, provide a new point of view or insight to change the angle on an issue, give a relevant example from my work to add understanding to the issue, or simply propose a solution that was very relevant and insightful. In other words, I wanted every client in every meeting to at least once think that I had given them some insight they did not previously have. Seeking these *aha!* moments can help G2 professionals show clients that they have the professional expertise necessary to be trusted advisors.

Demonstrating professional expertise is a much higher bar than simply meeting expectations. Clients are smart and educated people who often have significant knowledge about the topic at hand. While routine discussions, familiar questions, and general information may meet their needs and expectations, this level of service won't impress clients to the point where they will accept you as the lead advisor. You have to impress them with your knowledge and make a marked improvement on their case before they are willing to see you as more than a second chair. In some ways, you have to outshine your mentor.

Specialization

Outshining your mentor, who is often the founder of the firm, can be a daunting project. In my case, Mark Tibergien had an amazing talent for diagnosing core issues and communicating with clients. He also seemed to have worked with every firm in the industry and to know everyone. What was I to do with my five or six years of experience and less-than-polished communication style? The answer for G2 professionals is to specialize. Become the expert in an area or discipline that is very important to a group of clients and use that specialization to generate *aha!* moments.

In my career, I began by specializing in data and analysis. I became a fanatical collector of information. I made it a point to know all the statistics we generated in our reports and how they were compiled. I also gathered all the little numbers from all the engagements that we had: What is a normal referral fee? How much is a COO paid? What percentage of profits normally goes into a bonus pool? All these data points allowed me to impress clients with knowledge and get closer to the lead. Very importantly, these numbers were more than just trivia to clients. This was data and knowledge they needed.

Specialization can significantly accelerate your ability to become a trusted advisor. For example, if you specialize in working with Amazon executives as clients, you will find it much easier to assume the lead in those relationships. Likewise, specializing in working with professionals (e.g., doctors, CPAs, or dentists) will allow you to take command of those relationships and convince clients that you may be an even better person to work with than the founders, who don't have that specialization.

Time and again, I see G2 professionals who do not have any specialty. As a result, they have trouble taking the lead. If they don't specialize, their only credentials become reputation (which they don't yet have), experience (which they will always have less of than the founders), and hierarchy (where they do not hold an advantage). Ask yourself: "If I had to compete against my mentor, how would I ever win?" The answer should be obvious: "Specialize!" G2 professionals should seek a specialization area that will be productive in capturing an opportunity they see that aligns with their interests. Mentors and firms can help with that significantly. Such opportunities exist in every firm.

Presence

Presence is the ability to get the attention of participants in a meeting and direct that attention to a constructive purpose. It means getting heard and making an impression. Because presence is intangible and hard to define, it can be difficult to teach. However, it is a critical part of every client meeting and, ultimately, the client relationship. Presence is important for G2 professionals to attain in order to have success in taking the lead. Let's take a constructive approach and break down presence into its component parts:

- **Participation:** You can't make an impact in a meeting without participating. Over the years, I have seen associates who are perfectly content to silently sit in the back of the room and say little if anything during the meeting. While talking a lot can be a problem, not talking at all is always a mistake.
- **Position:** Don't fade away as soon as your mentor walks into the meeting. I once took my daughter to a teaching hospital for a doctor's appointment. The young doctor who spoke with us was very friendly, asked good questions, made a couple of very good comments, and seemed to be extremely competent. Then, a visibly older doctor walked into the room and the entire meeting changed. The younger doctor moved to a back corner and hunched over in his chair while the older doctor took a seat in the middle of the room. Before he even said a word, the hierarchy was established. The older doctor had the dominant position and his younger colleague never said another word. G2 advisors must not make the same mistake. They should remain in the center, stay in front of the client, and continue in an active seat. They must not become mere observers.
- **Body language:** If you want to have an impact on a meeting, you need to look like you belong and want to be part of that meeting. Body language that suggests that you are uncomfortable will severely undermine your credibility. I am not an expert on body language, and much has been written on the subject if you are interested in studying some of that theory. In short: Find a way to be comfortable in the meeting and project confidence.
- **Appearance:** Similar to body language, appearance has an impact on a person's perceived authority during a meeting. This is another topic that I am almost uncomfortable including, but it deserves mention. If you want clients to accept you as the lead, you need to look like you belong in the lead. This is not a style guide, but dressing up is always good policy,

even if the client or your colleagues go casual. I have never been to a client meeting wearing casual clothes, and I have never regretted the way I dressed.

Hierarchical Recognition

Clients instinctively perceive the hierarchy of the service organization and both consciously and subconsciously make decisions about whom to work with based on their understanding of who holds power. Explicit communication comes from titles and descriptions of responsibilities. Introductions such as "I run the investment committee for our firm" communicate hierarchy. As a general rule, clients will try to get the attention of the most-senior members of the team.

Some firms respond to this tendency by giving G2 professionals lofty titles, or even accelerating their career path to becoming a partner. However, such an approach produces no practical results. Clients can tell when a lead is not a lead. It will quickly become apparent to the client that another, more-senior advisor directs the engagement, and the client will seek the attention of that person. However, if an advisor is functioning well as the lead, there is no reason not to assign a title that showcases that ability. Most firms use titles such as lead advisor, lead wealth manager, or senior advisor to signal that a professional leads client engagements.

Transitioning the Lead to G2

One of the founders I work with once asked a question during a meeting that to me distilled the issue of how a G2 professional can take over a client relationship. The question was: "Should I, as a founder, step back to create space for G2s, or should G2s step in and push me away?" This is really the core of the issue. The answer is that both should happen. While the firm and its founders need to be purposeful in creating space, G2 professionals should not wait too long and create a bit of a push if necessary.

Define a Role for G2

In order for G2 professionals to have credibility with clients, they need to have a significant and well-defined role in client relationships, whether or not that role is lead advisor. Having a role in a client relationship means to be responsible for a portion of the client engagement, with that portion being visible to and accepted by the client. Examples of responsibilities include drafting and presenting a financial plan, allocating assets in a portfolio, or analyzing a private company in which the client has investments. G2 advisors should assume roles that allow them to showcase their professional skills and be seen as experts by clients.

Too often, G2 professionals are brought into client meetings without having any defined role to play. As a result, they barely participate and appear to clients as silent note-takers. Their silence undermines their credibility and presents them as people who should not be speaking much. Indeed, the lack of a defined role makes it difficult for G2 professionals to say anything at all. They often have to interrupt their partners when they want to contribute—an action that seems both overly eager and impolite.

Many firms have achieved good results by assigning a specific portion of the client meeting to the G2 advisor and letting the client know in advance of that responsibility.

Promote G2 Colleagues

The best thing an existing lead advisor can do to prepare the ground for an eventual switch of leads in a client relationship is to hype their more-junior colleagues. Comments that showcase the talents and expertise of G2 colleagues will go a long way toward convincing clients that other members of the team are credible professionals who can work independently. Naturally, the praise should be real. It does not serve any purpose to highlight expertise or knowledge that is not yet attained or complete.

Push the Envelope

When prepping G2 professionals to take over the lead in a client relationship, firms should be willing to push the envelope by giving them as much responsibility as they can handle. Pushing the envelope also requires the professional—and perhaps the client—to go out of the comfort zone. Testing the limits of how much G2 professionals can handle on their own is a great idea in theory but can be difficult to do in practice.

Many firms are reluctant to be aggressive when assigning responsibilities to junior colleagues out of fear that they are being unfair to clients. Asking less experienced professionals to handle client meetings on their own can seem like asking clients to pay the cost of training. These firms must realize that over time, clients will receive better results if they work with a team rather than just one professional. The accessibility of senior professionals will eventually deteriorate and not always match the expectations of the client. Firms have to ask themselves which is better: a highly experienced but unavailable senior professional, or an eager, talented, and highly available one who does not have a lot of experience.

Find the Right Clients

Many firms think that the best clients to transition to G2 are also the smallest. The logic is obvious: If some of these clients are lost, the firm can afford it. Unfortunately, this logic is flawed in many ways. First, often the clients transferred to G2 should not be clients at all. There is a difference between a small relationship that still meets the firm's client criteria and a relationship that should not be serviced. Delegating clients who should be let go to a G2 advisor is disheartening to the professional and does not generate any positive results for the client or the advisor.

A strategy that only delegates the smallest client relationships to G2 advisors also limits professional development. Small relationships offer very limited learning opportunities. It is difficult for a G2 professional to learn how to service a complex $50 million account when only working with $500,000 accounts. The client issues are different, and the lessons learned may not transfer well. A more productive strategy triangulates between the following three client categories:

1. **Clients who fall within the G2 professional's area of specialty:** This is the best criterion for identifying the right clients to transfer. If a firm has a G2 professional who is emerging as an expert on working with Boeing executives, then client relationships with Boeing executives are likely the best ones for the G2 to lead.
2. **Clients who already gravitate toward the G2 professional:** In any group of clients there will be some who naturally establish a good rapport with a professional. Maybe they have a similar style, share similar hobbies, or simply have schedules that match. Those clients are good candidates for transfer.
3. **Clients who present training opportunities:** Certain clients will stand out as a good training ground for new lead advisors. They either present cases that are instrumental in teaching or have the patience and willingness to work with new professionals.

Firms should prioritize these criteria when selecting the right client relationships for G2 advisors to lead in the early stages of the transition process. However, after the first couple of years of transition, as G2 advisors are progressing in their lead role, the criteria for their client relationships should converge with the firm's general criteria for accepting clients.

Resist the Temptation to Take Back Control

The biggest mistake firms make in the transition of a client relationship is giving into the temptation to rush in and take back a relationship at the first sign of trouble. After delegating a project or relationship to a junior colleague, things may start well and progress on track until an issue arises. Perhaps the previous lead receives an e-mail from the client that casts a shadow of doubt. Perhaps the client has a question that makes the mentor uncomfortable, or expresses some dissatisfaction with the work that the team delivered. The first instinct is usually to rush in and try to fix things. I have done this numerous times myself. I would review and revise reports, schedule a call with the client, and scramble to deliver more.

This kind of reaction is destructive. When you immediately take over as soon as an issue arises, you completely destroy the credibility of your team and communicate that you don't trust them to deliver your standards of quality. Should the new lead struggle, the right step is not to take back the relationship, but rather to coach: What is the best way to approach the problem? What can you do to fix the problem? What did you learn from the experience?

In many cases, you may find that new leads are perfectly capable of fixing problems on their own and do not need much help other than perhaps a little time. When they are not able to do everything on their own, your help should be behind the scenes, not in front of the client. In select cases, it may also be necessary to ask the client for some patience. To the degree that you have earned the trust of the client as a founder, you may use up some of your relationship capital to buy the new lead some confidence. Reassure the client that he or she is working with the right professional. Emphasize how much you believe in your colleague. Explain that your team is working hard to fix the issue. Your support for the team will use up some of your credibility, but that's an investment worth making.

To make client transitions possible, founders must change their mentality to one that considers having to take a client back as the worst-case scenario, even worse than losing the client. As a founder myself, I can tell you that this thought process is counterintuitive to most professionals, but it is the right approach to take if a transition is to succeed. After all, the time will come when you as a founder cannot work with any more clients. You simply won't have the capacity to do so. When that time comes, taking back a client and losing a client become one and the same. Imagine you are carrying a stack of porcelain cups in your hands, and you already have as many as you can safely carry. A new cup is introduced. Should you ask a friend to carry it, or put it on top of your tilting pile? If you add it to your stack, it is almost certain to break. Is it not better to ask a friend for help, even if the transition is a bit clumsy at first?

Set the Pace for the Transition

The transition from second chair to lead does not happen overnight. It tends to be gradual at first and then escalate. A typical schedule may be to ask a professional to take over 5 relationships in the first year, 10 to 15 in the second year, and another 30 to 40 in the third year. Notice the escalation: You want to begin slowly and monitor the results closely, but once you have established the process and the confidence of all involved, there is no reason to moderate the pace. You can go at full speed.

Training G2 professionals to take over client relationships should begin almost as soon as they reach the service advisor level. From the first day they enter into client relationships, they should begin preparing themselves to lead. I have practically never worked with a firm that had too many lead advisors. I have worked with many who didn't have enough. Successful firms teach how to lead as early as possible and try to advance professionals as often as possible. A good lead is hard to find.

CHAPTER 5

How Advisory Firms Develop New Business

Advisory firms have been growing fast over the past 20 years, and opportunities have been abundant. The typical advisory firm was founded in 1997 and had reached almost two million in revenue by 2006.[1] The last 10 years have only seen that growth accelerate. By 2016, the average revenue for independent advisory firms had reached almost four million.[2] This tremendous growth, however, has not come through regular and repeatable systems and methods.

Much of the recent growth has been driven by the personal reputations and networks of founders who will not be in the business forever and who may be difficult to replace. Older clients who are peers of the founders are also likely winding down, leaving firms at risk of shrinking if they cannot attract new business. Many clients have come from referral sources that either no longer exist or are now severely reduced. Custodian firms are no longer as generous with referrals as they once were, and accounting firms who once pointed many of their clients in the direction of advisory firms are now actively competing for the same business.

Most importantly, G2 professionals have been barely involved in this growth. Many arrived on the scene after the early stages of growth were already complete, so they lack firsthand experience in business development. Many G2 professionals were hired to service clients and promised that they would never have to *sell*. Many looked at the experience of the founders as singular, a thing of the past, much like the children of immigrants see the

---

[1] InvestmentNews Research, *Adviser Compensation & Staffing Study* (InvestmentNews, 2006).
[2] Ibid. (2016), p. 50.

experience of their parents as a fable of origins—part of history, but never to be repeated.

The most common criticism that founders have of G2 professionals is that they are *not entrepreneurial enough*. This is a masked way of saying *they don't sell*. They don't bring in new clients. Indeed, G2 has been mostly uninvolved in the growth of advisory firms. There are very few G2 professionals (i.e., nonfounders) across the industry who consistently develop new relationships on behalf of their firms. Many more have declared themselves *unable to sell* and have given up trying. Usually, their firms have accepted that G2 just doesn't have what it takes to build business.

Most of the troubles that G2 professionals face with respect to business development come from the fact that the experience of the founders is not repeatable. Let me offer a parallel: I learned to swim around the age of 8 or 9. I am not sure how I figured it out. Growing up on the beaches of the Black Sea, I played in the water nonstop. We kids—a big pack of hooligans ranging in age from 6 to 16—pushed each other, daring our friends to go deeper or jump from the keys. We did not know any exercises. We did not have any coaches. Somehow we figured it out, and I became a decent swimmer.

When my son turned 6 or 7 and I started teaching him how to swim, I really struggled. "Relax. Breathe. Move your arms and legs. Remember to come up for air!" These lessons of mine lasted a couple of years and had very little result, other than causing my son to grow frustrated with me and avoid the entire thing. When he entered high school, he joined the swim team. Within three months, he was swimming a very good crawl style. Within a year he was leaving me behind in our little beach race to the buoy.

Just as I was unable to effectively coach my son to swim, advisory firm founders have a very hard time understanding why G2 professionals cannot figure out how to bring in new business. This makes it hard to train them to do so. Founders learned how to bring clients to the firm somewhere in their history, but they were never formally coached or trained. According to the *2015 InvestmentNews Adviser Compensation & Staffing Study*, only 25 percent of all firms have a formal training program for new business development,[3] and the majority of firms rely on the founders to train younger advisors.

I really hope that I can convince G2 professionals and the firms in which they practice not only that "sales disorder syndrome" is treatable, but that it is not a condition at all. Rather, it is a misconception driven by a combination

---

[3]InvestmentNews Research, *Adviser Compensation & Staffing Study* (InvestmentNews, 2015), p. 130.

of history and the wrong approach. Let's begin by examining how and why advisory firms develop new business. Perhaps then we can find the answer for how to train it.

The Business Development Process

The business development process can be broken down into four components: lead, discovery, proposal, and contracting (Figure 5.1). A similar framework is broadly used by many professional service firms, including accounting firms and consulting firms. Let's examine each component separately as each requires a different set of skills and approach.

1. **Lead:** A lead is an instance where the firm receives an indication of interest from a prospective client and there is some form of contact that allows the firm to act on the lead. A lead can take the form of a phone call or voicemail, an e-mail, a form filled out on the website, or a conversation at an event. A lead may or may not be qualified (i.e., the person may or may not fit the firm's definition of a target client). Additionally, the person may or may not correctly understand what the firm does. As long as there is some level of interest in the firm and a way to pursue that interest, it is considered a lead.
2. **Discovery:** To pursue the lead, a firm needs to discover more about the prospective client. For discovery to happen, the lead has to show some willingness to cooperate and engage with the firm by agreeing to come to a meeting or participate in a phone call. During the discovery stage, the firm learns more about the needs of the prospective client and the

FIGURE 5.1   Process Framework for Business Development

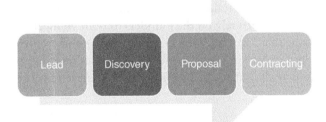

circumstances around those needs by asking questions, gathering relevant information, and examining data from past performance (e.g., account statements, plans). This is also a chance for the firm to qualify the lead: Is this the kind of case that fits our minimum requirements? How desirable is this prospective client? How much attention and resources should this lead receive?

3. **Proposal:** The firm articulates how it can help the prospective client during the proposal stage. This is a chance for the firm to describe its services, now customized to the needs of the client and positioned relative to the findings of the discovery process. For many firms, this may be a formal proposal document that details how the firm would service the client and tackle his or her needs. For other firms, the proposal is a separate meeting (after discovery) dedicated to presenting the solution. For another group of firms, the proposal is part of the discovery meeting, compressing the timeline of identifying needs and responding to them. Regardless of the form and timing, the proposal is considered a separate stage in the process, much like a doctor's office generally considers the patient exam and the drug prescription to be two different steps in a visit.

4. **Contracting:** Contracting is the closing stage of the process and the part that requires the most sales skills. Needs have been identified, and the solution has been proposed. Now is the time to finalize the logistics and price and get the client to sign the agreement so that the firm can proceed.

Many firms focus on the wrong step when training G2 professionals on business development skills. The tendency is to look at how G2 professionals can close, ignoring the reality that without a lead, a process for identifying the needs of that lead, and a proposed solution, there is nothing to close. Part of the reason firms struggle to train G2 professionals to develop new business is because the firm itself has very little process or discipline behind business development. Surveys show that 62 percent[4] of all advisory firms do not track the number of leads they generate and are therefore unlikely to have an accurate understanding of their success rate through the process.

Indeed, advisory firms are prone to overestimating their success rate at different stages of the process. Many firms claim that they close 90 percent of prospects. However, that rarely is the case. Often what happens is that

---

[4]See note 2, p. 69.

firms do not maintain accurate data on their pipeline. When asked about their success rate, they point to the last few meetings they had, which likely all led to success. In my experience, there may have been another four or five leads who never attended a meeting for every lead who agreed to come to the office.

According to the *2016 Financial Performance Study*, nearly half (46%) of leads generated by advisory firms do not become prospects.[5] In other words, they never engage with the firm. Imagine an initial phone call that never results in an appointment, or an introduction that never results in any other kind of contact. Of the remaining leads, 33 percent engage with the firm but never become clients. Fewer than one of every four leads becomes a client.

When and How Clients Act

Before any advisory firm gains a client, an individual must come to the realization that she should consider working with an advisor. Much like a gym cannot gain a new client until someone decides to take a new approach with physical fitness, an advisory firm cannot gain a new client until an investor considers making a change. Simply stated, if people do not care to exercise, gyms do not get any business. Likewise, if something does not drive investors to plan, manage, and preserve their finances and wealth, advisory firms do not attract clients.

The problem with the strategy of most advisory firms is that it is very passive. Firms wait for potential clients to decide to do something and then depend on the unreliable process of existing clients and centers of influence providing a positive reference. This passive strategy combines a low-probability event with an unpredictable outcome.

To be successful, firms need to be proactive. This means they must find a way to drive consumers to the realization that they need an advisor, and then have a method of communicating the firm's value to prospective clients who are convinced that they need a solution. Such strategies include the following:

- **Identify and work with client apostles:** These are the clients who will go out of their way to tell others about what you do.

---

[5] Ibid.

- **Focus on events and niche areas of service that drive action:** Examples include divorces, marriages, sales of businesses, and job changes.
- **Publish and otherwise spread a proactive message:** Disseminating your message through articles, podcasts, websites, and other tools can educate consumers to act on their situations by showing that solutions are available.
- **Position the firm as the center of advice:** Market the firm as a superior solution with a community atmosphere, where referring and recruiting others is part of the culture. I own, together with a partner, a small boxing gym in Seattle. The gym is very much a community, not just a place to exercise, and we notice how people go out of their way to bring their friends and colleagues. To have this effect, though, you have to start with a sincere desire to create a community. You can't fake it just because you want to get more referrals.

The Good-Intentions Prospect

Instead of employing proactive strategies, many firms rely on clients to initiate the process. As we will see, that rarely happens. Most prospective clients fall into the category of the *good-intentions prospect*. These are individuals who have never had an advisor but realize that they should consider working with one. That realization may carry a different sense of urgency depending on the prospect: Some prospective clients undertake an energetic search, actively seeking out the names of potential advisors. Others are more passive and do not put much energy into the search beyond making a few casual mentions to friends.

Exercise gyms are very familiar with these good-intentions prospects. They are known as *January clients*, showing up on January 3 with their New Year's resolution, a brand-new pair of running shoes, and a neon-colored jersey. They return on January 4 and 5, once more on January 24, and then never again until the next year. At my gym we do three times more business in January than any other month of the year.

Such prospects lack motivation, which presents a particular problem in the advisory industry. While it is easy join a gym, as they are relatively low cost and widely abundant, most people who intend to do something about their finances rarely take action. Few ask their friends for names of advisors, and even those who do seek referrals do not always call and set up an appointment. Consider doctors, for example. Ask yourself: How often has someone asked you to recommend a doctor? I have personally never heard that question.

Even though I really like my doctor, I have not made a single referral to him. A passive strategy creates very few opportunities to attract this type of prospect and move the prospect forward in the process.

The Proactive Prospect

There are also cases where the potential client is more proactive. Some prospects come to advisors with an urgent need. In such *event cases*, prospective clients have a higher sense of urgency and their criteria for selecting an advisor may be more specific and better developed. Depending on the nature of the event, the prospect is more likely to seek and compare options for an advisor. Such event cases are relatively rare but have significant relevance to niche practices. Examples include receiving an inheritance, divorcing, or selling a business.

Event cases are well served when the advisor also takes a proactive approach. While the event itself tends to drive the prospective client to action, there are usually centers of activity that advisors can use to proactively seek out such clients. For example, a business owner who is selling a business most likely works with a CPA and an attorney. This person is also likely to have used an investment banker. Finally, some business sales are announced in press releases. Proactive firms can use that as a reason to contact potential clients.

Another type of proactive prospect is the *unhappy client*. Unhappy clients are not satisfied with their current advisor and are looking to change firms. The cause of dissatisfaction varies and may include disappointing investment returns, slow responsiveness from the advisor, or a poor fit in communications style between the advisor and the client. Unhappy clients are likely to be more proactive in their search and gather more information on advisors. However, research suggests that only 3 to 5 percent of clients are unhappy with their advisors, and not all unhappy clients act on their unhappiness.[6]

The Curious Prospect

Finally, there are prospective clients who are already working with an advisor and are generally satisfied with their relationship, but who would change to

---

[6]Advisor Impact, "The Rules of Engagement," February 2013. Accessed April 16, 2017, from http://iiac.ca/wp-content/uploads/The-Rules-of-Engagement.pdf.

another firm if they discovered a new, interesting, and perhaps better way of tackling their financial lives. Many people who joined the CrossFit movement belonged to other gyms where they were regular, happy members. However, they were lured away by the novel approach of CrossFit gyms.

It is worth pointing out that the CrossFit methodology not only demonstrates great results for those who join, but also fosters a culture of community. This cult-like following encourages members to advocate for their gym. People go out of their way to tell their friends about their amazing progress and experience. As a result, CrossFit gyms have seen a quick and dramatic growth in membership. This is perhaps the kind of environment that advisory firms should replicate.

Existing Clients as a Referral Source

Regardless of what drives their intentions, most clients find an advisory firm through recommendations from trusted friends. This natural referral process is the lifeblood of the profession. Without it, the majority of firms would lose their ability to grow. The importance of the referral process cannot be exaggerated. According to the *2012 InvestmentNews* survey, 50 percent of new clients join firms through referrals from existing clients.[7]

Referrals from professionals such as attorneys and accountants are the second-leading source of new clients, contributing 17 percent of the total. Further behind, other sources of new clients include community involvement of professionals (8% of new clients), efforts of professional business developers (5%), community branding (4%), and Internet presence (3%). In other words, the propensity of existing clients to refer new clients to the firm may define the ability of the firm to grow. Similarly, the effectiveness of G2 professionals to develop new business may be tied to their ability to receive the recommendation of their clients.

There is a powerful reason why referrals are the best source of new client relationships. When clients choose an advisor, trustworthiness is the number-one criterion.[8] They are looking for an advisor they can trust with

---

[7]Matt Sirinides, "Most Advisory Firms Don't Have a Strategy for Landing Client Referrals," InvestmentNews, December 15, 2014. Accessed April 16, 2017, from http://www.investmentnews.com/article/20141215/BLOG18/141219955/most-advisory-firms-dont-have-a-strategy-for-landing-client-referrals.

[8]State Street Global Advisors and Knowledge@Wharton, *Bridging the Trust Divide*, p. 11.

their financial plan, someone who will help them protect the wealth they have created and want to preserve for themselves and their families. While trust is a logical criterion, it is also difficult to observe and scrutinize from the outside. Trust is something that happens much later in a relationship—a sense that develops after years of working together—and it is not easy to perform due diligence on such an abstract concept. Asking questions such as "Can I trust you?" or "Would you say you are trustworthy?" is not a very good strategy.

When prospective clients are trying to establish whom they can trust, they turn to people they themselves trust. This is the transitive property of trust:

If I trust you and you trust them, then I can trust them, too.

If $A = B$ and $B = C$, then $A = C$.

When a firm wants professionals to develop new business, it seems logical to begin with existing clients. Most of the time, however, firms do exactly the opposite. They ask G2 professionals to look outside of the firm for new clients rather than seeking ways to connect with existing clients on the inside. This fundamental disconnect between reality and intentions is the source of mutual frustration between the founders and the second generation. While G2 professionals are often victims of this poor business development strategy, they must also take responsibility for a very real problem: *If most new clients come from existing client referrals, how can someone be a very good service person but not a good business developer?*

Some Theories about Referrals

Referrals are vital to the growth of the advisory industry. As a result, much has been written on the subject, including the best way to entice clients to make a referral and perhaps accelerate them to do so. If happy clients refer their friends, relatives, and colleagues to the firm, how can someone be good at making clients happy but not good at getting referrals? There are several potential hypotheses worth examining here:

- Clients would refer new prospects, but the advisor never asks.
- Clients are not really happy; they are just content.
- Clients are simply not coming across opportunities to make referrals.

- Clients are actually making referrals, but the advisor is failing to capture them.
- Clients are passing on the story of the firm, but it is not resonating.

Each of these potential explanations is worth a look and a discussion of its own. I would like to review some of the many theories circulating, because each provides a possible answer to the question we asked above.

Stop Asking for Referrals

To begin with, let's dispense with a dangerous urban legend that exists in the advisory industry: Clients would refer more if you were only to ask them, or ask them in a certain way. I receive many e-mails from advisors whose signatures include something like "Referring your friends is the greatest compliment to our practice!" or "We are looking to grow our business and service more people like you!" I personally find these messages to be off-putting and awkward. I also doubt that they are ever effective.

The theory that an advisor must only ask nicely for a referral in order to get one is flawed. Whether it's phrased, "Can you recommend five people I should talk to?" or "We are looking to grow our business with great clients like you!" the result is the same. Clients become uncomfortable and may even be more guarded about referring than they would have been otherwise.

Steve Wershing, a practice management and marketing expert working in the financial advisory industry, wrote a book called *Stop Asking for Referrals*. Steve argues that asking for a referral is a great way to make clients feel defensive and awkward while achieving no result. Instead, if advisors want to receive referrals, they need to differentiate themselves and do more than just serve clients.

Social Capital

In *The World Until Yesterday*, the famous anthropologist, Jared Diamond, describes how tribes in New Guinea trade items with each other that they already own.[9] One tribe may trade vegetables to another tribe for tools, but this does not mean they do not already have access to similar tools.

---

[9] Jared Diamond, *The World Until Yesterday* (New York: Penguin Books, 2013).

Rather, they trade in order to enhance and build a relationship with the other tribe that may prove useful in hard times.

Similarly, we make referrals because they create social capital. Investing in our network and social standing makes us feel good about our position in society and can perhaps provide us with help when we need it. Referrals are fairly easy to make when someone asks us for one: Do you know of a good hotel in Bulgaria? However, making a referral without being prompted by a question is another matter. The things we promote without being asked are usually the same things that reflect very positively on us. For example, I might promote:

- My boxing gym (translation: Hey! I am a boxer!)
- A quaint little hotel or restaurant (translation: Hey! I am in the know!)
- A ski or wilderness experience (translation: Hey! I am adventurous!)

To entice clients to be more proactive with their referrals, a firm should try to create the same positive correlation. Clients need a reason to tell the story of the firm without even being asked.

Raving Fans

In *Raving Fans: A Revolutionary Approach to Customer Service*, Ken Blanchard and Sheldon Bowles provide an explanation for why clients sometimes go out of their way to make referrals and other times seem very passive in that regard. The authors argue that you cannot simply meet client expectations if you want to have a great relationship—you must exceed them. Exceeding expectations turns clients into "raving fans" who will promote your firm and its services to their social network.[10]

Sam Allred, who specializes in working with the next generation of partners in accounting firms, has a great story that exemplifies how exceeding expectations creates raving fans. A chef in a restaurant learns that one of the guests has numerous food allergies. He makes his way out of the kitchen, walks over to the table, and simply asks, "Susan, what would you like to have for dinner tonight?" He then proceeds to cook a delicious dinner (off the menu) for the guest and her party. Needless to say, the lady and her friends will likely rave about the chef and his restaurant to many others.

---

[10] Ken Blanchard and Sheldon Bowles, *Raving Fans: A Revolutionary Approach to Customer Service* (New York: William Morrow & Co., 1993).

Find Your Apostles

According to research from client feedback expert Julie Littlechild, 29 percent of clients make referrals to their advisors.[11] The number of referrals made per client, however, is not consistent. Some clients may refer once over the course of 10 years while others may refer two or three relationships every year. I'll refer to the latter type of client as an *apostle*; every practice has them.

Apostles are clients who go out of their way to tell everyone about their advisor. These advocates have much in common with the raving fan, but they also have another characteristic: a wide network of high-quality contacts that they are willing to share. Usually, apostles are successful people who themselves understand the importance of building quality relationships. They are very active in creating such connections for themselves and are open to sharing them with others. They are not always extroverted busy-bees. On the contrary, some may be rather quiet professionals, but they listen carefully and take interest in what is going on.

The client you want is not just name dropping all the time. Rather, apostles have a genuine curiosity about you and your practice and want to know more. That kind of person is also likely to know high-quality potential clients and be willing to share that network with you.

Playing Telephone

When we were kids, we used to amuse ourselves with the game of telephone. Everyone sat down in a line, and the first person whispered a word to the next person in line. That person then passed it to their right, and so on, until the word emerged on the other end. As it traveled down the line, passed from one person to the next, the word inevitably became distorted. A simple word like *crocodile* emerged on the other end as *textile* or *turnstile*. The same thing happens to marketing messages. As they pass from one person to another, they change and sometimes become unrecognizable.

I observed this phenomenon frequently at my former firm, Fusion Advisor Network. When I asked new clients who joined us what they had heard about the firm from those who had referred them, the message was far removed from what I thought it would be. For example, one client said that

---

[11] See note 6.

she was told we were a Seattle-based firm that had good marketing services. In reality, we just had a small office in Seattle (where I worked), and we had subcontracted a marketing expert to work with that advisor, but it was not an area of specialty for us. This is analogous to how a person who orders fish at a steakhouse may describe it as a seafood place.

Your marketing message will probably become distorted as clients pass it along to their acquaintances. To preserve the message, you need to train clients to deliver it. A simple and memorable statement can help clients accurately describe your firm.

The Reciprocity Principle

Finally, there is the *reciprocity principle*, which dictates that when we receive something, we instinctively look to give something back. The reciprocity principle is well known in social psychology and is wonderfully explained by Robert Cialdini in his book, *Influence: The Psychology of Persuasion*. Following the reciprocity principle, if we want to receive referrals, we should make some referrals, too.

Other Referral Sources

To summarize the last section, if we want to help G2 professionals generate more client referrals, we need to train them on how to create raving fan relationships, recognize their apostles and spend more time with them, create stories that clients can tell, and teach clients to communicate those stories. But clients are not the only source of referrals. Firms also receive leads from accountants, attorneys, and other professionals. As previously mentioned, 17 percent of all leads come from this kind of professional referral.[12] Of those, accountants and attorneys are almost equal in their value as referral sources. Other sources of professional referral are more rare.

It is worth noting that many of the largest firms in the industry have at one time or another in their history benefited from the referral network of a custodian. The retail branches of the custodians (e.g., Schwab, Fidelity, and TD) have referred hundreds of thousands of clients to independent firms. In fact, if we were to examine the list of billion-dollar firms in the country, we

---

[12]See note 7.

would likely find that more than half are or were at one time beneficiaries of custodian referrals.

With professional referrals, my experience has been that deeper is always better than broader. In other words, being closely aligned with one good source of referrals is a much better strategy than having more superficial relationships with 20 firms.

Beyond Referrals

Advisory firms have very few ideas of how to market themselves beyond referrals. The most commonly used methods are community involvement and nonprofit board participation. According to the *2016 InvestmentNews* survey, 65 percent of firms are active in the community and 57 percent volunteer on nonprofit boards.[13] However, only one-third of firms that use these methods consider them to be either very successful or extremely successful. The majority consider these methods to be only moderately or slightly successful. Similar results are achieved by another traditional industry staple: sponsorships. Forty-one percent of firms use sponsorships with most firms considering the strategy to be moderately successful.[14]

Very few firms are actually generating content such as articles or podcasts. However, when firms do employ a proactive, content-based marketing strategy, many have success. The power of content is not only that it steers good-intentions prospects to the firm after they have chosen to act, but also that the content can itself drive clients to act. In other words, a good article may not just provide a name to someone already searching for a firm; it can also drive someone into action who was still on the fence.

The Simple Mathematics of Reputation-based Selling

Having examined all the different components of the business development process, we can now construct a very simplistic mathematical model of how a firm develops new business:

Probability of gaining a new client = Stage 1 × Stage 2 × Stage 3 × Stage 4

---

[13] See note 2, p. 70.
[14] Ibid.

where:

Stage 1 is the probability of a prospect recognizing a desire to change.
Demographic circumstances such as age, children, etc.; others (advocates)
urging action or giving example; local economics; overall economy;
markets; legal environment; extraordinary events; overall reputation of
the industry

Stage 2 is the probability that a prospect received the name of the firm.
Marketing; online presence; community involvement; client referrals;
professional referrals

Stage 3 is the probability that the prospect receives favorable information from the firm.
Reputation; branding; online presence; collateral

Stage 4 is the probability that the firm presents itself well.
Business development meeting; proposals; sales skills

Think of each stage as a collection of levers that you can use. Using only
one lever will get you some results, but the best outcomes come from acting
on all four stages.

Principles of Business Development

We set out on this examination of business development theory and practice
with the intention of identifying principles that can help G2 professionals be
more effective business developers. Based on our discussion, these principles
are as follows:

1. **Begin with existing clients:** Learn to impress clients to the point where
   they are ready to provide your name in response to a good-intentions query
   (e.g., "Do you know an advisor?").
2. **Cultivate apostles:** Apostles will go out of their way to tell your story on
   your behalf. Identify which clients are your apostles, and find a way to
   create close relationships with them.
3. **Be an expert:** This is a badly overlooked principle. Many people focus on
   the social aspect of business development, as if it is all wining, dining, and
   golf. But as advisors, we work with people who can easily afford their own
   wine and golfballs. Focus instead on having something to say.

4. **Create content:** Content not only provides your name to prospects, but also primes the pipe by driving consumers to action.
5. **Get to know a lot of people, and get a lot of people to know you:** Reputation enhances the probability of success at Stage 2.
6. **Help your firm's marketing committee:** This will greatly increase the chances that those who are interested in the firm are encouraged to make contact.

Advisory firms have grown on the strength of demand and a wave of demographic factors. Founders have intuitively found the right way to create new relationships and get very good at business development through experience. G2 professionals have to find their own way to contribute. The next chapter will describe a productive strategy for doing just that.

CHAPTER 6

Be a Business Developer

The first time I went skiing I was 34 years old. My 9-year-old son expressed an interest in learning and, though I was perhaps a bit old to pick up a new skill, I did not want to miss the chance to ski with him. Growing up on the beaches of the Black Sea, I had not had many opportunities to hit the slopes. Still, if he was going to learn, perhaps we could take lessons together.

That first season of skiing was nothing but frustration and disappointment. Here I was, a grown man, tumbling down the mountain, snow in my pants, contorted into some of the most grotesque and humiliating positions you can imagine. I watched helplessly as my son quickly surpassed me in skill level. All I had to show at the end of the season was a pair of poles bent out of shape from falling all the time.

It would have been easy to quit at this point. All the reasons were there. "I am too old to learn. I could suffer all kinds of injuries to my limbs (and my pride). Perhaps I am just not meant for it. I am very good at other things, so why not stick to what I am good at and leave skiing to those who have the gift for it?" But I stayed with it and I'm glad I did. Had I quit, I would have missed out on some of the most amazing experiences of my life: countless hours spent on the lift talking to my son, the amazing slopes and unforgettable trips we shared, the first time we skied a double black diamond (a minor navigation mistake of mine).

Today skiing is one of my favorite things to do, and I now enjoy skiing with my daughter, who was just a baby when I started skiing. The point of this story is that when we try something new for the first time, we struggle and the temptation to quit can be powerful. We look for reasons to quit and willingly embrace them rather than continuing the struggle through another season. But struggle we must. Many new activities begin with frustration, but once we get good at something, we usually can't have enough. Business development is no different.

So many professionals find their early business development efforts plagued with discomfort and a lack of results. As a result, they quit and never go back to trying. At the beginning, it may feel like they are not meant for this kind of work and that any further attempts will generate nothing more but painful memories. If this has happened or is happening to you, resist the temptation to quit. Business development is a skill that everyone can learn, and as you improve you will find that you enjoy the activity. There are a few things you need to do to become a good business developer:

- Find a good mentor.
- Develop specialized expertise.
- Devote enough time.
- Approach the process with discipline.

If you stick with it, it won't be long before you are able to contribute substantially to business development.

The Four Stages of Learning to Develop New Business

Reflecting on my personal experience, I think there are four stages I went through before I experienced any success in growing a practice:

1. **Frustrating trial and error:** Like many young professionals, I tried to get involved in business development early on. Not knowing exactly how to go about it, my efforts followed what seemed to be the most obvious path: networking. I attended meetings and conferences, awkwardly looking for a way to pass my business card to people and get theirs in return. The result was a stack of business cards from accountants and CPAs who were also looking to develop new contacts. Rarely would I meet qualified prospects and, when I did, I had little to say that would catch their interest. This was quite discouraging, and I was quite ready to give up.
2. **Working with a mentor:** My attitude to business development changed when I found my mentors. One of the best ways to learn is by observing experienced professionals in action and participating alongside them in meetings. Following their example taught me how to approach the business development process, enabling me to participate constructively in the conversation. Finding a good mentor should be the first step for you, too.
3. **Managing a proposal process:** I eventually became responsible for the proposal process, which is simply the process of turning a conversation

about the needs of a client into an actual contract for working together. I was not yet responsible for generating leads, but once my partners identified a lead and, perhaps, had an initial conversation with the potential client, it was my responsibility to describe our services and propose a work plan and budget. Helping your more experienced colleagues turn leads into client engagements is good preparation for the more difficult task of generating leads.

4. **Generating leads:** Generating leads is the most difficult part of developing new business. It requires a reputation, which takes a long time to build. You must find your own *distribution channels*. You can build a reputation more quickly when your expertise is narrower. Focusing on a specialization or niche will suggest natural channels to spread your message while generalists may require many years to establish themselves.

Part of the reluctance we all have to participate in business development comes from the perception that it is a *dirty job* that involves tricking people into buying things they don't need or want. If this is how you see business development, it's no wonder you struggle to find enthusiasm for it. It's better to think of business development in terms of a puzzle.

Solving a Puzzle

Business development is like finding the solution to a puzzle. To extend the metaphor, business development is nothing more than a diagnostic process. Think about those medical shows where a doctor is trying to figure out what is wrong with a patient. The patient has familiar symptoms, but perhaps the typical medicine does not work. There are different treatment possibilities depending on the diagnosis and each patient's individual case. Which option is the best?

In business development, the client is the patient. Clients need your help, and it is your job to figure out how to help them. Your advice is the treatment, the proposed solution for something that is bothering a family, an individual, or a business. Much like medical advice, financial advice is not a discretionary luxury item that a consumer may or may not need. All consumers need it—some more acutely than others. The earlier consumers receive advice, the less likely they are to face a financial emergency.

The intention here is not to provide a *rah-rah* speech to motivate you to engage in business development. Rather, I want you to change your frame of thinking. If you believe what you do is valuable and that you are truly able to help people with their needs, then business development is nothing more than a way of helping someone. If you don't believe you help people and that people need you, then you are not in the right career in the first place. The notion of business development as a diagnostic process is very intriguing, but it may be difficult for you to learn that approach on your own. Look for a mentor who can teach by example and give you opportunities to be involved in the process.

Finding Your Mentor

My mentors in business development were two of the partners in Moss Adams: Mark Tibergien and Ed Drosdick. Mark was the head of the consulting division at Moss Adams and the leading expert on practice management for financial advisors. Ed was the head of the firm's technology practice and one of the more-senior partners. While they did not work together, they used a similar approach to business development. They were also both remarkably successful at creating new relationships on behalf of the firm.

Both Ed and Mark regularly took me along on business development missions. Sometimes it was lunch with a prospective client. Other times it was a phone call or a meeting at their office. Occasionally we met with an existing client who potentially had a new project. I got the chance to experience many different situations and to learn firsthand how Mark and Ed approached business development. More importantly, I got the chance to participate and contribute. That really helped me build confidence.

Having a good mentor is the difference between learning to ski on your own and having a good ski instructor. A good mentor provides you with a learning process, opportunities to practice, and introductions to future sources of new leads. It can be difficult to identify the right mentor. I was lucky to find mentors who proactively took on the task of coaching young professionals, but the choice is not always so obvious. There may not be anyone at your firm who is known for coaching others.

The right mentor is not necessarily a rainmaker. Rather, a good business developer is simply someone who successfully and systematically attracts new clients to the firm. What you are looking to absorb from your mentor is:

- An understanding of how to approach a meeting
- A sense of how to generate leads to pursue
- A strategy for working with prospective clients
- A process you can follow
- Chances to practice

Begin by identifying the best business developers at your firm and seek out their attention. Even if they don't see themselves as mentors, they may not be opposed to the idea of bringing others along on their new business activities. An offer to help with preparation, materials, or follow-up may be your ticket to the next prospect meeting or conference. Most people want to share what they do with others. Chances are that if you reach out, your request will not be turned down.

Learning to Ask Questions and Listen

There is a natural tendency to see a business development meeting as a stage for showcasing what we do and how we do it. It is easy to spend most of the meeting in a nervous outburst of information, trying to impress and convince the client. My mentors, however, took the opposite approach. They spent most of the meeting—sometimes all of the meeting—asking questions and intently focusing on the client's responses.

Business development meetings are your chance to learn everything there is to know about prospects. Who are they? Who is in their family? What are the relationships like within the family? What do they do? How is their career or business progressing? Does it bring them satisfaction? Is it stressful? What do they dream about in the next 5, 10, or 20 years? What keeps them awake at night? Chances are you know the right questions to ask, so ask them.

Asking questions in a prospect meeting should not only give you good knowledge about the client, but also steer the client toward potential solutions. Imagine you are playing the game Twenty Questions. All questions have *yes* or *no* as an answer. A good prospect meeting should be a lot like that game. Gradually but surely, you should be able to narrow down the field and identify what the client needs.

Not every prospect arrives at an advisory firm with a problem, so it can be easy to stray away from this kind of diagnostic thinking. That said, in any conversation I have with a potential client, I ask myself the following questions:

- What is this person experiencing that she wishes to change?
- What keeps this client awake at night? What does he worry about?
- What prompted him or her to act? Why did he or she choose to come to this meeting today and not a year ago or next year?

The answers to these questions are not always obvious. Clients may not know or fully recognize what bothers them. Approaching the same issue from two different angles is a good way to dig deeper. In most client interviews, I hope to ask an *aha!* question that digs to the heart of the matter and leads the client to some clarity or realization. Perhaps it is a question no one has asked before. Sometimes such questions are offered by prospects themselves. If not, keep asking yourself throughout the interview: What is missing here? What is something she may not have considered? What is an issue she may not have recognized is important?

A good interview should also reveal your knowledge of the field. The questions should be structured and well ordered, and they should show your understanding of the case. This is how you can showcase what you do. A long speech about your experience working with technology executives is not nearly as effective as a thoughtful question like: "It has been my experience working with technology executives that when they have this issue, they also have this other problem. Is that, perhaps, the case with you?"

Finally, a good interview will also tell you how to propose to the client. Clients will generally tell you how they want to work and interact with a professional. They will also give you their goals and their timeline. Clarify these key elements and reiterate them in the language of your firm's process and services. Many of the prospect meetings I attended with my mentors ended without us ever talking about our firm, our process, or our fees. Often, Ed or Mark would simply ask: "When would you like us to begin?"

Finding Your Specialty

Participating in business development meetings held by experienced professionals proved invaluable to me not only because I could observe their approach, but also because I could participate. Participation gives you the chance to practice and build your confidence. It also gives you the opportunity to find your role. Ideally, your role is constructive and contributes to the overall success of the meeting. To have such a role, you may consider specializing in something that is an important part of the client relationship.

It is much easier to define a role for a professional who is specialized. Specialization immediately builds credibility and gives your presence in the meeting a constructive purpose. Instead of clients seeing you as just a junior professional who is there to take notes, they see you as someone who is bringing an important skill and knowledge. For example, my mentors introduced my participation in meetings by saying, "I asked Philip to join us because he specializes in financial analysis and statistics." There are many areas for potential specialization. You should look for an area of specialization that meets the following qualifications:

- You are good at it and very interested.
- You are either an expert or can develop expertise relatively quickly. Being a fake expert does not do any good for your clients or your reputation.
- The firm needs more expertise in the area. You can complement your more-senior colleagues and supply them with knowledge or expertise they are lacking.
- It is very relevant to clients. There is no practical use in being an expert in an area of obscure knowledge in which clients have no interest.

One example of a specialization is the financial analysis and valuation of businesses. It always amazes me that many financial advisory firms claim expertise in working with business owners but never ask for any of the business information. What if you could perform benchmarking and financial analysis on the businesses of all the firm's prospective business-owner clients?

Alternatively, if your firm draws clients from large corporations, you could gain a deep understanding of stock options and other compensatory instruments. Specializing in these instruments—their rules, vesting, taxation, and ways to exercise them—could make you very valuable to corporate clients.

A more generic example of an area of specialization is healthcare expenses and healthcare options as part of a financial plan. All financial plans contain some healthcare component, and the analysis of options is very important and also perhaps beyond the knowledge of the typical advisor. Regardless of the specialization you choose, the idea is to be an expert and to use that expertise to create credibility at a time when you are not yet able to say, "I have been doing this for 15 years."

Developing a Niche

Niche-specialization is one of the fastest ways to build your business development skills and create opportunities for your firm. A niche market is a group of clients who have specific needs that are either poorly addressed or overlooked by generic planning and advice. While most firms may be able to service or cater to that market, a niche-specialized firm or professional will have a demonstrably superior approach and solution that clients quickly recognize as better suited to their needs. Even if your firm has a more generic competitive strategy, your personal niche-specialization can fit well within the overall firm strategy and will significantly accelerate your success rate.

Focusing your efforts on a niche market allows you to fully understand the clients with whom you work and how they make decisions. It also allows you to build a specific, practical plan to market to prospective clients rather than trying to appeal to a very broad universe. Finally, it helps you stand out from generic advisors who may be targeting the same group of clients.

A niche strategy can also shorten the time needed to generate leads on your own. In my experience, a more generic approach requires a successful career of at least 10 to 15 years at a reputable firm before you find yourself in a position where you can consistently develop opportunities. With a focused approach, that period can be shortened to between 7 and 10 years. Of course, for a niche strategy to be effective, you need to start with a good niche.

Identifying a Good Niche

The success of a niche strategy largely depends on the attractiveness of the niche. Becoming the foremost expert in a niche that is either too small or not yielding desirable clients is counterproductive. You should consider the following criteria when choosing a niche:

- **Passion and interest:** Everything in life and in business works better if you have passion and enthusiasm for it. Whatever the market potential of the niche, whatever the wealth and opportunity in it, you will always achieve more success by pursuing something you are sincerely interested in rather than faking interest in something you don't care about. Even if it seems that all the lucrative clients are on the golf course or the boards of nonprofit organizations, resist the temptation to go there unless you are an avid golfer or passionate about the charitable cause.

  Pursuing a niche market will take time away from the office and away from your family. It will require countless learning about the trends and dynamics that influence the niche. All of that is better achieved when you look for a niche where your normal interests intersect with your professional needs. I know many miserable golfers who regret their club memberships. Find something that allows you to meet interesting people and don't worry too much about whether they have money.
- **Presence and existing knowledge:** In many cases, your firm may already have a significant presence in your preferred niche. There could be several clients who are part of the niche that already work with your firm. There could even be another professional who already specializes in the niche.

You don't have to start from scratch. Leveraging the experience and expertise of your firm will give you a great start and accelerate your strategy.

- **Uniqueness:** The more unique the needs of a niche, the more important it is to specialize in it and the less the threat of generic substitution. Unique needs are key, not necessarily unique characteristics. For example, *Bulgarian business owners* sounds like a unique niche, but it's not really because this group is likely to have the same needs as other business owners. Business owners, however, have very different needs from corporate executives. The more unique the needs of a particular niche, the more fruitful and sustainable the specialization.

- **Growth and opportunity in the niche:** Look around your local market at the industries or other dynamics that are creating new wealth. Which sectors are growing and seem to be full of opportunity? Where is the local marketplace going? Growth isn't typically found at the golf course, where retirees gather to sip scotch. Instead, look for active people who wake up at 5 A.M. to do *important* things. These people are more likely to lead you to long-term success because they are the ones creating the future.

- **Competitiveness:** The most attractive niches may be highly coveted by other firms who are already well established in the market. For example, *business owners who have sold their businesses* is a niche with unique needs, but it is also a very crowded space. The same is true for niches such as *women who are in the process of divorcing*. There are thousands of professionals and firms pursuing this niche. The same goes for the *large and successful corporations*.

  A perfect niche is one that has not yet been noticed. It may be up and coming but still unnoticed due to forces that are purely local, such as industries or businesses specific to your area. It could also be due to trends that are not yet well established but have the potential to become a major part of the future discussion. For example, if you were starting a practice in Seattle, you might forgo the more obvious niche of *Microsoft or Amazon executives* and instead focus on the rich ecosystem of biotech companies that continue to grow and receive funding. This niche is not yet in the bull's-eye of Seattle's large firms and the growth potential is enormous.

- **Fulcrum:** A good niche allows you to leverage your marketing efforts. Is there a point of contact within the niche that acts like the fulcrum to a lever, allowing you to magnify your initiatives? For example, when Moss Adams was building its reputation in the financial services industry, this fulcrum point was the Financial Planning Association (FPA). The FPA provided a forum for many of its early practice management presentations, and the FPA study conducted by Moss Adams was the first benchmarking study in the industry. The ability to reach thousands of advisors who were all potential clients greatly magnified the firm's ability to reach its target market.

Typical points of leverage in the advisory industry include:

- Industry associations (especially for business owners)
- Leadership training and professional development groups (e.g., for business executives)
- Professional societies (e.g., for doctors, dentists, or CPAs)
- Specialized professionals (such as divorce attorneys, business brokers and investment bankers, royalty compliance accountants, and business valuation experts)
- Publications (both traditional and online)

Different niches have their own influencers and places where they congregate. Finding those points of leverage is part of your niche research. The best way to understand a niche is to follow those who are already part of it. An existing client or a colleague can be an invaluable resource, providing you with guidance on the best places to gather knowledge and meet influencers.

Create a scorecard based on the factors above to compare potential niches. The resulting balanced scorecard may suggest the best niche to pursue. While a firm can pursue multiple niches with success, you, personally, should focus your energy on only one niche. After all, if you specialize in a dozen niches, are you really specialized?

Understanding Unique Needs

As we already discussed, a niche is defined by its unique needs. Your efforts to build niche expertise should focus on identifying those unique needs and developing unique solutions. Take business owners as an example. The majority of the wealth of business owners is not liquid, but rather held within the businesses they own. Many firms understand this lack of liquidity but many do almost nothing to work with the resulting unique needs. Instead, they simply wait for the business to create liquidity. For wealth managers to work effectively with business owners, they need to understand the P&L, valuation, and vision for that company, as well as trends in the industry that affect it. A wealth manager who works with business owners should perhaps be thinking like a business consultant, not an investment advisor.

Issues that create unique needs also create opportunities for you to quickly develop expertise and credibility. Not many other advisors will know what you know, even if they have more experience in general. For example, Christopher Street Financial in New York specializes in working with gay and lesbian couples and supporters of the LGBT community. CEO Jennifer Hatch and her colleagues provide strategies to help couples who might otherwise not be well suited for the generic financial planning process to build their financial lives.

While unique needs can and should be researched from the outside when you are choosing a niche, the ever-important nuances will become clearer after you dive headfirst into the niche. The deeper your knowledge of the niche, the better your ability to structure unique solutions and the more compelling your specialized expertise.

Finding the Point of Leverage

A good business development strategy should yield a consistent flow of new leads rather than opportunistic, one-at-a-time chances. To create such a consistent flow, you need to find a source of leads that creates exposure systematically rather than by happenstance. Such points of leverage vary from niche to niche, but here are some of the more typical ideas that come to mind:

- **Industry associations** can be great places to meet the leaders of specific types of businesses. If your niche is business owners within a specific industry or broader sector, the industry association can be a great source of opportunities. It may be a particularly fruitful source if your geographic area has many businesses of a certain kind.
- **Large companies and their internal training programs** offer another source of leverage. Many large corporations systematically expose their executives and employees to training programs. Becoming a trainer or presenter at such meetings can expose you to a large number of the executives and employees of the company.
- **Universities and their business centers** can be a great place to meet business owners and entrepreneurs who are just starting out.
- **Venture groups, angel funding groups, and other startup groups** can be a fantastic way to meet some of the most innovative entrepreneurs in your area as well as the entire ecosystem of consultants, CPAs, and attorneys who work with them.
- **Continued professional education forums** can give you great leverage in meeting doctors, dentists, CPAs, attorneys, and others. Many of these professions have tracks in practice management and financial management that may pair nicely with your expertise in setting up retirement plans or in general managing the finances of the professional practice.

- **Leadership development programs** will put you together with other young executives and business owners who are getting ready to take the wheel of their respective organizations.
- **Specialized consulting or accounting firms** may focus on the same niche as you and perhaps already have a significant reputation in the niche. It is not unusual for such firms to seek alliances with similarly specialized advisors who can speak to the issues in the niche and are knowledgeable on the challenges that the niche faces.

Most of the avenues for leverage described above pertain to the business market and tend to describe niches based on what the client does. This is simply a reflection of my personal experience. I am a business consultant, so I have an easier time producing examples from my world. That said, you can find similar examples of niches defined by other factors such as culture, group affiliation, charitable causes, medical issues, and family situations. Regardless, every niche has a center or point where people go to meet others who have similar experiences and exchange information about opportunities and challenges. The best way to identify this center is to fully understand the ecosystem of the niche.

Building a Reputation

A reputation is the foundation of business development. Your reputation is your personal brand. Developing and enhancing your reputation should be an ongoing process of highest priority. Naturally, as you work with more and more individuals in a niche, your reputation will grow organically. This can be a very slow process, however, which is why business development often leads to results only much later in a career. Niches tend to accelerate the process, and your results will be even better if you look for opportunities to proactively showcase your skills. Writing and public speaking are two powerful methods for building a reputation. Each requires patience and persistence and is best approached as a career commitment rather than an initiative that will create immediate results.

Writing

Writing articles, columns, and blogs is a wonderful way to showcase your knowledge and engage with your target market. Your writing will reach hundreds—perhaps thousands—of potential new clients. The key, of course, is in the quality of the topics and the articles. If the topics are well chosen and well written, you can instantly add to your credibility. Time and again, I see advisors wasting opportunities for exposure by writing articles on topics that are too broad and quite unoriginal. Remember: Your clients have full access to all the financial publications and are showered with market updates and generic advice about retirement or wealth. Instead of repeating what many other articles have already covered, ask yourself: "What keeps my clients awake at night?" Think of the unique challenges facing your niche. Focus on the areas that define your niche and where general theory does not apply well.

For example, if you focus on business owners, don't write another article about investing in volatile financial markets. A more interesting article would be "The Dialogue between Your Personal and Business Balance Sheets," or perhaps "Should You Hire Your Children in Your Business?" The more niche-specialized you are, the easier it will be to find specific topics that will resonate with your audience and the more differentiated your voice will be.

If you do choose to write, please write your own articles. Many advisors outsource writing to ghostwriters. The result is a bland article that lacks ideas and a unique voice. Your writing should be an extension of your personality and your knowledge. The voice should be uniquely yours. Anything and everything unique about your practice will stand out best if you write it out on your own. Any attempts to hire others to do it for you are very transparent, and the results are invariably poor.

Writing takes time. It can be painful to look at the blank page with a deadline looming, but good writing is worth the pain. Next time you have an interesting client meeting, help a client avoid a mistake, or encounter a big problem, open a file and start writing about it. Don't write an article yet, just jot down some notes: What happened? Why is this important? What is difficult about it? What should clients know about it? What did you do, and why? Later, organize these notes into an article that generalizes the circumstances to apply to more people while preserving what is uniquely applicable to the niche. Using your unique voice and expertise will help you tremendously in building your reputation. Regurgitating what other people have already said will not.

Finding a place to start your writing career is not easy, but it's certainly not impossible. Seek out the editors of niche publications, blogs, or magazines. In today's media environment, niche publications often have to publish online content daily with an editorial staff of only two or three people. They always welcome quality contributions from writers who have a reputation and a track record. To develop that track record, start writing. Write something relevant and interesting. Don't shy away from small forums and unknown websites.

Anything you can publish is a step in the right direction. Success at this point is defined as publishing—*anywhere*—even if only two people end up reading it.

During the first couple of years, your focus should be on writing, publishing, and interacting with your audience. Expecting any results beyond this would be unreasonable and unrealistic. I have seen several young professionals abandon promising columns and blogs because they never "got any business." *Getting business* is not the idea. Instead focus on developing your reputation and getting experience in writing. Small blogs will help you find bigger publications. No one starts out writing for the *Wall Street Journal.*

Public Speaking

Public speaking, much like writing, can enhance your reputation tremendously and help you reach a broad audience. Public speaking is a great way to build your reputation because it allows your audience to see you and interact with you. As powerful as writing is, it does not allow others to experience your personality and way of communicating in a live setting. A good public speaker can draw the audience into a conversation that they want to continue after the podium time is over.

Similar to writing, public speaking begins with a well-chosen topic of discussion. Once again, this is where niches are invaluable. The unique needs of the niche should suggest unique topics of discussion. Focus on these unique issues rather than a generic presentation topic. Conference organizers can really help you with this. Spend some time with them researching the audience and tell them about your topics of expertise. Work with them to find the intersection between their audience's interests, your expertise, and the conference's themes.

Workshops and teaching opportunities are also a form of public speaking. Both offer you exposure to a broad audience and create credibility. Depending on the niche, such training opportunities may be a regular part of the niche landscape. Many professions have continued professional education requirements that include topics on financial management and practice management.

Public speaking is a skill that can be honed through practice and training. There are many presentation coaches available who can help you work on your voice, stage presence, content, body language, and presentation style. When you are first getting started, don't focus too much on the size of the crowd. Speaking in front of small audiences is perfectly fine, especially in the beginning. I remember my first presentation at an advisory conference. There were two people in the audience. One of them was the next presenter.

Following a Disciplined Process

A good business development process ensures that opportunities are not wasted and also creates efficiency. Having a disciplined process makes it easier for others to be involved and contribute to the effort. When we asked advisors in our annual survey whether they document the leads they generate, we were surprised to discover that close to 67 percent of firms do not.[1] What is more, about 50 percent of generated leads do not follow up on their initial contact or engage the firm. Only about 20 percent of leads are converted into clients. This result can be attributed to a lack of process.

Developing Proposals

I was trained in a business development process that centered on writing a proposal, or a letter that describes the services provided to clients, the pricing of those services, and the timing of each step. A proposal will also often contain a restated understanding of the client's objectives and a project plan for the engagement. While typical for business consulting firms, proposals are not usually part of the new business process for advisory firms. A minority of firms create any type of written communication that goes beyond the standard advisory contract. Some firms see the development of such documents as a compliance risk, an area in which I have very limited expertise. Still, to the degree that a written letter to clients does not pose legal or regulatory challenges, a proposal can be instrumental in helping you with your closing steps.

One of the best aspects of the proposal process is the fact that you have to write down your services and plans for the client. A proposal avoids the ambiguity of saying something like "We will help you with whatever you need"; instead, you can rely on a well-articulated description of what you will do and how. By forcing you to be disciplined in communicating to the client what you are about to do, a proposal also helps you better articulate your value proposition to clients.

A proposal also gives you time to pause and consider important pricing questions. If there are any pricing decisions to be made, developing a project plan as part of the proposal will help you make those decisions in a more thoughtful manner.

Finally, a proposal gives you a great platform to follow up with clients and discuss their expectations. Rather than explicitly asking them for a signature

---

[1] InvestmentNews Research, *Financial Performance Study* (2016).

or a check, posing simple questions allows you to nudge clients toward action in a very responsive way: Did you have a chance to review our proposal? Were there any comments on our proposal?

Asking for Feedback and Input

Another great thing about written proposals is that you can share them with colleagues. Peer review was a required part of the new business process at Moss Adams. To this day, I tend to share many (if not all) of my proposals with my colleagues. I also frequently share draft proposals with my wife, who is the chief marketing officer for a design firm. Hearing the perspectives of people who are in the business of professional services but not deeply entwined in our own terminology and assumptions is very helpful.

Peer review can help your business development process a lot. This is true not just for proposals, but for all client interactions. Peer review will make sure you are taking the right approach and using words that resonate. It may also uncover steps or suggestions you have missed. In addition, peer review can generate ideas that enhance your proposal.

Receiving feedback is a vital skill in new business development. Every client decision—whether it is to sign, wait, or decline—is a form of feedback. I only wish that every time my proposals were not accepted, someone would tell me why. What did I do wrong? What could I have done better? Unfortunately, clients never give us this kind of information. Our colleagues are the next best option.

Be Persistent

Business development requires patience to master. It requires discipline to stay involved. At times it takes some stubbornness to get through the more frustrating episodes that inevitably arise. Be persistent. The learning cycle is predictable.

At first, everything is hard and intimidating. You need some encouragement and motivation to just give it a try. Eventually, you begin to learn and progress quickly, and you grow excited. A little training, some mentoring, and a few opportunities lead to a few early successes. Now you are feeling progress but also the pressure of time. To improve, you need to devote even more time, and there seems to be so much more you need to learn.

Going from mediocre to great takes a long time, and progress is slow. You are familiar with this stage from your language lessons or golf game. Many people get stuck and stay on a plateau for the rest of their careers. To move past this stage, you need to devote considerable time and energy. When you are truly an expert, opportunities will seem to find you. You will learn more and more, always upgrading and improving your knowledge.

Business development should not be merely a part of your professional toolkit. It should be part of what you enjoy about being a professional. It is a puzzle to be sold, a new relationship to be created, and a new experience to be had. Persistence will make the difference between learning to enjoy business development and feeling you lack the knack for it.

CHAPTER 7

Managing People

Managing people is an integral part of being a high-performing professional in the financial services industry. It is impossible for advisors to deliver desired results to clients without the help of a capable team of people. To be a good advisor means to lead a team of people in servicing the client, including coordinating their efforts, setting their priorities, monitoring the results, prioritizing resources, and helping them when they need help. This, in essence, is a definition of management. Not being able to manage your team will limit your effectiveness as a professional. The same is true for those who become leaders in the operations and administration of the business. Management is an integral part of every position of responsibility.

Much time has been devoted to the myth that if you want to be a good advisor, you should let others manage and focus your time on clients. In fact, there are articles suggesting that advisors should not be involved in management at all and instead should hire full-time managers. While I am a huge fan of specialization and professional managers, management responsibilities can be delegated but should never be abandoned. On a good soccer team, strikers will come back to play defense when needed. On a good basketball team, the best shooter should run back hard to defend the team's basket. Letting others play defense while you watch will quickly get you kicked off the team.

Management is part of practicing—particularly in a team-based firm. However, it is also one of the biggest and earliest frustrations for advisors. Management requires a complete shift in mentality and priorities, and lack of experience can turn initial troubles into a lengthy ordeal. Having spent three to five years intensely focusing on professional knowledge and client service, G2 professionals suddenly find themselves responsible for the performance of a team of people. It is very difficult to go from trying to develop and improve your own performance to being responsible for what others are doing.

Management requires a lot of time and emotional energy, and even more so when things go poorly. A successful, high-performing team is easy to manage. Effective management is most necessary and valuable when there are challenges and difficult decisions to be made. Shifting your focus from clients to internal management is a difficult but vital task that will enhance your career significantly.

Defining Management

Let's begin by defining what management is. Much of the reluctance to manage may be attributed to a misunderstanding of what exactly it entails. Management as a function within an advisory firm involves the following responsibilities.

- **Coordinating the activities of a team:** This includes assigning specific roles or specific tasks.
- **Establishing accountability:** Team members must be held accountable for their responsibilities, including timeliness of completion.
- **Monitoring results:** Team results should be continuously evaluated, making changes as necessary to ensure that the client is receiving the right service.
- **Acquiring and maintaining the right resources:** A good manager is responsible for team members having the right amount of resources (e.g., technology, budgets, people) and time to complete their work.
- **Resolving conflicting priorities:** When there are tasks that compete for resources, a manager should be able to resolve those conflicts.
- **Providing feedback:** Performance feedback enables individuals and the team as a whole to improve.
- **Connecting the team to the organization:** A manager should ensure that a team does not work in isolation from the activities of the overall organization.
- **Making recommendations for the compensation and career advancement of team members:** While the manager should make recommendations on both promotions and compensation, the ultimate decisions may be made by the firm.
- **Hiring and firing when necessary:** Finally, a manager is ultimately responsible for staffing the team and correcting that staffing when necessary.

I have intentionally listed every management responsibility I can think of in order to arrive at a comprehensive definition of management. That said, not every manager will be responsible for every activity on this list, nor will managers have to accomplish every activity on their own. A good team may in fact be able to manage itself with minimal intervention from the manager. For example, team members will often hold each other accountable and provide feedback to each other.

The team should also be heavily involved in the hiring and firing process. There are organizations where those decisions are actually made at the team rather than the management level. Whole Foods is famous for its policy of only hiring employees once they pass a 90-day test with their future team. Modern management theory tends to favor and recognize self-managing teams. I would still argue that even the best teams need a manager, but the management role will be different on such high-performing teams.

While management should be located at the team level, the firm also has a large role to play. The firm should not appropriate the management responsibilities of a partner or lead advisor, but rather enhance and support them. A strong HR team or dedicated management function at the firm level can complement management in a variety of ways:

- The firm can provide managers with tools and resources that allow them to manage better and more effectively.
- The firm can be highly instrumental in training both managers and team members. While employee training at the firm level is no substitute for on-the-job feedback, it should be leveraged to support employee training at the team level.
- The firm can bring suggestions for team improvement through best practices and industry exchange of information and knowledge.
- The firm can help managers make hiring and firing decisions by providing coaching and a perspective on team member performance from people who are not part of the team.
- The firm can leverage compliance and HR administration capabilities to ensure that the team is performing in accordance with company and other policies and regulations.
- The firm can bring data to the team to help it better understand how it is functioning and aid decisions on capacity or staffing.

It is difficult to provide a standard, quantitative guideline on how much a professional should manage. Saying a person should spend a certain number of hours managing the team doesn't account for shifts in management involvement as teams evolve. A qualitative guideline will be easier to tailor to your team's needs at the present time. For example, I recommend that you treat your team as your most important client and spend as much time as necessary to make sure team members are performing at their highest level.

When I became a partner at Moss Adams, I received guidance that I should be spending about half of my time with clients and half of my time developing new business and managing my team. Accounting firms tend to be very mindful of how they spend their time by virtue of booking the billable hours. In my experience, this 50/50 split is reasonable for a partner. At the very least it's not a bad place to start.

Prioritizing Management and Communication

The first steps toward successful management are learning how to prioritize your management time and finding the right form and tone for your communications. Early in a professional career, it is common to feel besieged by the needs of those you manage, leaving you unable to do your own work. I remember that feeling distinctly. I had a calendar full of client appointments and an inbox full of client e-mails, but every time I had five minutes someone would come to my desk with a question or an issue. And the conversations were never short. Half an hour later, I would be late for my next call, never having finished the e-mail I needed to send and being forced to skip lunch again because there just wasn't enough time to eat.

Management requires time. Unfortunately, chances are good that time is the one thing you don't have, particularly at the beginning of your management career. You have a significant client load and are surrounded by more-senior professionals who are used to having you help them. In addition, you are still in the habit of doing rather than delegating. Add on top of that the responsibility to manage five other professionals, and it starts to feel overwhelming.

A potential solution is to train your team to understand when you are interruptible and when you are capable of giving them your attention and when you are not. This only works if you set aside sufficient time to be available to your team. For example, you could set aside a couple of hours each day as your *office hours* and steer your colleagues to seek you out primarily during those hours. For this to work, the allotted time has to be sufficient, and the schedule must coincide with the needs of the team. If most of the issues that require your attention occur during the morning hours, it is unreasonable to only set aside time in the afternoons.

Another technique is to set up regular team meetings and train your team to ask their questions and seek your guidance during those meetings. For example, scheduling a weekly project coordination meeting could eliminate the barrage of related questions that you might otherwise experience. This requires patient and persistent steering. If team members are not playing by the rules, asking questions as they arise rather than preparing for the weekly meetings, you need to find a way to coach them into not doing that.

Addressing Your Team

This brings us to the issue of tone and form. Finding the right form of communication is something with which I have personally struggled. E-mail is much easier to use than in-person communication. You can write an e-mail at your convenience at any time of day. You can even write an e-mail at home while watching TV. Unfortunately, e-mail does not lend itself well to many important communications.

To start with, e-mail is a horrible way to deliver critical feedback or communicate to someone that she has not met your expectations. The impersonal tone of typed text can come across as harsh. In the context of a critical message, words and phrases can often be misinterpreted. The very nature of the message can easily become inflammatory. Such communications are so much better in person, where body language and the context of the office protects the communication from becoming a runaway train that veers off the track of prudent conversation.

The same principle holds true when communicating significant changes or decisions. You never want to tell someone about her new salary or job description in an e-mail or memo. Such messages convey a lack of involvement and caring, and suggest that you may feel that the decision is somehow not right, since you would rather not deliver the news in person.

The tone of communication can also be an issue. If you use a tone that is too formal, you may come across as intimidating or lacking authenticity. Excessive formality can sound like you are too full of yourself. On the other hand, a tone of voice that is overly friendly will not convey the importance of your message and may prevent you from being taken seriously. Striking the right tone is a function of your office and personality. Find a tone that suggests that this is important to you and deserves everyone's time and attention without sounding like a memo from a Dilbert cartoon. This balance can be particularly difficult to find when you manage people with whom you are also very social.

Accepting Responsibility

Management becomes very difficult when things aren't going well, but that is also when it is needed most. To be a good manager you will need to accept responsibility for results that are not what you hoped them to be. A good coach accepts responsibility for losses and praises his team for victories.

Most professional services occupations are individualistic in nature. We build our own professional knowledge and use it with our clients. We grow our confidence and ability to perform well in the spotlight of a client meeting or presentation. We pride ourselves on our ability to speak to a client and make good decisions, even in tough circumstances. Managing effectively requires us to suppress some of those instincts. Being a good manager requires more humility than being a good advisor.

I remember a commercial for IBM that illustrated this concept well. A CEO-looking character stood up in a meeting and started berating his team of executives. "Our servers don't work! Our systems are outdated! Our people are not trained well! Who is responsible for all of this?" After a long, pregnant pause, one of the executives meekly answers, "Sir, you are." To succeed in management, you must be willing to accept that the results of the team are your results.

Personal relationships can make this very difficult. We often grow up as professionals alongside the same team members whom we will eventually manage. We go to happy hours together and feel a sense of camaraderie. We may even seek comfort by discussing what the company is not doing well. When we are promoted, however, we suddenly discover that we don't quite belong in these friendly conversations anymore.

It is perhaps possible to try to compartmentalize your relationship and be friends in one context and professionals in another. If you can keep those two roles separate and your colleagues also recognize the different contexts, the two are not necessarily incompatible. That said, if you find that one or more of your teammates repeatedly blurs the line between the personal and professional relationship, you have a very hard choice to make.

I have often had to deliver harsh criticism to people I see socially. On one occasion, I had to fire a personal friend. When managing means delivering bad news or negative feedback, you may find that your friends feel betrayed. After all, in the context of friendship, you are supposed to protect and support each other unconditionally, no matter what. Unfortunately, in a business context, you cannot ignore someone's performance and results, especially if that performance is hurting other team members.

My father, who has managed people and owned a business for the last 30 years, often tells me that "the captain spends a lot of time alone in his cabin." I used to think that this was an old-school truism that could be overcome by the constructive optimism of young people. Today, after many years of managing teams and businesses, and with all the scars to show for it, I am starting to concede the enduring truth in that statement. Management will create some distance between you and the colleagues who report to you. To be a good manager, you have to accept that distance. While you should still give your team the support of a friend, you must also be willing to demand the results of a good coach.

Providing Feedback

Susan Dickson, COO of Private Ocean and one of the coaches in our G2 program, gives all of her employees a book called *Difficult Conversations*,[1] in which the authors teach readers how to engage in communications that are both difficult and necessary. Mastering the skill of providing effective feedback is absolutely vital to management.

Feedback is not inherently negative. In fact, the most important form of feedback is positive. Praising employees for the good things they do is the best way to ensure that they will do them again. It can also be a fantastic way to compensate employees for their work. Research from Gallup indicates that praise can be just as effective as money in rewarding performance.[2]

Good positive feedback is directly related to the positive event. It does not have to wait for the next staff meeting or performance evaluation, although there is nothing wrong with repeating it there. It should be on-the-spot and very specific: What is it that the person did that you are praising? Specificity is important because it is easy for praise to be misunderstood. "Great presentation!" is a very good statement. Something more specific is even better: "Great presentation! The way you gave the client a chance to ask questions and

---

[1] Douglas Stone and Sheila Heen, *Difficult Conversations: How to Discuss What Matters Most* (New York: Penguin, 2010).
[2] Brandon Rigoni and Bailey Nelson, "Retaining Employees: Does Money Matter?" Gallup Organization, January 15, 2016. Accessed from http://www.gallup.com/businessjournal/188399/retaining-employees-money-matter.aspx?.

the way you patiently waited for her to get comfortable with the information was great!"

Positive feedback can only be effective if you don't overuse it. Offering constant praise, especially when it is neither earned nor warranted, undermines your ability to use positive feedback as a management tool. Let me give you an example. I grew up in Eastern Europe, and Eastern Europeans are notoriously blunt. I played rugby and whenever I made a bad pass, kicked the ball to the wrong spot, or made a run I shouldn't have, my coach would scream his lungs out: "What the heck were you thinking!" It was a tough-love approach for sure.

Here in the United States, in the present time, the approach is quite different. When my daughter and son started playing sports, I got involved in their soccer teams. I noticed that whenever a player kicked the ball out of bounds or made a bad pass, the coach would say, "Good idea!" or "Good effort!" However, the move was very rarely a good idea. Usually, it wasn't even an idea. Often, it was not the best of efforts, either. The kids knew it, too. Players know very well how a good idea sounds and what a good effort looks like. When they get praised for something that actually deserves criticism, they don't feel better about it. Rather, they just start ignoring the coach.

That is not to say that I am an advocate of screaming your lungs out in criticism. That, too, will cause your team to eventually ignore you. They may also start avoiding the ball as a consequence. On a soccer team, you will start to see players not wanting to receive a pass out of fear of making a mistake. The main point is that if you dispense praise when it is not due, you devalue praise that is earned. Only praise performances that deserve it. When they happen, go out of your way to deliver that positive feedback and reinforce it.

The other side of the coin is critical feedback. When things go wrong, you have to be willing to point out what went wrong and how it can be fixed. However, that is much easier said than done. We all struggle to deliver critical feedback because we feel badly about what we are about to say and are afraid of the reaction of the other person. Even when we are in a management position, we are concerned that the receiver of our feedback will react with denial, anger, or sadness. We don't want to be the source of those emotions.

I see something similar at the boxing gym. Novice boxers are worried—almost afraid, even—to throw punches at their sparring partners. Instead, they make a slow, punch-like motion, usually directed away from the heads of their competitors. This is no way to box. Frankly, it does a disservice to your sparring partners, who are there to train for real punches. Your partners want to slip and block real shots. They can tell you are not really throwing, which feels like you are not taking them seriously or that you don't respect their boxing skills.

Delivering critical feedback is a form of respecting your colleagues. It means that you believe in their professionalism and ability to take feedback constructively and not overreact or ignore it. It means you trust them to have the skills to correct what went wrong and not commit the same mistake again. It also means that you trust them to handle themselves in the right way when you know you're going to deliver a hard blow.

Nine times out of 10, the people you manage know very well that something went wrong. They know a meeting did not go as planned or an assignment was late. They are not surprised by your critical feedback. Chances are that they are even relieved to hear it. Poor performance that goes uncorrected hangs like a cloud over both the manager and the professional who struggles. Both can see it, and both worry about it.

The purpose of critical feedback is not to "land a punch," but rather to correct what happened. That's why the feedback is needed in the first place. It should never be a form of punishment or a tongue-lashing that penalizes the guilty. Instead, critical feedback should be a constructive lesson on how to fix what went wrong. For criticism to be constructive, it must answer three important questions, which are detailed in the following sections.

What Went Wrong?

While it is often obvious that something went wrong, it is not always clear what exactly that thing was. It is important to understand the issue precisely. For example, imagine you receive a document meant for a client, perhaps a short presentation that you are meant to deliver. You have an hour until the meeting, and you are looking at a document that is incomplete. Your associate can tell that you are very unhappy about the presentation, but she may not understand why. She is puzzled. How was she supposed to know about all of those things? She has only been working at the firm for a year while you have six years of experience. This is her first time preparing for this type of presentation.

It is easy for the associate to come away from this experience with the conclusion that the problem is that the presentation has missing elements. The real issue, however, is that she did not share the draft with you earlier. She should have given you the draft at least a day earlier, when you would have had time to explain what is missing and how to obtain the missing information. If you are not clear about what exactly went wrong, your colleague may feel that she was set up to fail due to her lack of experience. She may decide that your expectations are unrealistic.

How Serious Is the Problem and Why?

Sometimes it may not be apparent what is a serious issue and what is a minor mistake. I had a colleague who repeatedly did poorly presenting to an important client. He always seemed uncomfortable and unprepared for the presentations. He got three chances over the course of two years, and every time the result was the same. Based on the critical feedback I provided during our first two conversations, he came away considering the issue to be rather minor: "I am not a good presenter. Perhaps I need to improve my presentation skills." In reality, the issue was more serious. I should have communicated this message instead: "This is your best chance to establish your credibility in front of an important client. If you miss this chance, you are also missing the chance to play a role in this relationship and to move to the next position. This can severely limit or even end your career."

It is particularly important to communicate whether this is an isolated mistake or part of a pattern. Your colleague should understand when she starts to repeatedly make the same mistake, especially when that mistake leaves a negative impression of her ability to perform.

How Can the Problem Be Corrected or Avoided in the Future?

This question is the difference between constructive feedback and criticism. Criticism merely points out what is wrong while constructive feedback focuses on how to fix it. Think about the difference between an angry fan screaming at a player who misses a shot versus the coach who is contemplating how to turn that mistake into a teachable moment. Constructive feedback communicates a solution.

Returning to our first example, constructive feedback would include a message such as this: "In the future, when you encounter a topic or a project for which you feel unprepared, seek direction and input earlier. Give me a chance to review a draft and give you feedback while we still have the time to fill in the gaps. Not knowing something is not an issue. However, not seeking out input to fill in the gaps is a problem."

In a similar fashion, our second example could be handled like this: "You need to practice and prepare your presentations much better, particularly when you have a chance to establish yourself as a lead professional. Practice more and ask for suggestions on how to become better at these presentations.

We can provide presentation training, but you also need to prepare significantly better and not try to improvise important presentations."

Dealing with Poorly Performing Team Members

Poor performance must be dealt with. There is no way around it. One person performing poorly is not just an issue between that person and the manager. Rather, it is an issue between that person and the entire team. Colleagues who underperform require the team around them to work harder, or to even do their jobs for them.

One of the most important questions to answer in management is whether a problem is the result of a poor performance or a poor performer. Poor performance, on the one hand, can be isolated and is subject to circumstances. It is a temporary state. A poor performer, on the other hand, is someone who repeatedly shows poor performance. It is no longer a case of circumstances but rather has become part of the professional profile of your colleague.

Distinguishing between the two is not always straightforward. There isn't a *three-strikes* rule in business. The case may be further complicated when a colleague consistently performs poorly in one area but performs well in another. For example, Philip may be a very supportive teammate and well-liked by his peers, but he consistently shows a lack of knowledge in preparing a financial plan. When you are having trouble deciding whether someone is a poor performer or just struggling once in a while, ask yourself these questions:

- Have you repeatedly dealt with the same issue many times before?
- Has this person earned a reputation for struggling?
- Have you already lowered your expectations for this person?
- Do you have to work around the performance of this person when assigning projects?
- Do other members of the team avoid working with this person or understand that working with this person requires extra work?

Dealing with poorly performing team members does not always mean firing them. While that may eventually be necessary, it is not the only possible outcome. The first step in dealing with poor performance means that the person must understand the severity of the issue. Explain that this problem can be career defining, and perhaps even career ending, at the firm. The individual must have a clear understanding of what the problem is, as well as its scope.

This includes the damage that the specific poor performance inflicts on the team and on clients. Most importantly, the person needs to understand how to fix the issue and what the deadline for making progress is.

The conversation should have a determined tone. Be very direct about the problem and its solutions. Performance problems that are due to a lack of knowledge and experience are a bit easier to discuss. This is a very specific issue, and solutions are more apparent. Performance issues that are rooted in motivation, effort, or work ethic are more difficult to discuss and correct. In such cases, it is good to go back to square one and ask these important questions:

- Are you interested in this job? Is this what you want to do?
- Are you interested in and committed to this career?
- Are you satisfied with your own progress in this job?
- Do you realize you appear to have lost motivation?
- Is there something that we are not seeing that impacts your ability to perform?

When addressing effort and motivation, it is very difficult but important not to cross the line where your criticism becomes an attack on the person. "Philip, you are not showing the effort we expect" is much better than "Philip, you are lazy." Focus on patterns of behavior, how they appear to others, and how they impact the team.

While a good team will be supportive and distribute the work to help someone who is not able to handle a full load or is struggling with something, this is not a viable, long-term solution. If the team always has to account for a poor performer in its plans, or when a team loses faith in a team member and no longer believes that she makes the team better, it is time to make a change.

A good manager is in tune with the team. You shouldn't ask, "Do you think it is better to let Philip go?" It is unfair to ask your teammates to carry the burden of that decision. As a manager, you need to be able to read the more subtle signs: Does the team still support this person? Do they believe this person will ever help the team be better? Do they still respect any of the qualities of this professional?

Letting people go is one of the most difficult and emotionally burdening decisions of management, but it is also one of the most necessary. My former partner, Rebecca Pomering, was once asked during a panel discussion about a decision she had made that she most regretted. "I never regretted letting people go," she answered, "but I always regretted not letting them go sooner."

Performance Evaluations

Performance evaluations are a great tool for delivering feedback, tracking progress, and identifying recurring issues. They have also received a lot of criticism over the years to the point where many firms and large corporations are abandoning them altogether. Still, when done right, they remain a great way to gather and systematize well-rounded feedback on performance. A performance review done *right* is well written, thoughtful, and constructive.

To be effective in improving performance and guiding the development of a professional, performance reviews should not be used as a substitute for on-the-job feedback. As discussed earlier, when team members perform well or make mistakes, they should receive praise or criticism at the time of their performance. Waiting for the next performance evaluation to point out a mistake is very counterproductive. The same is true for commendations. Performance evaluations provide a chance to look at the big picture and identify patterns, gaps, trends, and overall direction rather than specific instances.

Performance evaluations must also be well written in order to be effective. There is a tendency to overengineer the form and create a long list of categories with sophisticated scoring. A short list of important performance categories that are well described works better. In other words, explanations are more important than scores. Numbers are not a very good way to comment on behavior and suggest improvement. A score of two on a scale of one to five is not very helpful or constructive without comments explaining what the reviewer saw in the performance of the employee. A well-written performance evaluation should offer comments in every section that achieve the following goals:

- **Explain the score:** There should always be an explanation for the score, particularly with very high or very low scores.
- **Offer examples:** The evaluation should speak about the big picture, but even a big picture is made out of smaller elements. What did the reviewer observe that convincingly indicates that there is a pattern or a trend?
- **Offer advice for improvement:** What can the employee do better? How can he or she improve?
- **Provide balance, but be direct:** There is no point in making up positive feedback when a performance is rated below expectations just to create an artificial balance. Likewise, there is no need to make up areas for improvement just because none are readily apparent.

Who Are the Reviewers?

Reviewers should accept full responsibility for their comments. Unsigned performance evaluations encourage comments that are less than thoughtful. In general, anonymity and management do not go well together. If a manager has comments on an employee's performance, the manager should be willing not just to sign those comments but also to discuss them face to face with the person being reviewed.

Performance evaluations should be completed by anyone and everyone who has meaningful feedback on the performance of an employee. One of the advantages of a structured evaluation process versus immediate feedback is that you can hear from many people on the same issue. The advantage gained from providing multiple perspectives should be balanced against the need to write complete and thoughtful reviews. If you have to write more than five or six reviews, you may start to resent the process. That's never a good development.

A performance review should be delivered by the person who is the direct manager or supervisor of the employee. At times, it may be difficult to identify that person. For example, an analyst may work with three of four lead advisors at the firm with none of them being the immediate supervisor. In such cases, each of the advisors would be a good candidate to deliver the review. Perhaps they could split responsibility for the reviews of the analysts. While some rotation of reviewers is a good idea, it can also damage the sense of continuity from one performance review to the next.

Bonuses and the Review Process

There is a strong case to be made for tying performance evaluations to bonuses. A person who earns high scores in performance evaluations should probably be receiving a good bonus. That said, the firm must be very careful about which element comes first. A well-working and accepted performance evaluation process is a great source of input for bonus plans. However, if the performance management process is not working well or is relatively new, tying it to bonuses may jeopardize both. Employees may sense that the evaluations are unfairly costing them money while reviewers may be reluctant to give low scores so as not to cause employees to miss out on bonuses. The only solution is to establish the function and tone of the evaluations outside of the bonus process. When it works, you can then use it for incentives.

Upstream Evaluations

We should briefly mention upstream evaluations. These are quite popular in many organizations, but they also present a significant challenge. For employees to be able to give feedback to colleagues higher on the organizational chart, they need some level of protection, specifically, assurance that their feedback will not be used to punish them or take away opportunities. At the same time, as already discussed, anonymity tends to destroy the constructive nature of the process.

Anonymous feedback is rarely good feedback. Stripped of the responsibility of explaining or taking ownership of a comment, employees often leave feedback that is not constructive, not substantiated, or just plain inappropriate. Even just a few such comments can badly injure the credibility of the process. Instead of anonymous upstream evaluations, I prefer an open door policy that encourages employees to speak one on one with a partner or even the CEO if they feel that they are not being treated fairly or if one of their supervisors is not performing well.

If your organization does upstream evaluations, as a manager you need to treat such feedback constructively and with respect. Rather than trying to guess who said what, consider what behavior is triggering the criticism and seek to improve it. Acknowledge that you have heard your colleagues. Don't be defensive about the comments and be willing to do better.

Being a Mentor

Managing an employee and mentoring are two very different functions. In fact, in many firms the person managing is purposely different from the person mentoring. While management is closer to supervising and evaluating, mentoring is closer to coaching and serving as an advocate. You should look to do both. Being a mentor will give you a better perspective on the thoughts and experiences of your team. Mentoring will also help you be a better manager, improve your relationships within the firm, and, most of all, establish yourself as a leader.

Mentoring is the process of guiding someone in professional development and helping that person find answers to some of the more difficult questions that are faced, personally and professionally. Mentors are advocates for their mentees. Mentoring is by definition supportive and focused on how the professional can succeed. A mentor should be someone with whom you can share your thoughts and concerns, free from the political implications that may arise from sharing that same information with your manager. Mentors can be a great resource of knowledge and guidance when it comes to answering important questions about your career:

- How can you acquire skills that you are missing?
- How can you overcome difficulties that you are facing?
- How can you improve relationships within the firm that are not working well?
- How can you find balance between personal and professional goals?
- What can you do when you are not sure this career, or this firm, is for you?

In your growth as a G2 professional, you have likely struggled with these difficult questions. Younger professionals who are coming up behind you will face the same challenges. Your experience and the answers you have found for yourself can be very helpful to your colleagues. Having a good mentor is invaluable in a professional career. We have all sought guidance or simply needed encouragement at some point. Members of your team need the same kind of support and advice you probably needed as you were maturing in your career. If you had a mentor, consider repaying that debt by becoming a mentor yourself. If you never had a mentor, you know how challenging that can be and why other professionals need your help.

Not all mentors have gray hair. In my career, the people who gave me the best advice were just ahead of me on the career track. Younger mentors have a significant advantage in being able to relate well to their team. Their notion of what it is like to be an analyst or paraplanner is not based on memories from 25 years ago but rather very immediate observations. This enables them to offer practical and actionable advice to those they mentor.

Younger professionals sometimes shy away from mentoring because they feel like they have not yet figured out their own careers. They worry that they will not have all the answers to questions that their mentees will have. It is important to remember that a mentor is not an official position but rather a relationship. In a good firm, a professional should have more than one mentor. Perhaps as a G2 professional you could serve as the mentor who deals with the more immediate steps in the career and the more immediate issues that the young professional experiences. A more-senior professional can then be the mentor who supplies the big picture.

Being a mentor will tremendously help your position as a leader in the firm. In my experience, when firms ask, "Who are our future leaders?," they rarely look at those who are the best business developers or the best experts. Instead, they look at professionals who are building a strong team, growing those behind them, and instilling trust in colleagues.

Being a mentor will also give you a close connection to the next generation. After all, your future success depends on your firm's ability to continue recruiting and retaining talented people. The more you can contribute to that talent acquisition and development process, the more secure you will be in your knowledge that when you decide to exit the business someday, there will be a talented and capable individual to take over your responsibilities and provide you with liquidity for your equity.

CHAPTER 8

Managing Up

The process of management is not limited to coordinating the goals and activities of those who report to us. An important side of management is the ability to steer the information, expectations, and suggested actions of those who are above us on the organizational chart. To be successful in a career, a professional has to both manage down (i.e., work with subordinates) and manage up (i.e., work with superiors).

The idea behind managing up is somewhat counterintuitive. Professionals often assume that the founders or executives of the firm somehow have a perfect view of all the information that they need to accurately make decisions or assess performance. Unfortunately, the opposite is often true. The CEO of the firm may not have good information on a situation or your performance. Younger professionals also assume that the burden is on the firm to gather accurate information. Again, that is not realistic and often not practical.

Beyond information flow, another reason to manage up is that often the leadership of the firm is either not fully aware or accurate in its perception of your interests, talents, or skills. Suggesting initiatives you want to be part of may be necessary to make sure that your responsibilities match your interests and that you are not assigned to the wrong projects.

Managing up is also a process of signaling your preferred pace. It is about letting the firm know how fast you would like to move and what challenges you are willing to accept. This holds equally true for both those with a lot of ambition who want to move faster and challenge themselves and those who prefer a slower pace and a chance to absorb changes. Without those signals, it is tempting for the leadership of the firm to equalize and assume that everyone will move at the same pace.

Finally, managing up shares an aspect with public relations. You need to manage the perceptions the firm has of you and what leadership believes to be your strengths and weaknesses. Especially in larger firms, the leaders of the firm do not have a good opportunity to observe the work of all professionals. Their impressions can be inaccurate or incomplete. They may not be aware of projects you have completed, work you have done, or successes you have achieved. Managing the information about your career will not only ensure you receive credit for your accomplishments, but will also give you a chance to receive help when you need it.

Speaking Up

Building your career in a firm is similar in many ways to building your presence in a market; you want to achieve recognition and develop a reputation. Before prospective clients will want to work with you, they have to know you exist and have a positive perception of you. Similarly, for your colleagues to see you as a leader, they have to first notice you in a positive way.

Your voice should be present in the internal dialogue of the firm and you should be seen as influential. Internal dialogue comprises all of the management meetings, committee discussions, and informal chatter in the office. It serves as an exchange of information and helps professionals develop and support various points of view on the firm's philosophy, values, and specific service decisions. It is vital that you speak up and be active in the many forums that exist in your firm. You should also develop well-thought-out positions on the topics that affect the firm.

Voicing Your Intentions

The worst staff issues that arise within firms usually stem from a lack of communication between professionals and leadership. Recently, I spoke with the CEO of a firm we work with, who told me about some concerns he was having about a colleague:

> Shawn is a good professional, but he is not a team player. He spends most of his time networking and building his name in the community, and he has little interest in any of the internal management projects or committees in the firm. He works alone and does not involve our associates in his work. Frankly, he seems to be building up his own reputation in order to leave the firm. Perhaps he wants to start his own firm, but we can't let him take our clients. We are not going to invest in building a business for him just to see him take it away.

I then had the chance to speak with Shawn. This is what he said:

I am at a loss to know what to do. I figure the only way I can be successful is to become a business developer, and that's why I have been working
primarily on new business. If I can bring in a lot of new clients, I can make
partner.

My problem is that the firm does not support me. I can't get any help
or any budget. I can also tell they are not happy with my performance and
I often find that they had internal meetings that I was never invited to.
Honestly, it feels like they want me to leave, but they just can't bring themselves to tell me.

As absurd as this situation may seem, it is not uncommon. CEOs and
other firm leaders often assume they can read the minds of younger professionals and guess their intentions. Compounding the issue, younger professionals
tend to think that the burden to communicate rests on the firm. Neither
assumption is true. This entire situation could have been avoided had Shawn
simply gone to the CEO and asked the following questions:

- What can I do to achieve partner someday?
- How can I contribute more to the firm?
- What corrections can I make?
- I would like to devote more time to business development. Can you help
  and support me?

If you want your career needs and ambitions to be heard and understood,
you need to take charge of the process and find a way to communicate
them to the leadership of the firm. Sam Allred, the CEO of Upstream
Academy, has trained over a thousand leaders in the CPA industry. He calls
this proactive approach to communication "giving up the right to remain
silent."

Finding the right person or forum for that communication is not always
easy. In a smaller firm (fewer than 10 partners), you should go directly to
the CEO or any other partner in charge of professional development. That
person may hold the title of chief practice officer or another title that indicates
management of all professionals. In a larger firm, you may need to find a
partner involved with professional development who knows you well. This
could be someone who is on the executive committee or highly involved with
career tracks and personnel decisions.

The tone of these conversations should be constructive rather than critical.
To make it clear that you are seeking guidance, do not open the discussion

with a complaint (e.g., "I am unhappy with ..."). Firms will rush to clarify, provide information, and steer the energy of good performers, but firms will become defensive and perhaps dismissive if they sense someone has an axe to grind.

Communicating Your Problems

It is important to communicate not only your ambitions, but also your struggles. Professionals often withdraw from firm life when they experience problems in their personal lives or feel they are not doing well at work. While it is tempting to suffer in silence, a better strategy is to find a mentor you can speak to about your difficulties. It is important for firm leaders to know if they can help you and how. If a problem is professional in nature, you may find that training, encouragement, and being surrounded by a good team go a long way. If the issue is personal, it may be more difficult to discuss, but you can express yourself enough to make it clear that you are not misunderstood or misrepresented.

I have encountered many cases where a young professional is introduced to me as a "future star." A glowing partner will describe to me how well Jane is doing, how much clients love her, and how ambitious she is. A year later, when I meet the same partner and ask how Jane is doing, the answer is puzzling. "Jane is not really a big part of our plans anymore. She is no longer progressing and does not seem interested in her career."

How did Jane go from star to pariah so quickly? What could have happened to change her? My instinct is to ask the partner for Jane's explanation. "We don't really know," is often the response. "We haven't talked." This is clearly a huge mistake on both sides. The leadership of the firm should know better and Jane, who probably senses a change in the partner's attitude, should speak up.

Being Treated Unfairly

I have also encountered situations where the firm makes an unfair assumption. For example: "Julie just had a kid, so she will not be interested in her career anymore." Such cases are alarming and just plain wrong. These assumptions can be directed at both genders. As another example: "He seems to be a lifestyle advisor. He's too busy with his kids." Such statements often reflect deep-seated firm values that are also quite wrong.

To begin with, diametric notions force a false choice: *You are either a family person or a professional. Choose!* If those really are the only choices available to you at your firm, you might be better off changing firms. If this happens to you, signal your intentions and communicate to firm leaders that such assumptions are hurtful—to individuals and to the firm's ability to recruit and retain people. The best outcome may still be leaving the firm. As much as I am a fan of communication, it rarely has the power to change the values of a firm. If you oppose the value system of your partners, you are not likely to succeed.

We will spend all of Chapter 9 discussing how to manage a balanced life. There are times when you just have to "bite your mouthpiece," as boxers will say. Still, if the prevailing attitude in your firm is that you can have either a career or a family, but not both, I would start looking for a way out. That is probably not the type of career you want. It's better to be at a firm where you can focus your energy on demonstrating to your partners or future partners that you are not only a good advisor, but also a capable leader.

Getting Involved

The best way to develop your management skills—and make your career aspirations clear—is to get involved in one of your firm's many management projects or standing committees. There are probably various options from which to choose. Most firms have a variety of standing committees that need more participation and projects that are understaffed. The best choices are areas where you have expertise and interest, but you should also consider helping in areas where you need to develop a skill or where the firm needs help. Signing up for a team that is in need of help demonstrates your commitment to the firm, which is a key part of managing up.

In most firms, the *glamour committees* tend to be the ones oriented toward clients, such as the investment committee or client services projects. The overlooked areas are usually the ones that have to do with training, organizational functions, or staff management. While these may seem to be a departure from the professional focus of the organization, these functions are just as valuable, and you may have the opportunity to establish yourself faster. If the investment committee is already fully staffed or overcrowded, look into areas that are perhaps less popular but equally important like recruiting talent or staff development programs.

Much like the process of developing a new business plan, management also lends itself to specialization. The same way you would specialize in a niche market, it is possible to specialize early on in your career in a management topic. The topic you choose should meet some of the same criteria we would apply to a market:

- Is it an area that is growing and of high importance?
- Is it an area overlooked by others and therefore not in high demand?
- Is it an area that will expose you to working with many of the firm's leaders?
- Is it an area where you can play a leadership role? (Perhaps you are better off leading a less popular project than being one of many professionals in a very crowded committee.)
- Is it an area that provides an opportunity to develop a skill set and knowledge that you can use through the rest of your career?

Young professionals often feel that they should be invited to join a project or a committee in the firm. Volunteering is a better strategy. It sends the message that you are dedicated, thoughtful, and looking to expand your role at the firm. If you identify a project or a committee that you want to be a part of, speak to your mentor or your manager and express your interest.

Remember, participating in internal management is another demand on your time. It is common to volunteer and then realize it puts additional stress on an already full schedule of responsibilities for clients and new business. That said, it is important that you show your colleagues that you are devoted to improving the firm. If you are going to participate in the firm management, dedicate the time necessary to do it right.

Taking Responsibility for Your Team

Part of the responsibility of being a leader in an organization is to advocate on behalf of your team. When you begin managing others and working with staff below you on the organizational chart, one of the best things you can do to enhance your career is to use your exposure to the leadership of the firm to promote your team. When you are sitting in a partner meeting, you are not there just to represent yourself and your own career and ambitions, but also to make sure that your team receives the resources it needs and the recognition it deserves. This approach is critical to successful upstream management.

You can advance your career in a professional services firm by advancing the careers of those with whom you work. Professionals who are known for building and managing a good team always enjoy success and the respect of their partners. In fact, especially in a large firm, a partner who is capable of training and developing other successful professionals may be just as valuable as—if not more valuable than—a lone-wolf partner who is developing a lot of business.

Supporting your team also means taking responsibility for the outcome when things don't go well. When a client is lost or a project is not completed on time, it is a sign of a good leader to take personal responsibility for the problem rather than blaming the team. Blaming others for the lack of success of initiatives in which you are involved never reflects positively on you. Instead, it undermines your relationships with others and erodes your leadership status.

Taking responsibility for your team is another step in the transition from the role of professional to the role of leader. In our professional training, we tend to focus on our own expertise and behavior and how others see us. We strive to be knowledgeable, showcase our expertise in front of the client, build strong personal connections, and be the star of the client services show. Good leadership requires us to do things that are perhaps counterintuitive: Give others the credit, take responsibility for mistakes that were not ours, and help team members succeed. A good leader will take the spotlight and use it to showcase what others can do.

Supporting Your Colleagues

It is impossible to have a successful and fulfilling career if you are not surrounded by colleagues who support and help you. This means you have to be equally supportive and helpful to those around you. It is an unfortunate reality in many firms that there are individuals who perceive a career as a race, where colleagues are competitors rather than teammates. While such behavior can be driven by personality—some people have a more competitive nature than others—it can also be encouraged by the firm's culture or environment.

Such career races are often not based in reality; they are imagined by a professional. Over the long term, the number of opportunities is limited only by the growth and success of a firm. In a firm that is growing and profitable, there is rarely a shortage of chances to step up and take a higher level of responsibility. In fact, there is usually a shortage of professionals who are ready to perform at the next level. If it ever seems to you that there is but one promotion available or one partnership to be earned, take a better look.

I have felt that pressure at times, but in retrospect, it became clear that I was putting pressure on myself. While starting out my career at the accounting firm Moss Adams, I feared that someone would get ahead of me in the line to be a partner. I tried to protect my spot and felt very competitive toward those around me who I perceived to be contesting it. I wish I hadn't tortured myself (and others) with such thoughts. Over the long term, you will have a better career if you are surrounded by talented professionals in a firm that is fast-growing and profitable. While being the star on a bad team may seem tempting, it is a short-sighted goal.

Looking back, every one of my colleagues who was ready to step up and play a bigger role eventually did. The people I once saw as competitors still have relationships with me today. Though we have scattered across many firms in the industry, we still maintain a connection. I have learned much from my former colleagues. Their presence only ever helped my career. They never hurt it.

Another common mistake is to be constantly critical of your colleagues. Naturally, there are times when criticism is necessary. However, if you are always the person with nothing positive to say about your peers, you will find yourself isolated and perhaps left out of opportunities. Building a good relationship and a spirit of camaraderie with your colleagues will not only help you to better enjoy your career at your firm, it will also open the door to many opportunities. Everyone wants to have the person who is always encouraging and supportive as a member of their team, committee, or project. And CEOs do not want to advance the career of professionals who seem to do little else but undermine colleagues. They realize that if you are always criticizing someone who is not in the room, chances are that they are next on the list as soon as they exit.

As your career develops, you will transition from having to prove yourself to firm leaders to being one of those leaders, working with your peers to run the business. Your present-day colleagues will become your future partners. Your cubicle-mate may very well be the next CEO of the firm. Not only will your colleagues advance as fast or faster than you, but the day will come when the former leaders will be gone and you will have to rely on each other. After all, it is not unlikely that someday you and a group of your G2 peers will take the collective risk of buying the firm from its founders.

Measuring Your Criticism

Talented and ambitious professionals too often get labeled as *negative* because they seem to be critical of every initiative and decision. Once someone is labeled that way, it becomes very difficult to erase that reputation and instead be seen as a constructive member of the team. Think of criticism like a potent spice. Without it, a meal will be bland and in need of improvement. However, put too much on, and a dish will become inedible. It is best not to be known as the person who douses everything with too much cayenne.

The desire to criticize comes very naturally to well-educated, smart professionals. The Socratic method of asking probing questions or doubting the effectiveness of solutions is an intellectually appealing way to explore an idea. Unfortunately, one of the best ways to get under the skin of superiors is to constantly question their decisions. When you're behind the wheel, the last thing you want is a backseat driver constantly asking why you chose a particular route. It's no different at the firm.

Two Types of Criticism

There is a difference, however, between *constructive* criticism and criticism in general. Constructive criticism stands out in two distinct ways: (1) It focuses on solutions rather than problems, and (2) it resists the desire to play devil's advocate. In most business situations, a problem can only be solved once a decision is made. Inaction is a decision in itself, so no matter what, an outcome will occur. Criticizing all actions and outcomes is not a constructive approach and it is a good way to get yourself kicked out of meetings. A better strategy is to propose solutions early enough that they can be adopted—or at least discussed during the decision-making process. Managing up relies on constructive advice rather than playing Monday-morning quarterback.

For example, "I don't believe we should be spending a lot of time and resources on social media because it has not been effective for us in the past" becomes constructive criticism when you conclude with a possible solution: "Instead, we should be focusing our efforts on A, B or C." In the absence of the second part, you are offering valid criticism but failing to address the problem. This can derail a productive discussion—or set you up to be shot down too quickly—because it opens the way for the dreaded response: "Do *you* have a better idea?" If you end up criticizing more than one or two of the proposed solutions, you will inevitably be seen as a critical voice who is not excited about anything. In contrast, if you offer an idea every time you argue against one, you can become the kind of professional people seek out and rely on. However, bear in mind that engaging in constructive criticism means you are also prepared to take it. Do not become overly attached to your own ideas. Use them as openings to enhance your understanding and influence in the firm.

The Devil's Advocate

Apparently, the Devil's Advocate was formerly an official office in the Vatican. The Devil's Advocate, usually a cardinal, had the role of arguing against the proposed canonization of a candidate, pointing out his failings and flaws. That may have been a role needed in Rome, but it certainly does not belong in a modern firm.

Playing devil's advocate is a common way of alienating colleagues. There are always professionals in every meeting who believe that their contribution should be to take the opposite position of every proposed solution purely for the sake of debate. Inevitably, they earn a reputation for being negative, difficult, and contrarian. As a result, they are often avoided and excluded from discussions, making it difficult for them to contribute positively. Colleagues will quickly write off the ideas of a devil's advocate, assuming they are based more on opposition than analysis.

The problem with playing devil's advocate is that you are arguing without a purpose, making points that are entirely intellectual and that hold no practical significance. The devil's advocate sabotages the efforts of everyone else without having any concrete goal in mind. If you are not involved in a project and are not willing to invest in finding an alternative solution, then don't entertain the position of shooting down proposals that everyone else agrees on.

Chess players are familiar with the "best-move-available" principle. This simply means that in difficult positions, you may not like the move you are going to make and you may lose pieces as a result, but it is the best move available. This is also often the case in business: You may not like what you are about to do, and the solution may be flawed, but there are no better options. It is in such situations that playing devil's advocate will earn you a bad reputation. No one enjoys picking between the rock and the hard place, but it often has to be done.

This is not to say that you should shut up and get in line. However, G2 professionals must recognize that making decisions is difficult. While criticism can be valuable, it should be mixed in equal parts with new ideas and alternative approaches. Without striving for that balance, you can easily earn the wrong reputation.

Managing Your Own Expectations

A lot of the friction between professionals and their firms occurs because both sides have unreasonable expectations of each other. As you grow your career, you need to communicate with your firm and manager about the expectations your colleagues have of you, but you also need to manage your own expectations.

A career is a marathon. One of the most common mistakes made by marathon runners is to rush out of the starting line and run the first six miles too fast. The race is very long and any energy you expend in the first hour will be badly missed a couple of hours later. The same thing can happen in a career. After you have been with your firm for five years, it may seem like the next year is the time to make or break your standing in the firm. I guarantee you that 10 years later you will barely remember that year while you will likely still be at the same firm and surrounded by many of the same colleagues.

The pressure of expectations comes from two sources: promotions and income. The two are closely tied together. As mentioned before, when I was five years into my career at Moss Adams, I thought that becoming partner would make me financially prosperous and bring me to the top of the consulting profession. Neither statement was true. When you become a partner, you find out that your income is still heavily invested in the business. You also discover that there is an entirely new career that starts at the partner level.

Having patience with income and compensation can be particularly valuable. Many founders perceive salary negotiations to be a sign of a lack of respect or commitment to the firm. Unfortunately, when professionals express concern that their salaries are not competitive, many founders label them mercenaries. This is not to say that you should not bring the subject up, but be careful how aggressive you are in such discussions. If you sense that the conversation is getting too tense, you may be better served waiting another year. I have worked with many firms that are deliberately very generous in the later stages of a career but very sparing in their compensation to early-stage positions.

Impatience can damage your relationships with colleagues and firm leaders by changing their perception of you into someone who is only interested in compensation. It can also lead to rash decisions. I watched a professional who was widely regarded as the future star of his firm leave because the salary increase he received was $10,000 less than expected. He was strongly considered for ownership at the end of the following year, received unlimited attention from the CEO, and was always one of the first choices to work on the top new accounts. He likely would have been the CEO of the firm in 10 to 15 years, but he left for another firm where he got the $10,000 raise, leaving all that opportunity behind.

It is easy to lose perspective when you spend years within one firm. Your relationships become very personal and emotionally charged. When you find yourself questioning the pace of your career progress, the rate of your compensation, or the amount of opportunity you receive, spend some time patiently discussing your expectations with the leadership of the firm. Make your concerns known, but do it in a constructive and patient manner. Most of all, remember that in the context of a 40-year career, one year is a relatively short and perhaps insignificant amount of time.

As a professional, the responsibility to manage your career is yours. While a good firm will help you by giving you the training and resources you need to succeed, if you find yourself stalling or moving too fast, accept that the burden is on you to make a change. Speak up and let your firm leadership know where reality falls short of your expectations and then work with them to find a constructive solution.

CHAPTER 9

Managing Yourself

You can't manage others until you learn to manage yourself. This is one of my favorite ideas from the renowned management consultant and author, Peter Drucker, and failing to understand that concept has sabotaged many careers.[1] Managing yourself consists of the following critical skills:

- Managing your life in a way that affords you the time and energy you need for your career
- Managing your personality, emotions, moods, and weaknesses to prevent them from becoming landmines that damage relationships or your reputation
- Communicating in the right way in all situations to enhance your ability to be a leader and help you maintain excellent relationships with your team

In the tenth year of my career, I came to the realization that my future career beyond that point would not be driven by my ability to be an expert, but rather by my ability to be a teammate, coach, and leader. To accomplish that feat, I needed to manage myself very differently than I had before.

Defining Balance of Life

Most professional service organizations today claim that they want their professionals to have balanced lives, but very few define what that means. Often, when firms profess their commitment to "balance of life," they really mean, "We want you to work a lot, and we can't really tell you to ignore your family, so we hope you figure it out somehow. Good luck."

---

[1] Peter Drucker, *Managing Oneself* (Boston: Harvard Business Press, 2008).

The expectations are growing on both the professional and the personal side. A professional career is very demanding. In many of the top firms in the industry, being successful means that you take on a large volume of client relationships, or the equivalent in operational responsibilities. You are also coached to be a leader and to train others. In addition, you are expected to develop new business. In the personal sphere, you are expected to actively participate in family chores, school functions, and community events in order to be a good spouse, parent, and community member. None of these responsibilities are negotiable. The pressure is high. This pressure tends to start building in your thirties and early forties.

Based on my personal experience—I have no theory or statistics to back this up—the best strategy to follow when those high-pressure years hit is quite simply to survive. There is no magic formula, and most of us find it impossible to balance professional and personal demands on our time without being frustrated and stressed out. The only way to deal with difficult choices is to accept them.

Much like a marathon runner accepts the fact that miles 20 to 25 will be nothing but pain and exhaustion, there are a few years in your professional life that will bring you the same level of challenge. There is really no way to avoid those few years of frustration, during which time you will be stressed out, pressured, and frustrated. The key is to hold out for mile 26. The crowd cheers, the finish line comes into view, and the joy of running returns.

Finding balance in this context means nothing more than spreading the damage as best you can. Try not to miss too many soccer games, but accept that you will have to miss some. Try not to miss too many big client meetings, but accept that you will not always be able to attend. At times you will inevitably disappoint people both at home and at work with your limited availability. You will also disappoint yourself with your inability to juggle it all. As anyone who has ever run a marathon can tell you, there will be times when you just can't run anymore and must walk. That's okay. What matters is that you don't stop. Similarly, there will be times when you are not the most ambitious professional in the office or the most dedicated parent at the soccer game. Again, that's okay. Just never stop trying to be both.

Balance of life sounds much nicer in concept than in reality. The reality is that if you set out with the ambition to achieve in every area of your life, you will pay a price. That price is a heightened stress level and a depletion of your personal energy. Walk into the little boxing gym that I go to in Seattle and you will notice that it is a very friendly place where people will embrace and support you. That said, make no mistake: The canvas that covers the ring floor is marked by blood stains. Boxing hurts, and the more you try to achieve, the more you will bleed.

I don't want to sound excessively gloomy. In the long term, your life will be quite balanced and enjoyable. As you grow in your firm, things will come together over time: Your responsibilities will stabilize, your productivity will increase, your ability to delegate will improve, and everything you do will become easier and more efficient. At home, the kids will grow up and need less of your time and help, responsibilities will fall into a groove, and everything will get better. You just have to get through that rough patch.

I hit that rough patch when I was two to three years away from making partner. All of my new business development and team management responsibilities started simultaneously, my son was still young, and my daughter had just been born. Because both my wife and I were reaching the same place in our respective professional careers, finding the right balance between our family and jobs was especially difficult and frustrating.

A smaller version of this experience hit me just this last year. With the Ensemble Practice in its fourth year and growing, it is reaching its capacity limits and demanding more and more of my time. Meanwhile, I wish I could spend more time at home with my family. In fact, I am writing this chapter on a plane to Phoenix, a day after missing my daughter's birthday.

In other words, I am in no position to advise you on how to find balance. All I can say is that there will be times when you have to "bite your mouthpiece and tuck your chin," as boxers say. You will find the right balance of life eventually. Just remember: It comes in the long term, not the short term.

Balancing Time

"So much to do, so little time" is the mantra of every G2 professional. The demands on your time are seemingly endless. You shoulder a massive client load to demonstrate your productivity, train and coach others, contribute to the management of your firm, and network and develop new business. Chances are that you are also an attentive mother or father, a loving spouse, and a good daughter or son. You go to PTA meetings, volunteer at the school, freeze your bones spectating at bad soccer games, and take in endless innings of Little League Baseball watching little pitchers struggling to throw a single strike. It is all expected of you. As they say, "If you are good at digging ditches, they reward you with a bigger shovel!" How are you supposed to tackle everything in 24 hours?

Balance can look very different from one professional to another. What creates balance in the life of one advisor differs from what creates balance in the life of another. So much of this discussion hinges on your family life, personal situation, goals, and ambitions. That said, there are certain components of a healthy life balance that are perhaps universally desired. Finding the time to cultivate them is difficult but essential:

- You should have personal goals that are just as ambitious as your business goals.
- You should surround yourself with friends and family who provide you with the relationships you need to feel connected.
- You should have the ability to manage your health. That may mean staying in shape or meeting your medical needs if there are special circumstances.
- You should have hobbies and interests outside the business. Not having any puts you at risk of having trouble connecting with others, including colleagues and clients.
- You should have presence in and be connected to your community.

Appreciate Flexibility

While professional service firms all struggle with the notion of balance, they also provide a valuable benefit that other kinds of firms don't: flexibility. Many times your busy schedule will require you to stay at the office late, begin early, or travel. Hopefully, this also means that there are times when you have the flexibility to leave early, start late, or take a day off. If intensity and long hours are the cost, flexibility is the benefit.

I have learned to appreciate and use the flexibility that my schedule allows. The best news is that you can usually anticipate when you will have flexibility. I know that Friday afternoons are quiet. I know that July and August are quiet. I know that not much is going to go on around the holidays. Whenever you sense that flexibility, you can definitely take advantage and schedule more time at home: an extra school pickup, an extra baseball practice, or even a family road trip you have been delaying.

Don't Let Others Distract You

The single biggest reason why you spend long hours at the office is conversations you have with colleagues. These conversations can easily consume hours of your day. They may start as a short exchange about a client but then turn into a full-blown discussion of the weather. We are human and we love to have conversations. They entertain us, they engage us, and they strengthen our relationships. Unfortunately, they also kill our schedule by consuming all the gaps between meetings and client calls.

While it is a bit antisocial, discouraging others from wasting your time is a great habit to have. Ideally, every conversation has a goal and a purpose. What information do you need? What decisions do you need to make? Beyond that purpose, it should be okay to interrupt your colleagues and ask them for a chance to return to your work. If you don't, the price you pay is less time at home and more late nights at the office catching up on the tasks of the day.

Schedule Time for Preparing and Writing

Most people need time and peace to write. Writing is also a very important part of our jobs. We write client e-mails, letters, minutes, and notes from meetings, blogs, articles, and research reports. Preparing to write and the task of writing itself both require you to set aside a block of time where that can be your singular focus. These blocks of time should appear on your calendar as appointments. If you do not formally reserve time on your calendar, you may never be able to complete the writing tasks you set for yourself.

Protect Your Time

One of the best things I have ever done to manage the flood of personal and business responsibilities is to add all of my nonnegotiable responsibilities to my calendar. Whether it is a client call or a soccer game, if I need to be there, I will put it on my calendar and let it be known I am not available. I literally block out my calendar to drive my daughter to school or attend a school play because I know from experience that if I don't, a phone call or a meeting will appear on the schedule.

At first it seemed a little awkward to fill up my work schedule with school plays, but having missed too many of those little family things that are so important, I started treating them like client meetings: time that is reserved and nonnegotiable. While such appointments can elicit a reaction from your colleagues—both your peers and professionals above you on the organizational chart—I have learned that I would rather face those questions than have to explain at home why I am missing another school function. No matter the culture of your firm, your colleagues will respect your personal appointments. After all, chances are that most of them have family, too, and are struggling with the same issues.

Train Others to Work with You

Another survival technique is to train your colleagues and family to appreciate how busy you are and to help you manage your schedule. A critical time in my work life is the Monday staff meeting, when all members of my staff gather together to discuss any projects, calls, or client deliverables that are pending. Following this meeting, I spend some time one-on-one with each of my colleagues reviewing projects that we share. A very important rule in Monday meetings is that all asking of questions, coordination, and scheduling has to happen at that time. Everyone must come prepared, and all responsibilities have to be allocated. It is definitely not okay to improvise at the last moment or schedule on the fly.

In a similar way, my wife and I (and we are both equally busy) have a standing Sunday "management meeting." This is the time to arrange for school pickups, soccer-practice driving, cello-lesson waiting, and everything else. It may sound a little overengineered to have management meetings in a family, but we find these meetings to be key to our survival. Before we started them, we had the frustration of the school play being booked at the same time as a client meeting, or the panicked texts at 3:00 P.M.: "Who is picking up our daughter from school? I thought you were!"

Gradually, both family and colleagues should understand that you need to plan, and that your ability to spontaneously join activities is limited. This may not be the best of situations, but again, finding the right balance of life simply means surviving (at least for a time). While I sometimes envy parents who have no trouble staying for another hour at the office or driving to an extra practice, finding a systematic way to balance your time can be essential in order not to miss the things that matter most.

Dealing with Weaknesses

The principle of "focusing on your strengths" is so prevalent in management literature and coaching programs that it has become second nature to business owners. Time and again, we use phrases such as "It's not my strength" or

"I'm not really good at that." This implies that since a task is not one of our competencies, we should avoid it, outsource it, delegate it, or even sweep it under the carpet. As a result, we rarely undertake any initiatives or projects that we do not perceive as being part of what we do well.

I often wonder if this method of behavior is a sign of sound strategy or mere conformity. After all, how do we acquire new skills if we never go outside of our comfort zone? If we stayed focusing throughout our lives only on things that we did well, we would still be arranging wooden blocks by color like we did in daycare. Clearly, we are capable of developing new skills. Things we are going to be very good at next year require a nascent and awkward effort today. So shouldn't we spend some time addressing our weaknesses and turning them into strengths rather than always dodging them and doing the same things we have become comfortable doing?

There is a perception we all share that our characters and the skillsets that we rely on for the rest of our careers are developed earlier in life (although it's unclear when this process is supposed to stop). We assume that our personalities and skills continue to form up to a certain point in life, after which we have little hope of changing and just play with the cards in our hands. In fact, there was a strong scientific following for this theory all the way until the middle of the twentieth century: Scientists believed that we form our major pathways in our childhoods and that our adult brains are more or less fixed. As Nobel Prize–winning neuroscientist Santiago Ramón y Cajal wrote in 1928, "In adult centers the nerve paths are something fixed, ended, immutable."[2]

As it turns out, this theory is wrong. Not only do we continue to build new pathways throughout our lives, but very importantly, we lose the ones we don't use. In other words, there is no neurological reason why we can't develop new skills. Stagnation is merely the result of us choosing not to invest in development. In addition, by not exercising certain skills, we progressively get worse at them.[3]

What does that mean in practical terms? All professionals should spend at least some of their time and energy focusing on improving their areas of weakness rather than steering clear of them. If you are not good at managing people, perhaps applying a consistent effort to improve your skills in this

---

[2]Santiago Ramón y Cajal, *Degeneration and Regeneration in the Nervous System* (New York: Oxford Press, 1991 reprint edition).

[3]The theory of *brain plasticity* is well documented and accepted and covered in many books, including Norman Doiges, *The Brain That Changes Itself* (New York: Penguin, 2007).

area would give you success and a better return on investment than hiring a professional manager. If you are not good at business development and sales, perhaps making an effort to be more involved in the new client acquisition process would eventually yield greater results for you and your firm than paying third-party solicitors. If you are not very organized in your work, perhaps disciplining yourself to follow a process would improve your practice and your own abilities more than just giving up and declaring yourself "an artist."

We often project this fixed-skillset thinking onto G2 professionals, who are usually very young and certainly not set in their ways. I have frequently overheard such comments made about young professionals at firms. For example, "She is not good with sales" or "He just can't manage people." While these statements may be made in a caring voice with the best intentions—"We recognize that he is not good at it, and we will help him work around it"—a better strategy is to challenge G2 professionals to improve in areas where they do not excel and encourage and support them in the process of building new skills.

Doing what feels comfortable and what we are good at is a satisfying and highly successful strategy in the short term. In the long term, however, letting our weaknesses define our strategy is often disastrous. After all, the ability to adapt, change, and acquire new skills is what drives evolution—perhaps in business, as well.

Thoughtful Communication

Many G2 professionals find themselves in a tough spot. Pressured by the demands of clients, colleagues, and partners, they end up frustrated and at times let those feelings out. As a result, they can be labeled as *difficult*, which introduces new problems and pressures. Trust me: I have been there many times.

It was a Monday afternoon, and I was angry. My whole body was angry. I could feel my pulse in my throat. I could feel my blood pressure in my head. My teeth were grinding. I had been on the phone since 8:00 A.M. There were dozens of e-mails in my inbox, but I had not had a chance to even glance at them. With no time for either breakfast or lunch, I substituted my meals with four cups of coffee (as I often do). The office was hot, and the AC was not working well. Every call I had had that morning consisted of things I needed to do and things clients expected of me. Everybody wanted something from me.

This day was a house of cards just waiting for someone to reach down and say, "Hey, let me look at this jack of spades here at the bottom!" And then the cards fell: I was double-booked. I began writing an angry e-mail to the colleague who had scheduled the appointment. It was all his fault. My schedule being crammed like that was his fault. I thought of a hundred ways to scold my colleague, each colder and angrier than the last. Negative thoughts raced through my mind, accelerating my rage. With every sentence I typed, the message grew more poisonous. Hitting send on this e-mail was going to be like letting out an angry roar.

But then, I paused.

We often think of our body as the vessel that carries our consciousness around. If the body is the car, our brain and our thoughts are the passengers. We treat our brain and our body as separate and very different things, but they are not. The body is not just our vessel—it is part of who we are. Likewise, our thoughts are not some higher form of existence, pure and untarnished. Stress is not just a state of mind. It is a state of the body, too.

Where does the anger come from? Does it come from self-righteous frustration with a colleague, or perhaps from a starved body signaling its needs? Does it come from an overcaffeinated nervous system trying to say, "Enough!" Or perhaps from an overheated and uncomfortable torso, sweating in a chair? Who is actually typing the angry e-mail? Is it the busy but constructive CEO, or the frustrated and overheated animal who is feeling a little scared and overwhelmed by his environment? How do we know which it is?

Take a pause. It is natural for our bodies to react. They are designed that way. And our minds are part of that system, too. They take part in the reaction. But we need something more than simple reaction if we want to communicate thoughtfully. We need action. Taking a pause creates the necessary space between reaction and action, between the thoughtless lashing out of the frustrated animal and the thoughtful action of a socialized being.

If you watch sports, you have seen this many times. At the moment of highest pressure, when the game is on the line, the athlete goes through a personal ritual: He bounces the ball three times, no more and no less. He wipes his forehead with his left hand and takes five deep breaths. He shakes his arms in a limbering motion, loosens his neck and jaw, touches his toes, and relaxes his back. Finally, he explodes into action and serves the ball, shoots the free throw, kicks the penalty kick, or jumps at the starting signal. Why do athletes perform these little rituals?

This ritual is the pause before the action. It is the chance to calm the body and mind and focus on your purpose. The ritual slows the breathing, relaxes the muscles, decelerates the heartbeat, and quiets the hyperchatter of the brain so that body and mind can be as focused and capable as possible and find the right action for the moment. The pause is the difference between the reaction and the action.

Awareness of our own emotions and their source can save us a lot of aggravation and prevent damage to relationships we need and cherish. While I am a believer in the value of conflict, mindless anger is not the same thing as a purposeful fight. So when you feel yourself on the verge of snapping, remember to pause, calm the frustrated animal within, and focus your energy on the action of thoughtful communication.

On the Value of Conflict

Conflict is everywhere in our daily lives. It can appear as the guy honking his horn behind us in gridlocked traffic, the person who cuts into the line at the airport, the coworker who disagrees with us, and the spouse who forgets to buy coffee. Conflict surrounds us. And though we experience conflict frequently, we tend to avoid it and hope it goes away instead of exploring it and using its creative potential. That's right: Conflict can be creative and constructive.

We love conflict when it happens to other people. We are entertained by TV shows and movies full of dramatic confrontations. We delight in laughing at the absurdity of behaviors that occur when other people clash. We get excited when our sports teams and favorite athletes square off against each other. We like taking sides, trying to find wrong and right and waiting for the emergence of winners and losers. We crane our necks at car wrecks, watch heated debates, and eavesdrop on angry conversations. We even snicker privately at the couple having it out in public. Simply put: We love drama. The heightened emotions that arise from such passionate interactions appeal to something inside us.

When it comes to experiencing conflict ourselves, we quickly lose our taste for it. We fight, flee, or freeze. Our breath shortens, our pulse races, our muscles tense, we clench our teeth, our emotions rise to our throat, and we lose control of what we should do or say. We often feel embarrassed and humiliated when we have to back out, but we also regret it when we confront another person who is ready for a fight. Conflict makes us uncomfortable.

Imagine you are in a meeting. You just presented an idea you have been working on for a month. You love your idea and believe it will really benefit your business. Then somebody across the table says, "That's a really bad idea!" How do you react? Are you calm and composed or is your heart skipping beats as you try to come up with some kind of response?

Businesspeople could learn a lot from boxers. Boxers know a little something about conflict: They practice it as their passion and sometimes as their profession. When they enter the ring, they experience confrontation in its most physical manifestation. Boxers know that if you let the fight-or-flight mechanism take over, you will not have a good fight. The out-of-control, raging animal is not a good boxer. Its reactions are delayed, its tense limbs are slow, its angry brain is unfocused and muddled. By recognizing the way the body prepares for conflict, boxers learn to be more comfortable in the ring and are more likely to land their punches.

Tricia Turton, my business partner at the boxing gym, has fought many boxing matches, both as an amateur and as a professional, competing twice for the world title. Tricia now coaches boxers to be better at conflict. She discovered that many of her clients are business owners and leaders who come to the gym not only for the fitness value, but also to experience the intense situations that boxing offers. They often feel that the intensity of the experience in the ring matches the intensity of the experience in the boardroom. They want to be better at conflict.

That's right: You can learn to be better at conflict, and that's a valuable skill to have. If you approach conflict with curiosity rather than giving in to the fight-or-flight response, you will discover how constructive fighting can be. Watch yourself and the other person when you encounter a confrontation and start recognizing the automatic signs. That in itself will make you a better fighter, whether in the boardroom or the cubicle.

Our country was born out of conflict. The universe started with a Big Bang. We are born crying our lungs out. Clearly, conflict can be constructive and creative. It brings the truth out of us and our relationships and then helps us build something newer and stronger. Research shows that couples who fight early in their courtships tend to have better and stronger relationships.[4] The ability to passionately disagree and find the truth in an argument is very valuable to any business or personal relationship.

Tricia calls this *sharing punches*—the ability to fight without hurting each other. The notion of sparring, or conflict under control, is very intriguing in business and in life. Boxers have to train to fight, but they don't want a

---

[4]Daniel Goleman, "Want a Good Marriage? Learn to Fight a Good Fight," *New York Times* (February 21, 1989).

training injury to keep them from the tournament. That's why they spar. In sparring, the punches are real but not meant to hurt.

Any relationship can be improved when the two people learn to spar. The ability to confront each other with arguments, passion, and emotion, but also to find that balance between your point of view and hurting the other person, is so valuable. Controlled conflict allows the strengths and weaknesses you each bring to the relationship to be brought to light while preventing you from hurting each other beyond repair.

Sparring takes a lot of skill. It requires recognizing the reactions of the body and keeping them in check. It also requires approaching conflict with curiosity rather than blind reaction. Most of all, it requires trusting the other person to do the same—to exercise self-control and not escalate the debate into a bloody and mindless fight.

Conflict is everywhere. While we tend to avoid it and frown upon it, perhaps we should embrace it instead. By learning to be more comfortable in the fight, we can harness the creative power of conflict. We make our relationships stronger when we learn how to share punches with each other. Appreciating the value of conflict is an important lesson to learn in business and in life.

Looking at Your Own Plate

In my native Bulgaria, people say that "happiness is doing a little better than your neighbor." As much as I agree with that, I would also add that the shortest road to misery goes through your neighbor's driveway. Beyond outright conflict, I have often found a layer of festering dissatisfaction in many firms caused by either a perceived or real lack of fairness in the way professionals are treated vis-à-vis their colleagues.

I can't believe how many times I have worked with successful professionals who were immensely bothered by the compensation, achievement, recognition, position, or advancement received by a colleague. This is going to sound like a page out of a self-help book, but I really want to offer this piece of advice to all G2 professionals: Define your own goals and measure your achievements relative to those goals rather than relative to the achievements of your colleagues. Any other mentality will leave you constantly dissatisfied and potentially very unhappy.

Not that my writing needs any more analogies, but I can't help but think of that moment at a restaurant when dinner arrives. Perhaps there are five or six of you around the table, and each has ordered a different dish. When the food is served, you look around and feel pangs of regret. "Wow! That beef looks so good! I wish I had ordered that instead of the chicken. My chicken does not look all that great. That fish also looks delicious. Why did I have to order the chicken? I get the worst dish every time!"

This kind of dinner-plate mentality will not serve you well in your career. By definition, in a successful firm, you will be surrounded by a number of high-performing, talented individuals who are earning accolades, promotions, and high incomes. In fact, the more successful the firm, the more likely you are to be surrounded by such people. Their achievements should inspire happiness and satisfaction, not disappointment. After all, their successes assure the continued success of your firm. Unfortunately, a part of you will always wonder whether they took those opportunities from you. Were you treated fairly? Have they gotten more than they deserve? Please, do yourself a favor and tell that part of your brain to let go. Look at your own plate.

G2 professionals often worry about career progression. If someone is hired ahead of them, or if a perceived peer is promoted first or earns an opportunity they thought they deserved, they get upset. Such thoughts can be very toxic and are also quite counterproductive. Careers at a successful firm are rarely like the counter at an airline service desk, where if someone cuts ahead of you he takes your spot. This is not just a matter of mentality. It is a matter of fact.

The only time promotions and advancements become a zero-sum game is in organizations where there is very little growth and someone must retire before there is another opening for a lead advisor or partner. This is not what advisory firms look like today. The typical firm in our industry is rapidly growing and changing. There is no shortage of chances, so this it's-me-or-you thinking does not apply. Firms need professionals who are ready to take advantage of those chances.

The person who pulled ahead of you may turn out to be your best friend. She just received the promotion you seek, so ask her questions. What did she do that you can also do? What does it feel like to be in the next position? What were the challenges that she faced that you will also face? What can you learn from her experience? In many ways, the best mentor you could ever have is that person who is just a little bit ahead of you on the career track. That is the person who can best relate to your experience because she still vividly remembers everything you are going through.

Dangerous competition also takes over when professionals get a chance to compare compensation, either explicitly or through an implicit analysis. It is inevitable that every person in a firm will try to guess how much everyone else is paid. When professionals become partners, they often find out how much everyone else in the firm is compensated. This can be a very stressful experience.

Once again, avoid looking at the plates of others. Instead, begin with an analysis of the market. What is the prevailing compensation for your position in the industry? How does your pay compare to your expectations? How does it compare to the market? How quickly is your income growing? Are you excited about the rate of change and the direction of your opportunity? Can you see exciting possibilities in your future?

That additional $10,000 or $20,000 you could win in a compensation argument with your partners will make very little difference to your sense of happiness or fulfillment with what you are doing in the long term. And the bridges you burn in that argument may very well be bridges you need. Those bridges may be connections to people who are instrumental to the progress of your career.

The line between being treated unfairly and feeling slighted is very fuzzy. Whenever you feel like you are getting the short end of stick, keep an open mind. There are three possibilities here:

1. Your firm is treating you poorly, and it is intentionally doing so.
2. You are feeling slighted, but realistically you are wrong and your firm is actually treating you well.
3. Your firm is not treating you as well as it could, but this is by omission rather than intention. Firm leaders have simply made a mistake.

If you ever truly believe your firm is treating you poorly and that it is doing so purposefully, you should not remain with that firm in the long term. If the leadership of the firm is really not giving you the recognition and compensation you deserve as part of a deliberate plan, then you are working in the wrong place. No matter how much you believe your career is tied to the firm, chances are you will be much better off starting someplace else. There is no circumstance in which you should work in a firm where you don't trust the leaders. This would be like getting in a car when you know the driver is drunk. Don't do it!

On the other hand, if you have some doubts about either the objectivity of your perceptions or the circumstances that led to the decision you disagree with, approach the issue with curiosity, goodwill, and good intentions. Protect the relationships you have in your firm because they are extremely valuable to your future success. Examine your own thought process. Could you be wrong?

While the first half of your career in an advisory firm is defined by your professional excellence and your ability to work with clients, the second half of your career—the half we talk about in this book—relies on your ability to work with others: your team, your partners, and your firm. The more you are able to manage your personal energy, motivate yourself, balance your stress factors, control your emotions, and root your sense of satisfaction to your own accomplishments, the more successful you will be.

CHAPTER 10

Owner, Manager, and Leader

As professionals master their craft and reach the highest levels of expertise and responsibility, they discover that in order to continue their career progress, they need to get involved in management and become leaders in their firms. The idea that those who are good at being advisors should focus on being advisors and those who are good at management should focus on management is overly simplistic and often harmful to both the firm and its professionals. Leadership is a quality rather than a position, and possessing leadership is both a privilege and a burden. Firms need many leaders from all parts of the organization.

Every professional should aspire to be an owner. That's the highest level of responsibility and achievement. While not all owners will manage, they should at least be well informed and perhaps involved. All should be leaders in some capacity, taking charge of various functions in different situations. Understanding what it means to be an owner, including your responsibilities as a manager and a leader, is critical to your career success. This also means that firms should be very clear with professionals on what exactly is expected of them and when.

Defining *Owner, Manager,* and *Leader*

Let's begin by carefully defining our terms. First, we will continue to use the terms *owner* and *partner* interchangeably to refer to someone who has a share of the firm and is actively involved in the business. The nature of ownership means that these professionals are invested in the success of the firm both professionally and financially. To introduce an analogy, if the firm is on a road trip, the owners are the ones who own the vehicle.

Managers drive the car: steering, controlling the speed, and ensuring that the vehicle remains operational and safe. For our purposes, *management* refers to the act of day-to-day decision making that allows the firm to operate.

If management is driving the car, *leadership* is setting the destination and navigating the path. Leaders make high-level decisions that have long-term consequences and determine the direction of the firm. Leaders also communicate the values of the organization to stakeholders (i.e., owners, employees, and clients) and continuously promote those values through their words and actions.

As simple as these definitions may be, there will still be some ambiguity between these three roles. As anyone who has taken a family trip can tell you, the driver and the owner of the vehicle will have just as much to say about the direction of the car as the navigator. Ultimately, all three groups are responsible for what happens in the car, so their responsibilities will inevitably overlap.

Management

Just as a car operated by an inattentive or unqualified driver becomes dangerous, a firm without competent management is a risky operation. Every firm must designate managers, the professionals who will make sure that daily and monthly decisions are made so that the firm can continue to operate well and serve its clients, employees, and owners.

Frequently, the owners of the firm—who are usually professional advisors—have some aversion to management. Acting as manager distracts from their other professional responsibilities ("best-use-of-time" concept) and can be quite aggravating, particularly when it requires dealing with employee behavior. For this reason, partners in many firms wish they could delegate management to somebody else.

Management in an Ensemble Firm

In a team-based firm, there should always be some involvement in management required from lead professionals. At the very least, advisors must manage their service teams to be effective. For firm management to be productive and maintain its connection to clients, it needs to find a way to involve professionals in various committees and management functions so that the voices of both clients and professionals are heard in every management meeting.

It's natural that some professionals prefer to focus on management because that's where their interests and talents lie while others are passionate about service and want to focus on working with clients. That said, all professionals—particularly owners—should stay connected to the firm's professional activities so that they can continue to feel the pulse of clients, even if they ultimately pursue a full-time career in management.

It's important to distinguish between management as a full-time job and taking a role in management. While key management positions should certainly be full-time, every practicing partner (and perhaps every lead professional) should have some involvement in management. Taking a role in management could simply mean that professionals lead and manage their respective teams, or it could involve actively participating in one of the many committees or project teams that make decisions on behalf of the firm.

Every professional should see management responsibilities as an integral part of the job. Directing the client service team is a key activity and absolutely necessary in order for the client to receive the right outcome. Participating in committees and projects is a necessary extension of making decisions on behalf of clients. No one dreams of having more committee meetings on the calendar, but without them firms can end up making some very poor decisions. It is kind of like going to the gym. While exercising may not be your favorite activity, you shouldn't skip it if you want to stay healthy.

Arguments about best use of time often keep practicing professionals away from such management responsibilities or implicitly excuse them from participating. As a result, too many decisions are made by a very small group of people who have inadequate exposure to their colleagues or clients. That's why it is so important for all professionals to participate in the management of the firm.

The reverse is also true: Dedicated managers can benefit from having some functional responsibilities, or at least sitting in on some client meetings. This keeps them connected to clients, their concerns, and their hopes. Tim Kochis, founder and former CEO of Aspiriant, took part in client meetings until his last day at the firm, even though his full-time job and primary responsibility was being CEO. During an interview at our G2 Training Program in February 2016, Tim insisted that doing so kept him grounded and connected to work with clients. This experience is necessary to fully serve clients and set the firm up for success.

Training Management Skills

Management skills can be acquired, and it is the responsibility of every firm to train its partners how to be managers, or at least how to participate in management. In large accounting and consulting firms, such training begins very early in the career path as firms systematically seek to introduce future partners to all aspects of running the firm. In such firms, professionals encounter their first management responsibilities as soon as they earn their first promotion. This is followed by an extensive emphasis on their professional ability to train and develop those who work with them and for them.

There is no reason why advisory firms cannot and should not do the same. Participating in management is not a distraction for the partners of a firm. On the contrary: It is part of the very experience of being a partner. *Participation*, of course, is a very broad term. It may mean anything from dedicating a significant amount of time to simply staying informed and providing input when needed. While it is impractical to expect every partner to be involved in every decision all the time, a good firm should ensure that each partner at a minimum participates in at least one management committee, has some employee responsibilities, and follows the work of the firm's management.

Managing is like parenting. While you can certainly ask others to participate—there will be teachers and babysitters involved—raising children is a job that ultimately falls to the parents alone. Granted, none of us enjoy changing diapers or disciplining children, but if we miss too many of these unpleasant moments, we will not have a deep connection with our kids. And at the end of the day, if you are not involved, you will likely have issues with the outcome.

Professional Management

While all lead professionals should play a role in management, this does not preclude the need for professional management. Professional management is absolutely necessary, and its importance increases with the size of the firm. Firms with over $1 billion in assets under management (i.e., super-ensembles) likely have a chief operating officer. In these larger advisory firms, management comprises many aspects and requires multiple managers. According to the *2015 InvestmentNews Compensation and Staffing Survey*, 58 percent of super-ensembles have a chief operating officer, 58 percent have a chief investment officer, 45 percent have a chief compliance officer, and 72 percent have a CEO.[1]

The critical question then becomes where firms find the best professional managers. I believe that when management—and especially leadership—in a large advisory firm comes from the ranks of the practicing partners who have grown their careers within the firm, the result is more likely to be a powerful representation of the firm's client service philosophy and values. These home-grown managers are well-steeped in the culture of the firm and are likely to incorporate it into the management process as they guide the firm into the future. In contrast, when the firm imports its future managers and leaders, the result is often a disconnect between the culture of the firm and the people who set its direction.

I am not trying to argue totally against hiring managers from the outside. There is no reason why some (or even many) managers in a firm should not come from the outside. These externally hired managers bring specialized knowledge and experience and can help the firm make better decisions. However, they don't know the firm as well, don't immediately have the respect and trust of staff, and won't immediately understand the culture. When all managers are outsiders, that can be very damaging to the culture of the firm and limit the effectiveness of management.

In fact, the greatest competitive advantage of independent firms may very well be that owners and managers are also advisors in the firm. This means that everyone making decisions has a very clear and recent view of what really matters to clients and what is in their best interests. If the management of the firm consists mostly of non-advisors, it becomes very easy to rationalize decisions that promote efficiency but destroy relationships.

Examples of decisions that create efficiency but damage relationships are numerous: raising fees beyond what is reasonable or competitive, firing small-client relationships regardless of potential or connections, or constructing portfolios based on ease of management rather than client needs. While these are good management decisions for the bottom line, they are very poor client decisions. Including the voices of practicing professionals in management provides that balance between efficiency and client interests. To return to our road-trip analogy, a car with only professional drivers is nothing more than a taxicab, and that won't get you very far.

---

[1] InvestmentNews, *Compensation and Staffing Survey* (2015).

Leadership

A firm needs more than just managers to be successful. It also needs leaders. *Leadership* is a term that is so frequently used that it has perhaps lost all meaning. My favorite definition of leadership is: the process of making difficult decisions, accepting responsibility for them, and convincing others to follow through. Difficult decisions exist in every area of the business and therefore a firm can practically never have enough leaders. There will always be a difficult decision looking for someone to own it.

Leadership is not a job. Rather, it is a quality and a responsibility. Some jobs imply leadership. For example, CEOs must be good leaders in order to be effective. Leadership is also not permanent. Leaders may become followers or vice versa. As General George Patton said, "Lead me, follow me, or get out of my way!"

Leadership is a burden. It means providing unwavering belief in the success of the firm, inspiring others even when you may need inspiration yourself, and always holding yourself to a very high standard. Only a few are willing to carry that burden. In fact, if only a few partners are interested in management, even fewer are interested in being leaders. Leadership has to come from somewhere, though; otherwise employees and clients can feel the lack of direction.

A few weeks ago we were hiking with another family. Our group was made up of four adults and three kids. At one point, the adults started arguing about which direction to go. We had a very sketchy map and a very ambiguous set of directions. We had spent maybe 10 minutes in a friendly discussion of direction when we noticed that the kids' faces were getting longer and longer. The youngest started crying, and the older ones started fretting. "We are lost," they whimpered. "We will never get home again!" This is what happens when there is no leadership in a firm. The kids get scared.

The Scope of Leadership

Leadership models differ in how centralized they are. Centralizing leadership creates a more decisive organization that can act and react more quickly while decentralizing leadership increases the reach of the organization and ensures that every aspect of the business receives attention. Effective leadership requires aspects of both. Leaders are not only decision makers, they are also ambassadors of the firm's values. Take the Knights of the Round Table as an example: Each rode on a quest to spread the values of Camelot. A successful firm will have a process for taking decisive action and then ask its partners to deliver that new vision to the rest of the firm.

CEOs and managing partners should always be leaders. The responsibilities inherent to these posts necessitate that professionals participate in articulating the vision of the firm and endorsing its values. However, the CEO should not be the only source of leadership in a professional services firm. Rather, all partners should participate in the process. Some firms try to emulate a more corporate management model. Many overdo the corporate part by reducing the role of partners to leading their respective teams and waving the flag of firm values.

I am not advocating that every partner should try to run the firm. Neither should the firm's management committee become a supergroup of many partners who discuss every decision and vote constantly, as was the case in the advertising agency depicted in the television series, *Mad Men*. A firm should both have professional managers and offer leadership opportunities throughout the firm for both partners and non-partner professionals.

Leadership beyond the Founders

The stamp of the founders is always felt, whether they are still part of the firm or not. Some of the habits the founders created may be less beneficial than others. Firms where founders were very reluctant to be leaders will likely be succeeded by a generation of future owners who share the belief that they should not be driving the car. Similarly, firms where the founders preferred to drive from the backseat are likely to create a group of future backseat drivers. The founders' behavior sets the tone for everything that is to come.

In my experience, there is no such thing as a founder who is not a leader. There are those who acknowledge their responsibility to lead, and there are others who lead from the backseat, but a founder is always a leader. Some just hate admitting it. The natural fragmentation of professional services makes it very important for founders to propagate leadership and seek the involvement of many leaders. Ideally there should be a leader in every client meeting and every team gathering, not so much to keep an eye on things as to set the right tone, establish a unified presence, and facilitate open communication.

Leadership is defined by the context of the group and the situation. Leaders can run executive committee meetings or simply command attention during a happy-hour conversation. Every professional should aspire to be involved in management and act as a leader. Exposure to management and leadership not only enhances a career, it takes it to a new level. Independent firms must cultivate people who want to be involved in growing, improving, and directing the firm rather than abdicating management and leadership to outside professionals. When that connection is made and leadership becomes an integral part of the advisor experience, the strength of the firm will be preserved as it transitions from one group of owners to another.

CHAPTER 11

Adding Owners: The Firm's Perspective

For any firm, adding new owners is a big deal. It should be treated as such and celebrated for what it is: a clear sign of success—for the business as well as the individual. When a firm adds new owners, it means that it is growing and thriving. Owners are highly capable professionals who contribute to the firm's success, and they provide a stable foundation for future growth. New owners should add to that stability by increasing the depth of the firm's ownership.

A governance model that sets partnership as a high bar is preferable to one in which such a promotion is easy. When everyone is a partner, the role is no longer special. A sequence of half-hearted promotions and low criteria for advancement undermine any title, and a string of advances like that make the ultimate role of ownership seem ordinary. Professionals who follow such a smoothened ordinary path are rarely motivated to make an emotional commitment to the role.

No one wears his T-shirt from the 5K race he finished, but everyone keeps forever their marathon shirt (some people have too many). There is no reason to award a medal simply for participation. If ownership is given to all professionals who participate in the firm for a number of years, it loses its specialness. When the partner title is diluted, people do not consider it to be a significant achievement. Earning partnership is important, so it should be difficult to achieve and those who demonstrate dedication and high levels of performance should be celebrated. In other words, my advice is: Design the selection criteria and process to make partnership an achievement.

At the same time, you should still help and support professionals who are on the track to becoming owners. I often see founders approach partnership status as some kind of gauntlet to be run, punishing G2 professionals every step of the way. Being a founder was difficult and required effort and sacrifice, but it is not necessary for every generation to start from scratch. On the contrary, founders should want G2 professionals to build upon what they created so that the firm can achieve even more.

Punishment and obstacles do not always come in the form of hard-to-meet criteria. Some founders prefer a passive-aggressive approach to punishing G2 professionals, effectively saying, "We have made it too easy for you, so it really does not mean much." They set the bar low so that partnership is easy to achieve, and then they provide little recognition or regard to those who meet the low standards. This is highly unproductive and demoralizing.

This is why it is important to design partnership criteria that are meaningful and require a real contribution to the firm. Set expectations high, and then support those who are trying to meet them. Encourage G2 professionals and help young colleagues along the path to partnership by giving them the knowledge and resources they need to succeed. When they finally cross the finish line, celebrate it! Their victory represents a success for everyone in the firm.

Criteria for Ownership/Partnership

The criteria for partnership should reflect the culture and values of the firm. The best way to design the requirements is to look at the values held by the firm and ask yourself how you would demonstrate that someone really reflects them. Most firms design partnership criteria that fall into these broad categories:

- **Contribution to the firm:** contributes to growth and clients, intellectual capital, or the creation of processes and systems
- **Productivity:** works with many clients, manages revenue, or oversees departments and teams within the firm
- **Leadership:** demonstrates the ability to lead by example and inspire others to follow
- **Character:** is held in high regard and well respected in the profession, firm, and community
- **Teamwork:** has been accepted and supported by peers in the firm and has been equally supportive and respectful

Is the Firm Ready?

While each firm will find its own way to measure and establish the partnership criteria discussed earlier, the most overlooked element of adding new partners has nothing to do with the professionals who are being considered for ownership. It has to do with the firm itself: Is *the firm* ready to add new owners?

In order for a firm to add new owners without reducing or diluting the income and ownership of existing owners, it has to grow. Without growth, the only way to add owners is to ask existing owners to reduce their income and equity by either selling shares or diluting existing shares. In contrast, a growing firm can issue new shares or even sell equity without having to ask existing owners to take a step back.

Growth is the fuel that drives career tracks, especially the step to partnership. Historically, advisory firms have experienced growth of 15 percent or more per year and have not had to be very careful about adding owners. There have always been enough revenue and profits to invite those most deserving to buy. However, starting in 2015, firms began to experience very slow growth, making partnership an important issue. The problem is that if the profits of the firm are not growing, splitting them among more owners simply means that everyone gets less—a process called *dilution*.

It is not unusual for professional firms in slower-growth industries such as accounting or consulting to design rules around the amount of additional revenue a firm needs to earn before it can add another owner. For example, a firm could have a rule that requires $1 million or more in new revenue to be added before a new owner can be brought on board. Alternatively, the rule could stipulate that the firm must add another $250,000 in EBITDA before a new owner can be added. Either of these rules would protect existing owners from dilutive additions. Keep in mind, however, that such rules may frustrate talented individuals who are contributing to the firm's growth.

To protect against existing owners resting on their laurels while not allowing new professionals to enter into ownership, some firms have created a rule that requires new shares to be regularly issued. For example, every two years the firm issues new shares corresponding to 5 percent of existing shares (the percent can be tied to the growth of the firm, as well). The new shares are sold to professionals based on their contributions, with a preference to new shareholders who meet the ownership criteria.

The result of such a scheme is that, as an owner, you have to either keep up or accept dilution. This process benefits those who are growing and discourages those who are standing still. Owners who are not buying new shares may find that their ownership stake is severely diluted after four or five years of taking it easy.

While the process of issuing new shares to encourage growth has its appeal, it also undermines the value of the equity of the firm. If you have to constantly buy to avoid dilution, this lowers the price of existing shares. Furthermore, there is the assumption that we can accurately measure an individual's contribution and reflect this in equity. In practice, this may turn out to be very difficult and political. Still, the idea is intriguing.

Being a Business Developer

The most controversial criterion in the partnership-vetting process is the ability to develop new business or *sell*. This is a skill that much of the industry lacks, and it is often purposely deemphasized by advisory firms. Founders at many independent firms despised the sales culture at the Wall Street firms they left, but they still possessed the skills necessary to win new clients. As a result, at many firms the founders did most of the dirty work of adding clients, which encouraged G2 professionals to focus on other business skills. Now, as the founders begin to retire, the next wave of advisors struggles to bring new clients on board because they lack the training and track record of selling.

This aversion to sales causes many firms to either not include or deemphasize business development in the set of ownership criteria. This is a very dangerous decision. Growth is vital for advisory firms. Growth is the fuel that powers careers and makes succession plans possible. Without growth, the erosion of assets and clients over time will slowly and painfully destroy any strategy or transition plan that the firm might have had.

While every firm and professional is enthusiastic about growth, few are enthusiastic about sales. Unfortunately, without sales there is no growth. Adding clients must be one of the core responsibilities of professionals in a firm. Firms have to find a path that allows professionals to develop their sales skills without feeling like it undermines their professionalism or damages their integrity. When firms embrace business development as part of their culture, professionals discover that it is not nearly as scary or difficult as they feared.

It is essential that firms clearly articulate the importance of growth and their business development expectations early in the careers of G2 professionals. It is not fair to start talking about growth only in the last year of the career track. At that point it is too late for people to do much to change the way they work. To avoid falling into this trap, firms should make a concerted effort to train professionals in business development at all stages of their careers. This allows people to grow their skills naturally, and it gives them time to become comfortable with this potentially awkward responsibility. Late in their careers professionals can become overwhelmed with client service responsibilities and do not have the time or resources to develop new skills. Early training in business development enables advisors to develop these skills before their list of responsibilities becomes truly demanding. Finally, without open communication about the importance of business development, younger professionals will not understand how vital it is. It is unjust for founders to avoid discussing business development publicly but grumble about the younger generation's lack of skills in private.

When firms do require new business development from their incoming partners, their expectations are a function of the firm size. Based on my experience, smaller firms may only require $15 to $20 million in new AUM per year from new partners, who may already have a track record of achieving that target in the last two or three years. Larger firms may set the target as high as $30 to $35 million per year for new partners. This target is also a function of the size of a typical client relationship.

One method to articulate a business development target for new owners is to think of a mature practice within the firm that is a little above average in productivity. Choose one of your more productive owners, but not the one with the most clients. Now divide that practice by 8 or 10. This is the amount of new revenue you should expect. For example, if a mature practice in your firm has about 80 clients with an average of $15,000 in revenue per client, an incoming partner should consistently bring in 8 to 10 new clients per year at that level of revenue, or a total of $120,000 to $150,000 in new revenue. This method requires partners to replenish their practices every 8 to 10 years, which means that they can sustain a growth of 10 to 15 percent. This is consistent with the experience of the industry.

Tenure Requirements

Tenure can be a sensitive subject and making it a requirement for being an owner is a difficult decision. On the one hand, the ownership/partnership model is meant to create loyalty and should therefore perhaps value loyalty. It also provides the firm with more time to gather information and observe a person before a decision is made on whether the professional behaves and contributes in the way the firm expects.

On the other hand, tenure requirements can hurt the ability of the firm to add highly skilled and credentialed professionals. In particular, it hurts the firm's ability to *laterally admit* or merge with partners who already have well-developed practices. Such lateral admissions are a very important growth mechanism for many firms, and not being able to offer partnership in the negotiation process can severely limit the opportunities available.

For example, I worked with a client firm that had a five-year tenure requirement for ownership. The firm recruited a very skilled and experienced executive who became a strong contributor. However, the five years moved more slowly than the executive thought they would. Much of the information in the firm and many decision-making meetings were reserved for partners, and the executive had a hard time doing his job because he did not have access to all the information he needed. As a result, he departed about a year and a half into his tenure, dissatisfied with not being treated as a partner.

In my experience, it is not a bad idea to require one or two years of tenure for partnership, with the exception that the executive committee can waive the requirement in special cases, such as a merger with a multi-partner firm. In these special cases, due diligence during the merger and the reputation and achievements of the professionals will serve as the test that replaces tenure.

Requirements for Non-Revenue Positions

The contribution of non-revenue positions is critical to the success of the firm and these professionals should be included in the firm's ownership. Positions such as chief operating officer (COO) and chief investment officer (CIO) are usually partners. Other positions such as chief compliance officer (CCO), CFO, and director of administration are also often considered for partnership. Investment management departments are important contributors as well and they frequently straddle the line between non-revenue and revenue-generating positions.

The key to adding non-revenue partners is to be judicious with the pace of such additions. Consider the revenue or profit rules proposed earlier in this chapter. Every time the firm adds another $1 million in revenue, it can consider adding a new partner. If there is a professional who contributed substantially to the growth of the firm and worked directly with the clients attached to that growth, it is very difficult to elect a non-revenue partner instead. That said, firms can certainly elect one non-revenue producing partner for every five or six revenue partners.

The criteria for non-revenue-producing partners should be the same as that for partners who work with clients. The only difference will be that under the contribution criterion, non-revenue partners will list their accomplishments in terms of management, operations, or administration rather than clients serviced and assets managed. The rest of the criteria, such as character, expertise, and teamwork, should be consistent across categories.

Example of Partnership Criteria

Here is an example of the information expected of partnership candidates based on the requirements of one of the premier firms in the industry:

1. **Detailed resume:** A complete resume that details the employment and educational history.
2. **Statement of interest:** A letter that explains what drives the professional's interest in becoming a partner. This letter may address questions such as: What does a partnership role mean to you? Where do you envision yourself in the firm's future? What role do you see yourself in to support this vision?
3. **Involvement in the firm's organization and culture:** A description of how the candidate participates in the firm's culture and contributes to the organization in terms of:
   a. Staff development
   b. Collaboration and teamwork
   c. Community and market involvement
   d. High-level client service
4. **Professional accomplishments:** A description of any professional achievements, including degrees and designations, professional society membership, recognitions, awards, and so on.
5. **Impact on the firm:** Every partner contributes to the firm's success in many ways, such as creating opportunity, managing relationships, supporting colleague growth, increasing our intellectual capital, and helping with management. A specific description and metrics that measure:
   a. Business development
   b. Relationship growth
   c. Client responsibility
   d. Marketing activities
   e. Expertise, knowledge, and specialization
   f. Management and leadership

Communicating Criteria and Managing Expectations

Ownership/partnership criteria are among the most important ways that a firm can communicate its value system and culture. There is no better way to reinforce the behaviors and characteristics of the firm's values than by tying them to ownership. Since these criteria represent the values of the firm, they should be well understood by all employees and widely publicized.

That said, when firms communicate partnership criteria to a wider audience, they should keep the language general rather than getting into specifics that are more technical. For example:

> To be an owner in The Ensemble Practice, professionals have to demonstrate that their knowledge is at the top of the profession, that they are able to sustain and manage great client relationships, and that they can contribute consistently to the growth of the firm through the addition of new clients. Future owners are also expected to help build and manage the teams they work with and lead those teams by example. Finally, they should exhibit the values of our organization by acting with integrity, showing intellectual curiosity and a passion for excellence and demonstrating excellent judgment in both professional and business situations.

This description is a much better expression of the firm's values than a more technical statement:

> Professionals need to contribute at least $200,000 in yearly new revenue and manage at least $750,000 in existing client revenue in order to be considered for ownership. They also need to manage at least four people on staff and complete their performance evaluations.

Such a specific statement is not necessary and may need to change too often to be useful. Of course, this only applies when communicating partnership criteria to the organization at large. Professionals who will become partnership candidates in the next two to three years do actually need to know the exact numeric expectations and goals.

Admission Process

The process of evaluation is as important as the criteria themselves. A good process is predictable, objective, and authoritative. Very importantly, candidates need to understand the evaluation and decision-making process and trust that they will be treated fairly.

The partnership admission process should reflect and respect the governance system of the firm. In many firms, partnership decisions are made by a committee of owners rather than one or two founders alone or all owners together. This committee reviews the information submitted, seeks additional information as needed, and then makes a recommendation to the executive committee or all the partners.

A good evaluation committee comprises three to five owners who have shown interest in developing people and contributing to their growth. Depending on the size of the firm, this committee can be larger or smaller, but it should always consist of only owners. After all, candidates for potential inclusion in the owner group should be vetted and evaluated by others who have similarly been considered.

Gathering the necessary data for making an informed decision can be challenging. First of all, many firms do not track individual data on business development and revenue responsibilities. If the firm wants to include this criteria in the admission process, it must gather that information on behalf of the candidate.

Many firms also overlook the importance of gathering recommendations from existing partners. While this step may seem unnecessary in a small firm, the words and reputation of an existing owner give a candidate's application more gravity and meaning. Recommendations can say a lot about candidates: Who are their mentors? Are their mentors willing to write about their abilities? Are the recommendations strong, or do they seem half-hearted?

If the firm gathers upstream evaluations, these can be reviewed during the admission process as well. For potential partners to be respected by others and seen as leaders, they should already have earned the respect of their staff. If that is not the case, negative upstream evaluations can provide the firm with a red flag that this candidate may not be a good fit for ownership.

In some firms, partnership candidates must be approved by all partners. While this is a very democratic provision, it is also one that I would caution against. The ability to veto a nomination can stymie other important decisions and create some very unpleasant circumstances. For example, I worked with a client firm where such veto power existed. One of the partners let everyone know that he planned to use the veto against a partnership candidate. He made it clear that his issues had nothing to do with the candidate. In fact, everyone highly respected the potential partner. Rather, his issues had to do with other decisions, past and future, and he wanted to use his veto power as a bargaining chip for revisiting and renegotiating those decisions.

Clearly, such political moves speak to a partner group that has some issues to resolve. Even if you believe your firm would never face these types of problems, I would caution against creating veto powers in any large group of owners. The power to freeze an important decision should not rest with one person. Perhaps veto power could belong to a minority group of owners, but it should never belong to just one.

Adding Family Members as Partners

In many smaller firms, founders hope that their children will want to join the business and take over someday. This is an understandable aspiration. However, adding family members as partners is like adopting a pet tiger. While it can be done, it is extremely dangerous. If you decide to bring your children or other family members into the business, you should understand that this creates a significant problem for employees and partners who are not part of the family. Very few professionals are comfortable spending their careers at a family firm. People who are not members of the family take the risk of not being treated well or of seeing their achievements not be adequately recognized. There is also a certain atmosphere in family firms that makes many professionals uncomfortable.

If you do add family members as partners, it is important for the process to be aboveboard. Family members should go through the same process as everyone else. If you are a small firm that has not yet added new partners, this is a great opportunity to articulate the criteria for partnership and make it clear that others who meet the same criteria can reach the same goal. If you already have partners, follow the established admission process and be as transparent as possible.

If you follow a well-defined partnership process and apply it consistently to family members, there should be no doubt in anyone's mind that your son or daughter has earned the right to be a partner. However, you should also remember that just because your daughter is now a partner, she does not have the right to inherit all your shares or become the CEO. This mistake can quickly destroy a firm.

The allocation of shares that are bought or transferred should be governed and managed by the firm, and rarely should there be a direct transaction between shareholders that is not approved by the firm. Such direct transactions can dramatically change the landscape and culture of the firm. They also undermine the trust between the founders.

I worked with a client firm where a father decided to gift half of his shares to his son and declared that upon his retirement he would sell his remaining shares to him. He would then become the CEO of the business by virtue of having a controlling interest. "I will never leave my son as a partner in a firm where he does not have control," he said.

His existing partners were beyond outraged. The founder was leaving them in exactly the same position he was determined to help his son avoid—a position without control. They also realized how little the founder trusted them. To make matters worse, they did not think very highly of the son. Within months, a good firm was in disarray. Conflict was everywhere. A pending merger fell through, and the partners likely made a rush for the exits. While such a result is tragic, it is also very predictable.

Firms that have a well-established and transparent partnership process can avoid this scenario. For example, I worked with a client firm where one of the six partners retired and sold his shares to the firm, rather than to a handpicked successor. This is what their ownership agreement required. His daughter, who is in the business but not yet a partner, did not receive any of his shares. She is highly regarded and very talented and will be a partner soon. When she does make partner, she will be treated the same as every other partner. No one will question her credibility, success, or role at the firm because she will have earned every step of her career progress on her own.

Laying the Foundation for New Partners

Chapter 13 discusses at length ownership and governance from the perspective of G2 professionals and new founders. It also contains a comprehensive due diligence checklist for new partners to complete as they read through the partnership agreement. While a lengthy discussion of governance here would be redundant, I do want to point out a few items that a firm should determine before adding new owners.

First and foremost, firms should train new owners to understand firm governance before they become partners. When I interview new partners at a firm, I often find that the reality of partnership has not lived up to their early assumptions about firm governance. They thought that they would be present at every decision and consulted on every issue, and they are disappointed that the firm took their check for the buy-in and never invited them to the decision-making table. Training new partners to understand the dynamics of ownership and management is a good idea—especially before they become partners.

Second, when new partners buy into the firm, there should be a mutual understanding on how they can exit. Review the provisions of exit and make sure they are consistent with the firm's philosophy. For example, imagine that Philip becomes a partner in your firm. Five years later, he announces that he is leaving to become an executive at another firm (perhaps a competitor). How would you deal with his equity in this situation? Would you buy him back? If so, would you pay full price? Would you penalize him for leaving? Would you pay him right away (and would you have the money to do so)? A firm should not be a prison, but if partners can leave without warning and receive a full price and full liquidity, then a firm is potentially facing some very significant issues if it ever experiences crisis.

Finally, new partners want to know they are represented in decision making. Firms need to show them how they are represented. It is not a bad idea to review the structure of the board of directors or executive committee with a view toward adopting a representation model where new partners get to elect at least some of the people who govern the firm.

Tackling Buy-In Financing and Valuation

Most firms today provide financing for new owners to buy into the firm. This financing can take the form of a loan from a bank that is guaranteed by the firm, or it can be a direct loan from the firm to the buying owner. The majority of firms prefer the bank option as it allows the selling shareholder to receive the price in cash and creates a third-party relationship between the new owner and the lender.

At present, the availability of lenders and loans is high. There are several specialized lenders, such as Live Oak Bank, who extend loans to financial advisory firms. Local banks compete for the business of advisory firms as well, with loan terms that are very favorable to buyers. A number of our clients have secured 7- and even 10-year terms on such loans. Loans with longer terms allow new buyers to acquire the equity primarily through the dividends associated with the equity bought.

This makes a key point about valuation. Ideally, the valuation of the firm is set at such a level that the new owners can acquire their equity by primarily using the dividends that flow as a result of the purchase. For example, suppose that Philip acquires 5 percent of The Ensemble Practice, which has EBITDA of $1 million and is valued at six times EBITDA. The dividend associated with Philip's purchase is $50,000 (5% × $1,000,000), and his purchase price is $300,000 (5% × 6 × $1,000,000). Philip's payments on a 10-year loan at 6 percent interest will be roughly $40,760. This means that his dividend (profit distribution) is actually more than his payments.

To be more thorough, we should mention that Philip's dividend is taxable. Depending on his tax rate and the loan year, he may have a deficit on the loan. For example, if his effective tax rate is 35 percent, then his net after-tax cash available will be $32,500. Still, the interest portion of his loan is likely tax-deductible, making it easier to eliminate any deficit.

Ideally, the net result is a valuation where the buyer does not go too deep out of pocket and the purchase is affordable. That said, some firms want the buyer to have some skin in the game. This can be accomplished by requiring a minimum down payment, where the firm will not finance more than 90 percent or so of the purchase price. It can also be done by shortening the loan term so that the buyer has to use some compensation to buy.

This second approach tends to favor potential owners who come from well-to-do backgrounds and can therefore borrow or otherwise afford such down payments early in their careers. In my opinion, the sheer size of the loan and the risk associated with it is enough skin. For most professionals, this is the largest or second largest loan they will ever take (after their house). They will also have to go without growth in their income for quite some time. That is sacrifice enough.

I am not a valuation expert, and valuation ratios are very vulnerable to circumstances and time, so I will resist the temptation to offer any rules of thumb. That said, you should approach the valuation with the following criteria in mind:

- **Make sure it is affordable:** You are offering equity to your best people in order to retain and motivate them. If the price is too high and it is too difficult to buy the equity, then the entire strategy becomes ineffective.
- **Reduce the deficit:** A firm should be sensitive to new owners having to go deep into their compensation checks to pay for equity. You can help new owners by managing the terms of financing in addition to managing the valuation.
- **Create reciprocity:** The valuation and terms for those buying in should be the same as for those who are selling. This is only fair. Set the price at a level that is affordable to the buyer without punishing the seller.
- **Give up control:** In many cases, the founder or founders sell shares out of a *control position*, which means that the shares allow them to make voting decisions on their own. Valuations will assign a *control premium* to those shares that can range anywhere from 15 to 50 percent of the value of the same shares if they were not exercising control. It is impossible to sell that control premium to G2 professionals, and it is not fair. As a founder, you can sell that to another company, but not internally. In return for giving up that value, you gain better liquidity and control over your own exit process.

- **Be careful with technicalities:** If you are working with valuation experts on the value of the firm, pay special attention when navigating the following difficult issues:
  - **Don't confuse enterprise value with the value of a share:** You are selling a small percentage of the firm, not the entire firm. The small percentage is in a minority position. The value of one share is not equal to the enterprise value (i.e., the entire company) divided by the number of shares.
  - **Avoid revenue-based valuations:** These can create a dangerous disconnect between profits and purchase price.
  - **Be careful about multiples applied to a single year of results:** Last year's profits can be a very good indication of the future, but they can also be very vulnerable to circumstantial changes such as hires or windfalls.
  - **Scrutinize discounted cash-flow models:** Discounted cash-flow models are theoretically the best way to estimate the value of a firm, but they require making several very important and extremely sensitive assumptions. Be particularly careful with the discount rate. A small change of 1 percent can dramatically change the value estimated.

When the valuation process is well understood and accepted by all partners in the firm, it leads to sustainability. Ideally, the process should be revisited every two to three years in order to reflect both external changes in the market and internal changes at the firm.

Onboarding Partners

New partners will need an introduction. It is a great idea to use the full power of the firm's PR machine to tell the world about new partners when they are added. This should include sending an e-mail or letter to all existing clients and centers of influence as well as issuing a press release to industry and local publications. Many business journals have a section for *people on the move* that is designed for exactly this. Publishing an announcement in a journal is a great opportunity to boost the reputation of the new partner and the credibility of the firm.

Most firms have an annual retreat, and it is a good idea to schedule the announcements around that time so that new partners can attend and be recognized for their new position. This is true even in firms where the annual retreat is open to the entire firm rather than being restricted to partners. Announcing new partnerships ahead of the retreat enables new partners to step into their roles in an inviting, relaxed setting.

Partner onboarding is a good opportunity to elevate the responsibilities of new partners, perhaps suggesting additional committees or task forces where they can participate. To become partners they already had to demonstrate a high level of involvement, but this is the firm's chance to steer their energy to where it is most needed. Partner onboarding is also a chance to discuss where new partners will have a voice and where they will not. This can be a useful reminder about the governance structure of the firm, and that not every partner participates in every decision all the time.

The firm should not be in the business of managing the taxes of its partners, so new partners should generally pick their own CPAs and tax experts. That said, new partners often struggle with the tax reality of being an owner, and the firm should help. Perhaps the firm could maintain a list of recommended CPAs for new partners, or at least repeatedly suggest that they find their own CPA. With a little help, new partners should be able to efficiently tackle the tax issues that arise in the first year of receiving a K-1.

Finally, new partners need to be trained on how to be partners. Every new partner should have a mentor. Perhaps the person who has guided them this far is still available, but in case a change is needed, new partners should be encouraged to seek the advice and guidance of those with more experience. I once asked Bob Bunting, the former CEO of Moss Adams, what happens to a professional's career after partnership is achieved. "It is not the end of your career," Bob said. "It is the start of another one."

CHAPTER 12

Buying Equity: The G2 Perspective

Becoming an owner will surprise you no matter how much you have prepared for it. The financial consequences of the decision will probably overwhelm you at first, but while those are quite significant, they will quickly fade into the background of your life. While buying equity in a firm is a financial transaction, it is most of all a statement that you will pour your talents, energy, passion, and time into the business for many years to come. Much like buying a house, you are financially investing most—if not all—of your money into the idea that the firm will be your home. It may even be the last firm you ever work for, and many partnership agreements are designed that way. When you buy equity in a firm, you are committing your career to that firm.

I remember making partner at Moss Adams and how excited I was to be recognized as one of the top professionals at a very large, successful, and prestigious firm. I remember becoming an owner at Fusion—the second firm of my career where I had an ownership stake—and not knowing exactly what that meant or what it was worth but nevertheless feeling excited about a new adventure and trusting that my partner would never steer me wrong. I remember selling a percentage of my current firm, The Ensemble Practice, to my first partner and realizing that the firm was no longer just mine, and perhaps that meant it was now a *real* firm. Buying equity was expensive and scary to do. Selling equity to a partner was surprisingly financially insignificant.

Every year I talk to G2 professionals who have the opportunity to become owners in their firms but decide to decline the offer. They see the opportunity more as a daunting risk and perhaps even a crushing liability. They worry about the markets and are afraid that the industry will change. In these cases, the founders haven't articulated a clear plan for the future, and so prospective G2 partners aren't sure where the firms are headed. These fears are legitimate. Still, I will spend this chapter trying to convince you to become an owner. I am very biased on this topic for three primary reasons.

First, our industry needs G2 professionals to be owners. We are a stronger industry when our firms are owned and operated by the same people who serve clients. Second, your firm needs you to be an owner. Any firm is better when its best and brightest people are the ones thinking about what to improve and how. Finally, you need to be an owner. No matter how rough the seas, you are better off near the helm than below deck.

Professionally, I grew up in an accounting firm, so I tend to think of buying equity as making partner or joining the partnership that owns the business (usually in the form of an LLC or an S corporation). Some firms avoid the term *partner* and instead prefer *principal* or *shareholder*. Throughout this text, I will use the term *partner*, but in most cases it can be easily substituted with other terms in common use. Regardless of the term used, the decision we are examining in this chapter is whether to invest a significant amount of your personal capital to become one of the owners of the business.

As always with investment and other financial decisions, it is prudent to consult your tax advisor and legal counsel. While many firms do not negotiate the terms of ownership—you essentially accept an existing agreement—it is critical that you understand the terms and consequences of your decision. This chapter will describe many of the common features of ownership of which you should be aware, but it is not meant to be a substitute for the legal and tax advice you will need.

What Does It Mean to Be an Owner?

Before you can make a decision on whether you should purchase equity and become an owner, you need to understand what it means to be an owner. Gaining a thorough understanding of ownership and what is expected from owners will allow you to make the right decision and be more comfortable with the risk associated with investing so much of your personal capital in the firm.

There are two common philosophies to buying equity in a firm. The first is based on a partner model. In this philosophy, owners are the best professionals within the firm, and making partner is a sign of achievement, success, responsibility, privilege, and some level of control. The partner philosophy is used by the vast majority of accounting firms, law firms, and financial advisory firms.

The partner philosophy considers the benefits of ownership to go in both directions. The top performers get a chance to buy ownership in the firm, and the firm secures their talents and efforts for the long term. In such an environment, G2 professionals need to prove that they are *ready to be owners*, as it's often described. The qualifications for ownership are fairly demanding, as discussed in Chapter 11.

Usually, the partner philosophy expects partners not only to be involved in a professional capacity, but also to be leaders of the firm and help manage and govern it. In such a system, partners lead by example and demonstrate to others the values of the firm. Firm executives are usually selected from within the partner group, and while partnership does not necessarily equal control or decision-making power, the partners sit on most committees and elect those who govern on their behalf.

An alternative to the partner model is the corporate system. In a corporate system, ownership is completely and intentionally separated from the functional responsibilities within a firm. Very importantly, it is also separated from leadership and management positions. It is not uncommon in such corporate firms for employees in any and all positions to be shareholders and either purchase or receive shares through compensation programs. In these cases, there is no special significance to being an owner other than pride (hopefully) and any associated tenure requirements.

On the plus side, the corporate system allows firms to broaden ownership and freely import talent from the outside. People are hired to do a job and they automatically receive an ownership stake commensurate with the position. Professionals in high-level jobs don't need to spend five years or more proving their skills and character to the rest of the firm before becoming owners.

A drawback of the corporate system is that it tends to produce a high number of shareholders, which can complicate the compliance process around entry and exit and make proper governance difficult. It also views employees as free agents. It is not necessarily assumed that professionals will work at the firm for the rest of their careers, which is a common premise behind the partner philosophy.

The vast majority of advisory firms today pursue the more traditional partner philosophy, but some of the largest and more acquisitive firms espouse the corporate system. The factors to consider when deciding whether to become an owner will differ depending on the philosophy of your firm. For example, the amount of capital invested and the restrictions on that capital are usually more significant in the partner model. In contrast, the corporate model often provides for a more frequent and fluid entry and exit, and the amount of capital committed is not as significant. That said, do not make any assumptions about ownership at your firm before asking some very important questions.

Key Questions to Ask

Before you begin asking questions about ownership, make sure that your timing is appropriate. Ideally, your firm has developed a career track and you have reached the last stage before ownership. (See Chapter 2 for examples of career tracks.) If you are at an earlier stage, leaders of the firm may be reluctant to answer your more detailed questions, and understandably so.

Many firms are proactive with their partner candidates and will approach them at the right time, anticipate their questions, and provide any information they request. However, if you believe that the time has come to talk about ownership and firm leadership has not yet approached you, the best thing to do is talk to your mentor and ask, "Has the time come for me to be considered as a partner?"

If the time is right for you to make a decision about becoming a partner, consider the following questions and make sure that you understand the answers provided by your firm:

- What does it mean to be a partner/owner/shareholder in our firm?
- Which is the right term to use and why?
- What do we expect from our partners?
- What are the criteria for becoming a partner?
- Who makes the actual decision?
- What is the timeline? When are such decisions made?
- What is the process for making the decisions? Should I be supplying any information to support my case?
- Is there something I can do to present my case better?
- What should I do to prepare myself to be a partner?
- What will my business card say? What can I tell clients about my new position?

Beyond questions that have to do with the nature of the promotion to partner, there are a number of more technical factors that you should also consider before making a decision:

- What is our form of incorporation: LLC, S corporation, or (very rarely) C corporation?
- Do we have different classes of shares or units? What class will I participate in?
- How much equity can I buy? What is the maximum and/or minimum? How was this number determined?
- Can I see our financial statements for the last three years? (These do not need to be detailed down to individual compensation or income numbers, but some level of P&L would help.)
- Have we done a financial performance benchmark? If so, can I see the results?
- Can I see a table of our current ownership? Who are our shareholders today?
- Will I have access to the shareholder agreement or membership operating agreement? (These two documents govern many of the rights and privileges of owners.)
- Do you expect every new owner to accept the existing agreement, or is there flexibility in discussing the terms?
- How is the firm valued, and have we done a valuation? If so, can I see a copy of the report?
- What, if any, credit is available for me to purchase shares? What are the terms? Does the firm guarantee the loan?
- Can I see the balance sheet of the firm itself?
- What is our income distribution policy? How do we distribute cash? Who makes that decision, and how often is it done?
- Are we aware of any shareholders who are selling shares in the next three years? If so, who are they and what is their ownership?

These are all very good questions to ask, but you must endeavor to ask them in a respectful and patient way. It is important to realize that these are very invasive questions and answering them requires your firm to provide you with a lot of information. Just gathering the required information may not be easy for the firm. While this information is very relevant to your decision, it is also subject to a cost-benefit analysis: How much value does it bring, and what is the cost of collecting it?

If your firm offers you the opportunity to buy equity but does not give you access to all of the information previously described, how do you make up your mind about how much is enough? As a rule of thumb, if you cannot see some kind of P&L and cannot read the operating agreement you are supposed to sign, you should be very uncomfortable. Much of the other information can be gathered either with some research or through discussions with your peers inside and outside the firm. Such research will actually benefit your understanding of how your firm compares to the rest of the industry.

Should You Buy Equity?

There is a saying that MBAs never start businesses because when you really analyze it, it makes no sense to do so. The same goes for buying equity. The answer to the question "Should I become an owner?" is not found on a spreadsheet. Rather, buying equity takes a leap of faith. Ironically, though writing a check to acquire ownership in a company can be seen as the most financial of transactions, deciding whether to pick up the pen will likely come down to questions not easily answered with money.

Time and again, I have spoken to G2 professionals who are paralyzed by the unpredictable long-term nature of the investment decision. Will the stock market change? Will advisory fees come down? Will the industry consolidate and make it impossible for us to be successful? Will robo-advisors take over? Will our founders sell the firm? How can we ever buy out our founders?

These are all important questions to ponder, but they often have no truly constructive answers. Answering them correctly would require a level of foresight and forecasting that no one has. Instead of analyzing possible outcomes to death, it is better to simply accept that buying equity requires a leap of faith and then ask yourself how much you believe. Here are some questions to get you started.

Do You Believe This Firm Will Be Successful in the Next 20 to 30 Years?

The answer here is not a forecast but rather a gut feeling. At this point you have spent 5 to 15 years of your career at this firm. You have seen it go through a lot of changes and situations. You have experienced the good and the bad. Does your experience and your professional instinct tell you that this is a good firm that will continue to do well?

Let's break down the term *successful*. To be successful in the long term, a firm needs to do the following things:

- **Be profitable:** If the firm is not profitable, why would you invest in it?
- **Grow:** Does the firm have the necessary growth to maintain momentum and position in the marketplace?
- **Attract and retain people:** Can the firm create opportunity, grow the skills of its professionals, and retain its best people?
- **Differentiate itself:** Does the firm stand out in its ability to attract and service clients?
- **Develop great client relationships:** Beyond just retaining clients, does the firm consistently engage clients in ways that build community, dialogue, and referrals, as well as promote the exchange of ideas?

Do You Want to Spend the Next 10 Years of Your Career at This Firm?

Buying a firm is a lot like buying a home—not only are you investing in a property, but you will also likely be living there for a good long while. If you can't imagine living in the house, there is no price that will make it a positive experience for you over the next few years. Ownership decisions are very long term in nature. You will discover that your equity does not become financially viable and lucrative until you have spent at least seven or eight years at the firm. If you are not enjoying your professional experience working there, you will not like being a partner.

Do You Trust the People Running the Firm to Guide It and Make the Right Decisions?

The governance of a firm is ideally a carefully thought-out process that creates checks and balances at every step and serves the firm's shareholders, clients, and staff. However, the process is only as good as the people who are executing it. In other words, if you don't like the driver, don't get in the car. No car, no matter how well it is built, can protect the passengers from a bad driver. When you look at the current and future leadership of the firm, do you trust the people in charge to find the road to success?

Are You Excited to Be Part of the Partnership Group?

When you look around at the partners at your firm today and professionals who will likely still be there 10 years from now, is this a group you are excited to join? Don't just look at the founders. Look at your peers and ask yourself if you want to spend the next 20 years of your professional life in their company.

Do they share your values? Do they relate to your ambitions? Do they see the world, the industry, and the firm in the same way you do?

You may be partners with the founders for another 10 years or so, but you will be partners with the other G2 professionals at your firm for as many as 30 years or more. Take a good look at them. There is a tendency for G2 professionals to only seek the attention of the founders and ignore or downplay the importance of the relationships they have with other G2 partners. Don't make that mistake.

I remember going to new-partner training at Moss Adams. I was one of about 40 or so partner candidates who were locked up in a lodge in the mountains for three days of classes on leadership and management. Up until that time, my mental image of a partner was someone in his fifties with quite an impressive professional career who seemed to have all the experience in the world. When I finally met my future partners, I was excited to find out that I could relate to them and even hang out with them.

My future partners were my age, had kids the same age as mine, drove cars like mine, shared many of my interests, and enjoyed hanging out at the bar or going for a hike. And it was not just a social group I discovered. This group also had ideas about the future of the business that were a lot like mine. They saw some of the same problems I did and wanted to change many of the things I wanted to change.

Does Working and Interacting with Clients Give You a Sense of Fulfillment?

At this point you should have already determined whether you enjoy your job and want to continue in your current profession for the foreseeable future. Nevertheless, this is a good opportunity to reflect and perhaps change careers if you are unhappy with what you do on a daily basis. If you are not fulfilled by what you do and the people with whom you work, don't make plans to spend the next 10 years doing it.

Can You Envision Living on Your Salary as You Patiently Invest in the Business?

Buying equity usually means that you experience either no change in income or some decline in the first three to five years. Whereas the buy-in is usually structured in such a way that you don't have to compromise your current life at home too much, if you are relying on bonuses or dividends from ownership to fund your lifestyle, you will be sorely disappointed.

If you need to continue growing your income in the next five or six years in order to meet your lifestyle needs, you may not be in a good position to buy equity. On the other hand, once you have completed the initial buy-in, equity usually becomes a source of lucrative cash flow that can fund many of the things you personally want to do. You just have to be patient.

Buying equity is a personal decision that only you can make. You must be convinced that it is the right thing to do. If you turn down the opportunity to become an owner, the next question becomes, "Can I be successful in this firm without being an owner?" The answer will vary from firm to firm.

Firms invest a lot of emotion and resources into developing the partner track, and there is no doubt that the leaders of the firm will be disappointed if you decide to turn down a partnership opportunity. It will also become apparent that there is something at the firm that troubles you. You will likely not lose your job or face repercussions by refusing to buy in, but you may find that your growth stalls out and your ability to be involved with the firm diminishes. Opportunities to work with the top clients or participate in training or key committees may be tough to come by. After all, turning down equity signals that you may be leaving, so the propensity of the firm to invest in you will decline.

Most firm leaders will try to downplay such scenarios and reassure candidates that there is no damage done from declining the opportunity. That said, in my experience the reality is that they will likely turn your picture to the wall should you refuse the offer, despite assurances to the contrary. I apologize for making such a grim assertion, but you should fully comprehend the gravity of the decision.

The only scenario where declining may prove inconsequential is if you ask for the decision to be deferred. Especially in the face of personal financial decisions or circumstances, most firms will have no problem if you ask for the decision to be delayed by a year or two.

The Characteristics of Equity

Once you make the decision to buy, it is time to examine what you are buying. Broadly, the characteristics of equity can be split into three categories: income, control, and value (Figure 12.1). We will discuss each in turn.

Income

Income is simply the percentage of the profits generated by the firm. In most cases, if you own 10 percent of a firm, that means you own 10 percent of the profits of the firm. That said, income is not always the same as cash, and that's

FIGURE 12.1 Characteristics of Equity

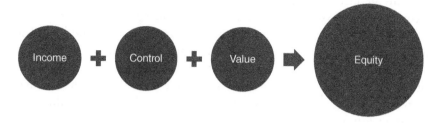

important to understand. For example, a firm may generate $5 million in profits but only distribute $3 million of cash to owners, retaining $2 million for reinvestment in the business. This means that as a 10 percent owner, you would receive income of $500,000 (10% of $5 million), but only $300,000 in cash (10% of $3 million). The remaining $200,000 would be used to support your equity stake in the business. It is important to remember that you not only get to receive the cash, but you also may have some tax liabilities associated with it.

Since virtually all firms in the advisory industry are pass-through entities such as LLCs or S corporations, all the income is passed through to the owners *whether or not* cash is actually distributed. In other words, using the above example, you would owe income tax on $500,000 even if you only received $300,000 in cash. This is why it is critical to understand the way your firm manages its cash distributions.

There are several scenarios where a 10 percent owner may not receive 10 percent of the income. Most of the time, this is due to a corporate structure that has different share classes. For example, there could be a preferred share class that receives the first $3 million in profits and then the other share classes divide the remaining profits. Applied to the same example, that would mean that the income to common shares would only be $2 million ($5 million less the $3 million in preferred dividend). As a 10 percent owner, you would only receive $200,000. Share classes with preferred dividends are often used in some of the acquisition models in the industry, and you may encounter them if your firm is affiliated with one of the large national networks.

Control

Control can be a very complex issue in the context of ownership. In its simplest possible form, if you have 10 percent of the units or shares, then you also have 10 percent of the vote when shareholders make decisions. However, the reality of control is rarely this simplistic. You need to understand how different decisions are made at your firm, who makes those decisions, and what level of control you have over the process by virtue of being a shareholder.

Many decisions must be made while running a business and not all of them require shareholder input. For example, the decision to buy a new office printer is not usually voted on by owners. Company executives are vested with the power and control necessary to run the business, and shareholders reserve the right to vote only on critical decisions. Thus, one of the most important features of corporate governance is how executives (e.g., CEOs, COOs) are appointed, who monitors their performance, and who approves their annual budget.

Decisions can be voted on in different ways or by different structures. Some may require only a simple majority. Others may require a super-majority or even a unanimous decision. And a supermajority vote does not always mean the same thing: The number of votes needed can be two-thirds of votes, or three-fourths, or really any ratio higher than 50 percent plus 1. To make matters even more complicated, some shareholders may have the right to veto a decision regardless of how others vote. For example, founders often reserve the right to veto the sale of the company even if they have been outvoted by their partners.

Some firms may also use voting and nonvoting shares. It is not uncommon to see G2 professionals first acquire nonvoting shares that later convert into voting shares upon the completion of some criterion, such as fully paying for the shares or achieving a certain number of years of tenure at the firm.

Finally, some decisions are reserved for the board of directors or the executive committee appointed by the board. The voting mechanism here can be complex. Board members may be voting on behalf of shareholders who have given them their votes, or they may be empowered to vote based on their own decisions. Board voting may also follow different rules for majority or procedure. Elaborate board rules of governance can be seen at some of the large firms with over 50 shareholders or in some of the acquisition deals that use preferred share classes. Sometimes a preferred share class with only 20 percent ownership may have almost full control of the board.

Value

Finally, owning 10 percent of the firm usually means you will receive 10 percent of the proceeds if you were to sell the firm. However, complications arise when we consider scenarios where we are not necessarily selling the entire firm.

Can you sell your 10 percent of the firm when you retire? What if you leave the firm before you retire? How will your shares be valued? And so on. And as we saw before, there are potentially special rights that can go to a share class, such as the right to sell first, match offers to buy, or be the first to be paid.

Keep the categories of income, control, and value in mind as you examine the actual terms of the ownership agreement. You will need to obtain a copy of the shareholder agreement (for S corporations or C corporations) or the member operating agreement (for LLCs). Reading through the agreement carefully, perhaps with the help of an attorney—which I highly suggest—can allow you to understand your situation as an owner.

Understanding Your Ownership Agreement

Let's now review in detail some of the common features and characteristics you will find in the typical ownership agreement.

Classes of Owners

It is important to identify whether your firm has different classes of shares. If it does, what class of shares are you buying? What are your rights and privileges? What rights and privileges do other classes of owners enjoy? While different classes are relatively rare, it is still worth looking at some of the main features of this type of arrangement. To begin with, differences in rights should dictate differences in valuation between the share classes:

- Voting shares should be worth more than nonvoting shares, everything else being equal.
- Shares that get paid first are worth more than shares that are paid later.
- Shares that have the right to sell first or match offers to buy shares are worth more.

The list can go on and on. Most firms will reflect this analysis in their offers to G2 professionals, but just in case your firm doesn't, keep an eye out for the firm selling nonvoting shares at the same price as voting shares. Sometimes firms do that out of a lack of due diligence rather than intentionally.

More importantly, if your firm is using different share classes, you may have some doubts about whether you are really becoming a partner after all. If you can be trusted to write a check and invest in the firm, why shouldn't you be trusted to vote on issues of importance? Sometimes nonvoting shares are a steppingstone and a vesting mechanism toward regular shares after a period of time. Other times, however, they signal an extreme reluctance to share control of the firm with G2 professionals. If that is the case in your firm, it is a very significant red flag.

A discrepancy in rights can be very alarming, especially when it is combined with significant restrictions on leaving the firm and getting your money back. Be very leery of a firm that uses nonvoting shares but then punishes you if you ever decide to leave. This punishment usually comes in the form of a very low valuation of the units or terms of payment that are severely delayed. Nonvoting shares are much more acceptable if you can leave and sell your shares back to the firm with relatively few restrictions. This at least allows you to "vote with your feet" if you can't vote with your shares.

Who Governs and Manages the Firm?

Understanding the corporate governance of your firm is not limited to searching for red flags. Rather, it provides you with an education in how the firm works. There are several interesting and important questions to ask here:

- Do we have a board of directors? If so, how do we choose the board? How often does the board meet, and what are the typical items on its agenda?
- How do we elect executives? When do we make changes? Are there term limits or are the posts indefinite?
- What are some of the more important committees in the firm? Can I be involved in them? If so, how?
- How do we make critical decisions such as selling the firm or merging with another?
- Is there an annual shareholder meeting? If so, when is the next one? (What is the typical menu for dinner, and can I order something different if I don't like the filet mignon?)

Restrictions on Leaving

The terms and conditions of leaving the firm are perhaps the most important area of due diligence. The easier it is to leave the firm, the easier it is to buy into all the other provisions of ownership. On the other hand, the easier it is to leave the firm, the more likely you are to see your fellow partners running for the exit in times of trouble. As the case is with everything else in business, it is a matter of balance. Also keep in mind that these terms apply not only to you, but also to your partners. They may choose to exercise them, and that can be to your detriment.

Restrictions on leaving the firm take two forms: restrictive legal covenants and restrictive terms for cashing out your equity in the firm. I will not spend much time discussing restrictive legal covenants, as they should be reviewed by an attorney. The rules governing them and their enforcement vary a lot from state to state, and you should examine them very carefully. While I have very little expertise in the legalities of these types of restrictions, I do want to stress that the more restrictive an agreement, the more carefully you should review it and consider all of its implications. The freedom to vote with your feet is a very valuable trump card in any ownership agreement. The basic list of agreements is as follows:

- **Non-compete agreement:** As suggested by the title, you agree not to compete with your prior partners should you leave. The competition may be restricted in terms of both time (e.g., one or two years) and location (e.g., within the geographic footprint of your firm). The covenants I have seen can also be very broad in terms of what constitutes a competing business. As an advisor, you may find that you are essentially not allowed to work for any financial services company, so please review carefully.
- **Non-solicitation agreements:** These restrictions prohibit you from inviting clients to work with your new business upon leaving the firm. If you have no intention of taking clients from the firm, this is less of an issue, but still read carefully. If there are clients who actually belong to you—either clients you personally brought to the firm or even friends and family you invited to work with the firm—now is a good time to document those as exceptions, if possible.
- **Client purchase agreements:** Some firms require that you compensate the firm if clients follow you to your new firm after you depart, even if you did not solicit them to do so. This is meant as an additional protection for the firm, since proving solicitation is not very easy to do. That said, client purchase agreements trouble me, as they restrict the choices that clients make and thus don't seem to be ethically sound. Still, it is a common practice, and it's not for me to argue with it.

The other type of restriction is on the capital you have invested in the firm and the ways to get it back. While your firm has your capital, it has a very strong trump card to play in every argument. If you violate any of the other provisions of the ownership agreement, you may find it hard to get your money back. There are several potential circumstances where you might leave the firm:

- **Friendly departure:** In this case, you find something else interesting to do and leave the firm smiling and shaking hands. There is no potential competition between your new role and your old one, and your partners wish you well. Usually, such friendly departures are not restricted and you should be able to get your invested capital back. However, the terms of being paid back may be a bit tricky. Firms often reserve the right to pay over a period of time in order to avoid severe hits on their cash flow. The valuation in such cases is not usually punitive, but it may not be the highest available.
- **Death or disability:** In the case of death or disability, firms usually take on the obligation to buy your shares back at full value and pay your family. Typically, this is funded with life insurance and the valuation is as high as practical.
- **Retirement:** In many firms, this is the designed mode of departure. You have spent your entire career at the firm and have made preparations to transition all business to other professionals. This is usually the highest valuation and the best of terms. In this context, leaving in any other way is less attractive.
- **Getting fired or violating the agreement:** Unfortunately, there are times when you may leave without much smiling and the handshakes are few. Your partners could choose to let you go, or you could try to leave in violation of other terms of your agreement. If that is the case, you will find it hard to recoup your investment, and you may lose a lot of your capital—particularly any appreciation. This is another reason why you should review these terms very carefully with the help of an attorney.

Accepting restrictions is difficult. Not only are you risking a lot of money, but you will also have to accept that you may not be able to work anywhere else for a while. Such is the nature of partnerships. If it is any consolation, your partners sign the same agreement. The fact that they are equally restricted gives you a lot of protection and security.

Restricting the ability for partners to leave means that if the firm were ever to hit hard times, its best people would not run away to better prospects. Rather, they would stay to fix what is broken. It means that everyone will comply with the rules and regulations set by the firm because getting into trouble can be devastating. It means that the firm can unite the partners behind the best interests of the firm, even if some are reluctant to do so. You may resent the wall around the garden when you are standing on the outside, but once within you learn to appreciate it. Of course, as any ancient civilization could tell you, walls will stop neither time nor people. But it is in our natures to keep trying.

Approving Shareholders

Deciding who can be an owner in a firm is not just a matter of having established criteria for achievement. It is also a very important part of the ownership agreement. Here are some critical questions to consider:

- **Who can approve (or deny) new partners?**
  Every firm should have well-articulated criteria for who can be a partner (see Chapter 11), but these qualifications eventually have to be applied to a specific candidate. Usually a committee of partners, or at times all the partners in the firm, vote on incoming candidates. But what if the rules are such that one partner can boycott the addition of any future partners? I have seen this happen in practice. One partner was disgruntled with the direction of the firm and had several issues with the firm's strategy. He expressed his dissatisfaction by blocking the addition of any future partners, since the operating agreement of the firm required a unanimous vote. Needless to say, the process became incredibly aggravating for everyone involved.

- **Can someone be an owner without working at the firm?**
  There are many hypothetical situations where someone could continue to be an owner while choosing to no longer work at the firm. For example, Philip could leave Seattle Wealth Advisors for Bellevue Asset Management and still retain his shares in Seattle Wealth. Is that okay? For most firms, the answer is a resounding "No!" In another scenario, Philip retires and chooses not to sell his shares, so his partners must continue to send him dividend checks. Why not? Many firms are not comfortable with this scenario, either.

- **Can partners transfer shares without the approval of the firm?**
  As an incoming partner, ideally you are joining an agreement that provides for stability and the careful vetting of future partners, and one that doesn't allow any one partner to alter the course of the firm. Thorny situations can arise when partners do not need approval to transfer shares to someone else. One such scenario is divorce. What happens if one of your partners gets a divorce and all of a sudden her estranged husband is your new partner?

Here is a second situation that can be even more upsetting: A firm has four shareholders, one of whom is the founder and owns 60 percent of the business, thus giving him almost full control. The founder's son joins the business, and after five years of working at the firm, his dad makes him a partner and the president of the firm. He will eventually sell all of his shares to his son, making him the new CEO. Needless to say, the other three partners are not happy. They did not sign up to be partners with the founder's son, who has yet to prove himself as a professional. I have worked with a client firm that faced this same situation.

Firing Partners

For the partnership to function well there should be a mechanism where if one partner violates the agreement, behaves inappropriately, or otherwise threatens to damage the firm, that partner can be voted out of ownership. However, this process should not be an easy one. It must be fair. Read this portion of the agreement carefully to ensure that the terms do not allow for the removal of partners who merely disagree with the management of the firm or have a dissenting opinion.

Changing the Agreement

A commonly overlooked area of scrutiny is provisions that deal with how the ownership agreement can be changed and who can make those changes. If the agreement is relatively easy to change and only requires a simple majority of votes to do so, then all other provisions are subject to changing and can potentially be rendered ineffective. As a G2 partner, you should be keenly aware of the existing structure of the change provisions, though you may not be in the best position to demand modifications. Still, you should understand the implications inherent in the existing agreement.

Issuing New Shares

The issuing of new shares will dilute existing shareholders, everything else being equal. That is why it is so important to understand how new shares can be issued and by whom. The issuing of new shares should be governed by similar provisions to those that apply to adding new owners. In particular, scour these provisions for any language suggesting that shares will be issued frequently in the future or used for compensation or other purposes.

For example, I work with a client firm that issues 1 percent new shares each year, granting those shares to partners who have contributed the most to business development. The effect is a slow but steady dilution in the equity of existing shareholders who are not part of the program. Over the course of 10 to 15 years, such a program can make a significant material impact, creating a differential between partners who contribute to new business development versus those who do not.

Contributing Capital

As unpleasant as it may be, every partner should theoretically be prepared to face the notorious capital call. If and when the firm runs out of money, each partner should either contribute capital or face the prospect of losing some ownership. Though capital calls remain very rare in our industry, I distinctly remember how many partners in 2008 had to forfeit compensation and make other arrangements in order to keep their firms viable. For this reason alone, it is good to understand your obligations to the firm when tough times set in.

What Happens If We Sell?

Many G2 professionals fear that they will become owners only to see their firms sold to other entities. While a change of ownership can dramatically change the course of the firm, it is better to be an owner when the firm is sold than not to be. The position of ownership gives you a much better view of the negotiation process, arguments for and against the deal, and, ultimately, the outcome. If nothing else, it allows you to benefit from the equity you have helped create.

Regardless of the legal voting mechanisms that are in effect when a deal is being negotiated, most acquirers prefer not to have to deal with a vocal partner who opposes the transaction. Being an owner allows you to voice your concerns in a way that is heard, even if you are not necessarily able to block the deal. It also provides full transparency into elements of the deal that you would otherwise not be able to access.

One drawback of being a partner during a sale versus not being a partner is the ability of the acquirer to enforce any non-compete agreements. This is something that should be discussed with your attorney. If you are an owner who received consideration for your shares, it may be much more difficult to leave the firm than if you were an employee who signed the agreement merely to secure employment.

Small Firms and Family Firms

Because of the modest number of partners involved, small firms present some particular challenges that deserve attention. Having a small number of shareholders may mean that voting powers change more rapidly. In addition to sudden shifts in voting dynamics, small firms will usually have a less formal governance structure, so sometimes their decision making can be a bit ad hoc. Founders and large shareholders may be in the habit of running the firm alone and forget to consult with their new partners.

In a small firm, you should be particularly careful with provisions in the agreement that can impact the makeup of the firm. This is especially true when the firm involves family members. For example, I consulted with a client firm that comprised one founder working closely with a G2 partner. The two had a very good professional relationship and had established a smooth pattern of making decisions and dividing responsibilities. All of this collapsed suddenly when the founder's daughter joined the firm. The founder quickly started promoting the idea that his daughter would soon be partner and his eventual successor. Needless to say, the G2 partner became nervous, and the relationship deteriorated to the point where he left. This all happened within one year. Interestingly, the founder's daughter left a few months later to pursue a completely different career.

As a G2 professional, you need to respect the fact that founders often see their firms the same way parents see their children. The firm is precious, it is theirs, and they have an instinct to control and protect it. These emotions are magnified to a barely manageable degree when family gets involved. It is very difficult to point out to founders that automatically adding their children to the business is not automatically acceptable. It is essential to find the right balance between expressing anxiety and preventing the issue from escalating.

If the issue erupts into a conflict, the instinct of the founders will likely be to side with their children and fight against others. This does not serve anyone's best interest. Instead, start a meaningful dialogue by asking the following questions:

- Where do we see the firm going in the long term?
- Which people do you want to involve in the ownership of the firm?
- What contributions and skills should someone bring to the table to be an owner?
- What is the best way for your children to follow the career path of the firm?
- What can I do to help their progress?

- How can you balance the best interest of the firm and the best interest of the family?
- There are many excellent resources on managing the relationship between family and business. Can I suggest some?
- I feel a little anxious that I am going to be the non-family partner. Can we speak about my fears?

Owner Compensation

Owner compensation has a significant impact on the profitability of the firm and, therefore, also on the cash flow of the owners. I will not be discussing here what owner compensation should look like in a typical firm. (If you are interested in that topic, there is a chapter devoted to it in my book, *The Ensemble Practice*.) However, as a G2 professional, you should have a very good understanding of the ownership compensation process and how it will affect you.

Begin by asking, "What is the compensation philosophy of our firm? Is it different when we apply it to owners?" Ideally, the same criteria that drive compensation for the rest of the firm should apply to partner compensation as well. The compensation logic should begin with position definitions that focus on functional responsibilities. For example, what is the position of partner? Is a partner a lead advisor who also happens to be an owner, or is partner a different position altogether? Different firms make different decisions here, and it is important to know where your firm stands.

Most firms use salaries as the primary compensation method. If that is the case at your firm, your next question to should be: "What is the range of salaries that owners can earn?" This range should ideally be validated by external research (i.e., benchmarking). Very importantly, it should also be consistent with the rest of the pay in the firm. The position of each partner in a particular range should be correlated to elements like productivity, expertise, experience, business development, staff training, and contribution to management. Actual factors will vary by firm and depend on its strategy and values.

Next comes the incentive question: "Can partners earn incentive compensation, and if so, how?" Some firms do not have incentives for partners, using the logic that the profit distribution is the ultimate incentive. Other firms prefer to offer incentive compensation as a way of signaling to partners that some types of contribution are very valuable. Some firms use balanced scorecards to drive incentives. Other firms have business development incentives that cover partners. Whatever the case, you need to know and understand how you are being paid.

Finally, it is not unusual for partners to have a different benefits package or flexibility to allocate a portion of their compensation to benefits. Some firms give partners a specific dollar allocation that they can use to purchase a benefits package or receive as income. Many firms, however, do not differentiate between partners and staff and offer both the same package. There are a number of compensation structures, so be sure to understand how partnership will change your individual situation.

What If the Ownership Agreement Isn't Right for You?

Having listed many of the different provisions of the ownership agreement that can affect you, we should also discuss what happens if you don't like what you read. It can be a very painful situation when you like and trust the firm but find the agreement to be somewhat onerous. Bring up your concerns in a productive way. Seek out your mentor or the person you have the best relationship with and express your hesitation.

As always in such dialogue, it is best to focus on the firm and how the issues you see will affect other professionals. Convince leadership that making changes will better serve the entire firm and does not stem from purely selfish motivations. It is possible that the leadership of the firm overlooked something or did not fully appreciate the G2 perspective. It is also possible that the attorneys drafting the document went too far in interpreting the desires of the firm and made the document too restrictive.

If you can convince the leadership of the firm that most G2 professionals will struggle with the terms, you may have a chance to drive the changes you need. That said, keep an eye on the number of partners in the firm. If you are one of the first two or three G2 partners, you have a very good chance of negotiating a change. If you are in a firm with 20 other partners who have already signed this same agreement, you have to either take it or leave it.

Understanding the Valuation and the Price

Entire books have been written on how to value an advisory firm, and there are many articles and research papers covering the marketplace trends. My intention here is not to review the valuation but rather to focus on the practical aspect of translating the valuation into a stream of payments you will make.

Ideally, your firm has commissioned a valuation report from an expert and has used that report to arrive at the value that is used for your buy-in. However the report was compiled, here are some important questions to ask:

- **What is the relationship between the EBITDA (profit) of our firm and the valuation?**
  This relationship will drive the financial dynamics of your buy-in. The valuation report should highlight that relationship and should also provide comparable statistics from marketplace transactions that have been observed for firms of similar size.
- **What financial data was used?**
  Different valuation methodologies are used: discounted cash flow forecasts, marketplace multiples, and so on. All of them require a base of historical data for forecasting or the application of multiples. Choosing the right base is often just as important as the multiples or discount rates. For example, for many firms there is a significant difference between x times this year's EBITDA versus x times the average of the last three years of EBITDA. This is not an invitation to argue with the valuation so much as a call to understand it.
- **Was there a minority-interest discount applied?**
  Most valuation reports calculate an enterprise value, or the value of the entire business as a going concern. The enterprise value less the value of debt borrowed by the company equals the equity value. There is a well-known body of cases that show that the value of a controlling interest in the firm is higher than the value of a minority interest. In other words, the price-per-share someone would pay for the entire firm will likely be higher than the price-per-share someone would pay for 5 percent. Not all experts agree on this theory and not all agree on what the discount should be. My only point here is that if the report calculated an enterprise value, it is valid to ask how that value translates into the per-share price at which you are buying.

After scrutinizing the valuation, it is important to get a sense of the relationship between your payments for the equity and the dividend you will likely receive after the purchase. For example, let's say that you are buying a 5 percent interest in a firm that is valued at $9 million and has $1.5 million in EBITDA.

In this example, let's assume that your firm helped you out by guaranteeing a loan for the purchase price of $450,000. This is a 10-year loan with an interest rate of 5 percent. (As a side note, I chose these numbers because they are easy to work with. Please do not use them to form any expectations.) The annual payment on your loan will be $58,277. In the first year, $22,500 of that will be interest. The dividend you receive from the firm will be 5 percent of $1,500,000, or $75,000.

You will owe taxes on the income, but the interest portion of the payments is likely tax-deductible (you will need to verify that with your tax advisor). This means that you will have taxable income of $52,500 ($75,000 less $22,500). Let's say that your effective tax rate is 35 percent, and since you live in Washington State in this example, you don't have to pay state income tax. This leaves you with $56,625 available to make your loan payment ($75,000 less an income tax of $18,375, which is 35% of your taxable income of $52,500). Your loan payment of $58,277 is almost the same as your after-tax dividend.

This is a rather simplistic example, but it allows us to explore some of the more important dynamics at play here, especially the relationship between the loan payment and the dividend. In a buy-in, this relationship is much more important than the valuation methodology and the associated multiples and discount rates. One of the best things a firm can do to help G2 professionals is to help them secure long-term financing on the loan. Long-term financing at a relatively low rate can make it even easier for G2 professionals to buy in than a relatively low valuation multiple.

I should perhaps manage expectations by saying that in most cases, the first one to three years of the buy-in results in a negative cash flow to G2 partners. However, the cash flow should ideally not cost so much that you have to make difficult compromises with your personal decisions. If the firm continues to grow its cash flow, the dividends will outpace the debt payments. If the cash flow stays flat, the gap (if any) will actually grow as the interest portion of the payment declines.

Organizing Your Personal Finances

The first tax season after becoming a partner is always a very unpleasant surprise. Hire a good CPA as soon as you learn that you are going to be an owner. You will need your CPA not only to help you examine the conditions of buying in, but also to prepare for your new tax return. Your tax return becomes much more complicated as an owner, and your tax liability is a lot less predictable. Depending on your firm's form of organization, you will receive either a K-1 form or K-1 and W-2 forms.

To prepare for your first tax return as an owner, work with your CPA to understand the amount of income your firm is likely to allocate to you and the changes in deductions that will result from the purchase. For many professionals, tax liability can increase. A lot of that can be offset by the deduction taken to pay interest on the financing, but a good estimate helps a lot.

Depending on your firm's registrations and business, you may discover that you need to file taxes in different states. Again, this will increase the complexity and cost of your return. As a result, you may find the first tax season to be a tough one. It is a good idea to budget a significant increase in the amount you pay your CPA.

You should also talk to your firm about the right way to make estimated payments. As an employee, your estimated tax liability was deducted from your paycheck. As an owner, you are now responsible for making quarterly payments. Those payments are likely significant and you should understand how you can budget for them and set funds aside. Some firms help their partners prepare such estimates and make quarterly distributions specifically designed for the estimated tax payments. Other firms let partners tackle those on their own. If your firm does not offer assistance, you should consult your CPA to create a good process.

As already mentioned, benefits packages can change when you become an owner, particularly your 401(k) plan. If your firm uses employee matching and/or profit-sharing plans, you can make significant additional contributions to your retirement plan. This is one of the great benefits of ownership. However, it may require you to make contributions from your income and you should understand what those are. Some plan features such as profit sharing may require that all staff are allocated a contribution proportionate to their compensation, which means that a portion of your income will be allocated to retirement. This is something you should prepare for and understand.

Beyond the First Purchase

When I first became a partner, I didn't have much of an appetite for buying equity. I was just doing what everyone else was doing. In my thirties, I passed on chances to buy equity and instead opted for more income. Then the day came when my partner and I successfully sold the firm we had created. From then on, I couldn't buy enough equity.

I work with several firms where the founders were older and transitioned out between 2006 and 2008. These firms are now run by G2 partners. Their role in the firm is no longer defined relative to the founders, but rather in terms of their leadership responsibilities. They have stopped thinking of themselves as G2. This successor generation may have been very anxious to buy their first tranches of equity, but now they can't get enough. The ability to buy more equity and increase ownership in the success of their firms has become a prize and a reward rather than a responsibility.

Your first purchase of equity will be the most difficult one, as it is rife with emotions, pride, and anxiety. But chances are good that you will make other purchases in the future. Depending on your age and the makeup of your firm, you may be buying shares for many years to come. As they say in Bulgaria, "Appetite comes with eating." Try it. You will love it.

CHAPTER 13

The Ownership and Governance Foundation for G2

The foundation of prosperity is poured out of stability and opportunity. In order to successfully develop future generations—G2 and beyond—a firm must be able to assure those professionals that if they commit their careers to the firm, the firm will reciprocate by never drastically changing and never ceasing to look for opportunities to grow. Before building their homes in the neighborhood, G2 professionals want to know that the site is not located on a floodplain and will never be rezoned for light industrial use.

Involving G2 professionals in the ownership and governance of the firm is a way to create that stability and ensure that sense of opportunity. Many founders struggle with the notion of relinquishing control and become annoyed when G2 professionals inquire about their succession plans. These frustrated founders misunderstand the question. Typically, G2 partners do not mean, "When are you going to retire and sell us your shares at a steeply discounted price?" Rather, they want to know: "If we commit our careers to this firm, can you promise us that we are not going to end up working for a bank or an insurance company because you could not figure out a way to create liquidity for your equity?"

The suggestions for corporate governance in this chapter apply to firms that want to prioritize the development of their next generation. If you want to grow a lawn in your backyard, there are certain things you need to do to the soil. However, not every homeowner desires a lawn. The advice that follows is not meant to be universal, and firms that want to maintain the control of a concentrated group of individuals may disagree with many of the steps in this chapter. Then again, owners with that intention are unlikely to be reading this book.

Constructing a well-functioning governance structure does not necessarily require founders to relinquish control of their firms. Rather, good governance simply means that a firm has a clearly defined and transparent process for making the most important decisions that affect the future of all professionals in the business. G2 professionals will not hesitate to commit their careers to such firms, as they will have no reason to fear that they are tying themselves to the mast of a ship that is sailing to the wrong port—or worse, one that is sailing to no port at all.

Career Investment

The unique nature of career commitment in the advisory industry puts additional pressure on ownership and governance decisions. Leaving the firm is almost unheard of in the advisory industry. This especially applies to professionals with a high level of responsibility and performance. Among the firms I have worked with, fewer than 5 percent of lead advisors and almost no partners ever leave their advisory firms to go to another. The emphasis on client relationships and very significant restrictions placed on taking clients upon departure effectively mean that lead advisors are likely to spend their careers at the same firm.

Indeed, most firms expect their top advisors and operations leaders to commit their careers to the firm and ask them to sign restrictive legal agreements that prohibit them from leaving. These professionals are asked to evolve their careers in the direction desired by the firm, limiting their ability to change careers or go to other firms. The firm also expects them to devote a tremendous amount of time to help grow and manage the business.

Firms should recognize that they are putting their best people in a conundrum. The career investment is very high: Before G2 professionals ever write their checks to buy equity in the firm, they have already made a massive investment in terms of emotional energy and time. It is unfair to ask G2 professionals to make such an investment without assuring them that they will be protected.

In order for them to feel comfortable (and even enthusiastic) about investing their careers in the firm, they need to see a decision-making and governance process that protects them from sudden changes in strategy or direction. Otherwise, G2 professionals may be left with the impression that the firm is asking them to book passage on the Flying Dutchman: "You can never get off this ship, you will have to do a lot of the work, and we won't tell you where it is going."

Stability and Governance

Involving G2 professionals in the ownership and governance of the firm ensures stability. The less a firm has to deal with concentrated founder positions, the more it can focus its eyes and resources on the future. There is a decisively different tone in the strategic planning meetings of G2 firms, as they do not suffer from the time horizon limitations inherent to a still approaching founder exit. Firms that have not already dealt with the exit of the founders and are unsure of how it will occur are somewhat frozen in their plans.

Think of a city before a coming snowstorm. It is expected to snow heavily on a Friday and winds will be high. The residents all know that it will be tough going for a few days and that they may have to stay home without electricity. Everyone is stocking up on gas and noodles, and any planning for the future does not extend beyond Friday. The same thing happens at a firm that is expecting the imminent departure of its founders.

Founders do not have to relinquish control or give up their business in order to achieve stability. Stability arises when founders create a system of promises and obligations that reasonably assures the next generation that the firm will not suddenly change its course, culture, or nature. Examples of such promises and obligations include the following:

- Selling or contractually committing to sell shares in the business to the next generation
- Selling enough ownership to relinquish supermajority control of the business
- Creating a board of directors and/or voting mechanisms that check the power of the founders
- Contractually limiting the ability of passive investors to own the business, including private equity and/or family
- Committing to an exit plan in which the founders sell their shares to the business or successors at reasonable terms
- Establishing and empowering an executive function that manages the firm
- Openly and directly discussing succession and ownership with the next generation and avoiding conversations or decisions where they are not involved

Broadly defined, *governance* is a combination of structures and processes that a firm designs to fit its vision and strategy. For example, a change in governance is often necessary to put important management decisions in the hands of professionals who focus on and specialize in making such decisions (i.e., dedicated executives). More specifically, governance in an advisory firm answers the following questions:

- What does it mean to be an owner, and what do we expect from our owners?
- How do we make decisions as a firm, and what governing bodies are empowered to make those decisions?
- What principles will we follow as we face changes of ownership on both a small scale (e.g., partners coming in and out) and large scale (e.g., mergers)?
- How can we ensure that the firm takes on an air of permanence that convinces clients, staff, and owners that their commitments to the firm will be reciprocated?

The process of revising a firm's governance can and perhaps should include G2 professionals. Involving G2 professionals early in the governance and ownership of a firm has dual benefits. It not only moderates the effect of concentrated positions, but also puts G2 professionals at the helm for decisions that will help the firm grow faster and perform better.

Elements of Governance

Most texts dealing with corporate governance focus heavily on public companies, the role of the board of directors, and the interaction between shareholders and management. However, my experience working with advisory firms has been very different. In the context of relatively small, privately owned firms, governance comprises the following elements:

- **Fiduciary attitude toward the firm:** Governance begins with everyone acting in the best interest of the firm. There has to be an understanding that the best interest of the firm supersedes any individual agenda, including that of the founders. Without this premise, nothing else in the governance documents makes any difference.
- **Accountability:** All people in the firm, including controlling shareholders, are accountable to the firm and other shareholders. Without a process of accountability, all measures of decision-making and control become meaningless.

- **Vision and strategy:** What will the firm look like in the next 10, 20, or 30 years? Who will articulate this vision for the future? Will strategy be set by a charismatic leader, a collaborating board of directors, or a broad group of shareholders and perhaps stakeholders (such as employees and clients)? These are fundamental questions that every firm should be able to answer.
- **Shareholder entry and exit:** The criteria for new owners, as well as the manner in which owners enter and exit, define the relationship between owners and their commitment to the firm.
- **Management and executive powers:** The running of the firm may be in the hands of select professional executives or distributed among many partners. Whatever the management model, it should be clearly defined.
- **Momentous events:** Finally, there are big decisions that can define a firm: merging, buying or selling, removing shareholders, or electing a CEO. Such decisions are critical in nature and the way those decisions are made has a profound impact on all other aspects of governance.

Each element of governance deserves a significant and lengthy discussion. We will try to do them justice by discussing each in turn.

Fiduciary Attitude: Putting the Firm First

Many of the issues discussed in this chapter belong in a shareholder agreement or operating agreement, but a fiduciary attitude is not something that can be legislated. Rather, it is a state of mind. Acting in the best interest of the firm is an absolutely necessary condition for any of the other governance provisions to be effective. Good governance depends first and foremost on having a fiduciary mindset.

The reality is that founders often maintain control of their firms until they retire. That control can be explicit and take the form of majority ownership, or it can simply imply that founders exercise a profound influence across the firm that trumps all shareholder agreements. Given the fact that founders retain so much control, they must show G2 professionals that they are focused on what is best for the firm if they expect these young professionals to trust them with their careers.

Of course, founders rarely act against the needs of the firm intentionally. Unfortunately, they often have a difficult time separating their own desires and ideas from the firm. I say this from experience. Founders believe that they know what is best for the firm, and what's good for them personally must also be good for the firm. However, they must understand that as the firm grows, it develops its own needs. Its future becomes separate and distinct from that of the founders.

Founders can either recognize that separation or resist. Founders who adopt a fiduciary attitude and put the interest of the firm first set a powerful example for their partners to admire and emulate. Alternatively, founders who resist waste a lot of time and energy fighting the pressure to change their behavior or release control of the firm. The inevitable result of such resistance is a firm that is divided between G2 professionals and founders. Feelings of dissatisfaction and alienation between these two groups eventually impact the firm's growth performance and ability to service clients.

Accountability: Making Everyone Responsible

For any management or governance method to function, all members of the team must be held accountable for their behavior and their results. Without an accountability process, behavior eventually erodes and individual agendas begin to take precedence over the firm's best interest. Imagine what happens when individuals form a waiting line: Some lines are self-policing with each individual taking some responsibility for making sure that no one cuts to the front. Other lines require an official to enforce the rules and prevent individuals from jumping the line (for example, when boarding a flight by group). However, absent any method to identify and discourage those who don't want to wait their turns, any line will erupt into chaos and conflict. When no one is held accountable, many will try to cut in and everyone will be suspected of noncompliance.

Accountability is absolutely necessary for governance to function. All levels and structures of governance require some form of discipline for their decisions and directions to be taken seriously. However, accountability is not just useful as a stick. It can also be a method of encouragement and reward. If those who perform well and behave according to the team goals are identified and held in high regard, this will encourage the same behavior in others.

Without an accountability mechanism, behavior breaks down. As noncompliance and cheating tend to be self-reinforcing, the more they occur and are observed by team members, the more likely these behaviors are to spread. Returning to our waiting-line example, most people do not cheat and try to cut ahead on the line unless they perceive that everyone else is already doing it. If you need proof of that statement, just observe what happens next time you board a plane by group number.

Advisory firms prefer to maintain an element of free will when it comes to governance, so they tend to avoid structures that define professional positions in terms of who reports to whom. Unfortunately, this inclination to promote freedom often leads to a lack of accountability. As a result, firms have trouble executing their own plans. In the absence of any control structure, partners tend to do their own thing, and the ability of the firm to accomplish its goals—particularly those that are more difficult and require partners to stretch—diminishes.

While accountability is a mechanism and part of the structure of the firm, it is also part of the firm's culture. Firms with a culture of good governance promote accountability at the highest levels. There should be a sense that decisions made by those in leadership positions are transparent. All leaders, managers, and owners are accountable to each other and to specific structures in the firm. Typically, these forms of accountability are as follows:

- **Owners/Partners:** Owners report to the CEO or another executive position. Their results are usually highly visible to the entire partner group or firm, and therefore missing goals or not producing results can be readily observed. The results of owners can be further scrutinized by committees (e.g., growth committee or investment committee), and so there can be an additional mechanism of accountability there. Ideally, a firm performs evaluations on its partners, and these evaluations reinforce desired outcomes. Note that many of the accountability mechanisms that affect owners are not part of the legal governance of the firm but rather its culture and management.
- **Executives:** Executives (e.g., CCO, CIO, CFO, etc.) usually report to the CEO of the firm. The CEO reports to the board of directors. One of the most important functions of the board of directors is to elect a CEO and work with the CEO to oversee the implementation of the strategic plan. Owners elect the board, and the board in turn makes sure that the CEO and other executives remain accountable to the firm. This is the very important connection between ownership and control that minority G2 owners seek, and it can be particularly important when the firm is run by a founder-CEO.
- **Board:** The board is accountable to the shareholders, or the owners who elect it. There needs to be a mechanism for electing board members that allows minority owners to feel represented at the governance level. This mechanism can also provide valuable feedback to founders, who may otherwise lack a sounding board or a check on their power.

Vision and Strategy: Framing a Constitution

A firm is at its best when it pursues a vision: a sense of destination, a goal, a state of what the firm will be when it matures. This vision inspires professionals to commit to the firm and provides direction for decisions. The ideal governance structure allows the firm to effectively articulate and pursue its vision. Once a vision is defined, it is the job of the board to select a CEO and work with the CEO in the pursuit of that vision. Without a vision, the governance structure becomes abstract and loses meaning, and professionals may assume that the firm and its employees are nothing more than tools in the hands of owners. No one wants to be a tool.

Most founder-controlled businesses struggle to articulate a long-term vision. As a founder of a business myself, I know from experience how troubling it can be to formulate a vision that extends beyond the immediacies of the present. Usually, the first vision of a business is to simply survive. Once some security is obtained, perhaps this vision expands to include growing and attracting good people. However, founders often have trouble looking past these basic requirements to a grander vision because they are unable to imagine a business in which they no longer play a large role.

By their very nature, vision and governance look far into the future. They require making statements about where the firm will be in 20 or 30 years—a perspective that is very difficult to achieve. The temptation is to try to forecast, which is impossible. The only constructive approach for a firm is to develop constitutional principles. The U.S. Constitution has served the country well for over two and a quarter centuries. It has done so not by anticipating the modern world, but rather by defining fundamental values and principles that continue to apply to the country today. Every firm needs a constitution—statements that define it well past the point in time accessible to forecasting.

According to Jim Collins, author of *Built to Last*—perhaps the best-known text devoted to the importance of vision to the success of a company—a good vision consists of two components: an "envisioned future" and a "core ideology."[1] Advisory firms too often focus on the envisioned future ("What will we look like when we grow up?") and neglect the crucial step of developing a core ideology.

---

[1] Jim Collins and Jeremy I. Porras, *Built to Last: Successful Habits of Visionary Companies* (New York: HarperCollins, 1994), pp. 219–240.

Articulating a vision is a great opportunity for founders to leave their mark. Unfortunately, many forgo this chance and believe that the responsibility of defining the future of the firm rests with G2 professionals. While this may ultimately be the case, if founders want to retain influence and leave a legacy, developing a vision in terms of constitutional values and principles is their chance to do so. Otherwise, firms can get stuck in a situation where founders are not yet willing to surrender control of the firm but still expect G2 professionals to define a vision for the future.

Shareholder Entry and Exit: Defining Ownership

Professional services firms offer equity to their top professionals because they want to create a mechanism of involvement that goes beyond compensation. In an environment where professionals have a significant influence over clients and a profound impact on client outcomes, firms realize that they must offer professionals more than compensation for time spent in order to retain and motivate them. This is why all the top professional services firms have partners, even those that have gone public and have shares traded on the stock exchanges. This list includes McKinsey & Company, Goldman Sachs, and Deloitte, among many others. If you want to win over your top professionals, you need to make them owners.

A key part of the governance documents of a firm involves defining ownership, who can be a partner, and how shareholders enter and exit the firm. Many questions require discussion in this context of who can join the ownership group:

- What does it mean to be an owner?
- Can our firm have passive owners (i.e., owners who do not actively work at our firm)? (The answer to this question has a profound impact on the retirement options for the founders.)
- What are the criteria for new owners?
- Who selects the new owners and what is the process?
- How do new owners buy into our firm? What financial resources does our firm provide?
- How do shares or units become available? Who will sell?
- Can our firm add owners from the outside (i.e., a lateral merger of professionals)?

In addition to identifying the criteria for joining the ownership group, firms must also address what the role of owner comprises. Many of the relevant questions go back to creating a sense of accountability among the ownership group, and how that accountability will be exercised:

- Is *owner* a job description?
- Do owners need a different compensation method?
- Do owners receive bonuses? If so, how?
- Are all owners expected to manage? If so, how?
- Should all owners be leaders?
- What happens if an existing owner is not fulfilling his or her responsibilities?

I prefer governance structures that define ownership in a restrictive manner. In order for partnership to hold a special significance in the career track, it must be reserved for those professionals who have contributed the most to the firm. Conferring special status on ownership acts as a motivator as well as a test of skill and commitment. This philosophy of exclusivity is shared by many firms.

For example, Goldman Sachs has 484 partners as of November 2016, which represents only 1.4 percent of its workforce.[2] McKinsey has around 1,400 partners out of 12,000 employees (11.7%).[3] Deloitte globally has 5,170 partners out of 78,642 employees (6.6%).[4] While this sense of exclusivity is also present in the advisory industry, it is perhaps not as strong. For example, at Aspiriant, one of the leading advisory firms in the industry, 56 out of 175 team members have ownership in the business (32%).[5]

When evaluating prospective partners, firms should translate their values into a scorecard for determining who should be an owner. When ownership criteria express the true values of the firm, the highest contributors to the firm will embody those values by meeting the criteria and becoming owners.

There is another school of thought that tries to get ownership into the hands of as many employees as possible, essentially making everyone an owner.

---

[2] Olivia Oran, "Goldman Names 84 New Members to Partner Class," Reuters (November 9, 2016).

[3] McKinsey & Company, "Who We Are," McKinsey.com. Accessed April 11, 2017, from http://www.mckinsey.com/about-us/who-we-are.

[4] Deloitte, "Facts and Figures," Deloitte.com. Accessed April 11, 2017, from https://www2 .deloitte.com/us/en/pages/about-deloitte/articles/facts-and-figures.html.

[5] Aspiriant, "Our Exceptional People," Aspiriant.com. Accessed April 11, 2017, from http:// aspiriant.com/our-exceptional-people/.

This model is often found in firms where the majority of ownership belongs to one founder who is eager to see all employees involved without risking a dilution of control during her or his tenure. It is not uncommon in such cases for governance documents to be written in such a way as to give the founder control of the board and essentially permanent CEO status. This is not meant to be a criticism, but rather a clarification that while the model may look democratic, in reality it functions very differently. After the founder exits, the model can become more democratic, but control usually falls to a select group of managers.

One of the most important decisions to be made is how owners will exit the firm and to what degree a firm will restrict their exits. The more restrictive the exit, the more the firm can expect to retain talent in tough times. Unfortunately, restrictions often apply to professionals who need to leave due to health reasons or other unavoidable life changes. Restrictions can also trap a perpetually unhappy shareholder who always acts as the dark cloud in the climate of the firm. As always, firms should find a balance when formulating answers to the following questions:

- How do owners retire? How will our firm reacquire their equity?
- How will our firm tackle the retirement of the founders?
- What happens if an owner quits the firm?
- Will our firm seek mergers or acquisitions? How will those generally be executed?
- Are there cases where our firm may consider changing ownership, either by merging with another firm or by selling to a third party?
- Who should approve changes in ownership and how?
- Is our capital structure sustainable as it is designed?

Many firms reward professionals who work at the firm for a long time and retire only after careful preparation by giving them a strong valuation and favorable payment terms while discouraging professionals from leaving early and without much notice by offering a lower valuation and slower payments. In extreme cases, owners who don't prepare adequately for their exits or those who leave to go to competing firms may find they have lost all of their capital.

Between entry and exit, owners will likely change their ownership stakes over time. Some will buy more shares to increase their ownership and some will choose to sell. Firms may want to consider if they should compel certain owners to sell and others to buy. Indeed, it is not uncommon for firms to manage the buying and selling of shares between owners and perhaps arrange the order of buyers and sellers based on performance. There are many such ideas, which we will discuss separately.

I have worked with numerous firms that deploy elaborate governance schemes. Some firms create different classes of shares that carry different rights (e.g., voting versus nonvoting shares). Other firms are owned by private equity, and control of the board looks very different from the way profits are split. For example, minority shareholders (who are usually passive investors) may have control of the board. Such complicated voting and governance schemes serve a purpose and exist for a reason, but firms should think twice before applying them.

If the whole idea of including professionals in ownership is to create a strong connection between them and the firm, these fancy control schemes undermine that connection and defy the primary purpose of offering equity. What is the point of bringing on partners if you then proceed to tell them that they are not quite partners because you are only offering them nonvoting shares?

One could argue that 3 percent owners should not worry so much about voting versus nonvoting shares since their votes don't carry much weight. However, this statement flies in the face of all cultural expectations. Problems also emerge when firms with nonvoting shares attempt to recruit or merge another independent practice and make the merged partners "non-voting partners." The response is usually unequivocal: "No way!"

Management and Executive Powers: Hiring Dedicated Managers

As a firm grows, it will eventually need to put management responsibilities in the hands of dedicated managers who spend most if not all of their time on the business of the firm. This pivotal moment usually occurs somewhere around the $1 billion in AUM mark, if not sooner. When a firm reaches this level, it discovers that its many clients, staff members, processes, technologies, finances, opportunities, vendors, and projects have created such complexity in management that the firm requires professionals dedicated to those functions. While we may feel comfortable driving our own cars, most of us would never attempt to drive a bus. Large vehicles that transport many people require professional drivers, and large firms require professional management.

Every advisory firm needs a functional leadership model. While not every model involves a dedicated CEO, for most growing firms the identification and empowerment of a CEO is key to executing the firm's vision. Leadership often means making difficult decisions. The difficulty of these decisions favors the emergence of a single leader. Many larger firms gradually convert their governance models from partnerships to more corporate structures for this very reason—and that's a good thing. In my experience, lack of effective leadership is the root cause of many issues that cause stagnation and friction in large firms that were previously successful before stalling after reaching a certain size.

When asked how they make management decisions, most firms give one of two answers. They either sit down as partners or follow the orders of a benevolent dictatorship (no firm ever admits to a non-benevolent dictatorship). The first statement describes a culture of consensus decision making while the second statement describes a top-down culture where founders take the lead. Very rarely will a firm describe its model of governance as a CEO and a team of executives. Clearly, the advisory industry prefers to distribute management responsibilities among the existing leadership in a firm. Unfortunately, that style of decision making can be sustained only up to a certain size.

The presence of dedicated management ensures that strategic projects are executed and firm-level initiatives are given attention and resources. Without dedicated management, it is very easy for the firm to focus too heavily on the daily business of serving clients to the detriment of making progress on strategic initiatives. Dedicated management also means that those who manage have both an interest in managing and the skills to do so. Unfortunately, firms are often controlled by people who have no interest in managing but have not empowered the managers to act. As Tom Murphy, who mentored Warren Buffett in management, puts it, "Don't hire a dog and try to do the barking."[6] When setting management responsibilities, a firm should ask the following questions:

- What are the management positions that our firm should have today and in the future?
- What are the responsibilities of each executive position?
- What are the powers and responsibilities of the CEO? Who will be the CEO? To whom does the CEO report? Under what conditions should the CEO be replaced?
- Does our firm need a president? What are the responsibilities of the president?
- Does our firm need a COO?

---

[6] Max Nisen, "The Man Who Taught Warren Buffett How to Manage a Company," Quartz.com (October 23, 2014).

- Does our firm need a CIO?
- How is a budget created and executed? Who approves the budget and how?
- Who can make hires? Are some hires subject to a different process?

Momentous Events: Forming a Board and Executive Committee

A governance structure that promotes the continuity and sustainability of the firm will use the board of directors as the mechanism for giving shareholders representation at the highest level of decision making. As the firm and ownership group grows, it quickly becomes clear that the firm cannot function with all owners coming together to make decisions. Such partnership models are often impractical. Ideally, decisions are allocated between a management team that focuses on the business and a board that focuses on strategy and vision. The board then effectively becomes the collective voice of the owners at the highest level.

A good board should have no more than seven members. Five is even better. The composition of the board should strike a balance between very large shareholders (typically founders) and smaller minority owners. When board members are elected solely based on ownership percentages, there is a risk that smaller shareholders (typically G2 owners) may feel left out in the governance of the firm. Various mechanisms can be designed to include minority owners in the decision making of large firms, such as reserving a specific number of board seats for smaller shareholders.

It is also healthy for the seats on the board to rotate periodically. If it is always the same board members working with the same CEO year after year, the connection between the owners and the governance structure can be lost. Putting at least two seats up for a vote every two years ensures a healthy inflow of ideas from the rest of the partners. It also creates opportunities for emerging leaders to be exposed to the highest level of decision making. Typical board decisions include the following:

- Setting a strategy and vision for the firm
- Selecting a new CEO and working with the CEO on her or his succession plans
- Changing the CEO, if needed
- Voting on behalf of shareholders on critical issues such as:
  - Selling the company
  - Changing the operating agreement or other significant agreements

- Dismissing a shareholder
- Making significant changes in capital structure (e.g., borrowing money)
- Merging or acquiring
- Issuing new shares or new classes of shares

This list can also be delegated to a more nimble executive committee (EC) appointed by the board. An EC is elected by the board to act on behalf of board members. Traditionally, an EC offers a more responsive structure than the board, especially in cases where the board is too large to meet frequently or members are not easy to convene. The EC can also consist of board members who have a more focused skill set that can serve important decisions well, such as mergers and acquisitions.

Some of the very large firms in public accounting and other service industries assign the EC the task of working with the CEO and tackling strategic projects, whereas the board meets less frequently and only on issues of governance (rather than management). This allows board membership to be more permanent and inclusive of external professionals, whereas the EC is elected internally and has more technical knowledge and experience. A typical EC is tasked with the following responsibilities:

- Bringing together the key executives of the firm to define a long-term vision for future
- Defining and executing a strategic planning process
- Identifying the top priorities for the firm
- Reviewing and making critical strategic decisions, including merger-and-acquisition opportunities, changes in strategic contracts, changes in pricing, and other impactful decisions that cannot be made by the CEO or other executives alone
- Interviewing candidates for executive positions and reviewing the appointment of key executives, including the CEO, president, director of marketing and client service, COO, CFO, and CIO
- Evaluating the performance of each executive (particularly the CEO) and providing feedback
- Reviewing and approving executive compensation, including the compensation of the CEO
- Defining and administering incentive compensation plans for executives
- Approving all new shareholders
- Approving a budget each year and monitoring its execution at the highest level

- Working with department leaders to identify and approve key hires and approving a plan and compensation for their hiring
- Providing the CEO and other executives with a forum for discussion and feedback on decisions that are of high importance to the firm

Note that the list of activities associated with the EC is long. This leaves the board to only meet and act when momentous events require critical decisions to be made. I will leave the actual structuring of the EC and the board to the advice of your attorneys, but I do want to emphasize that the board is a great place to create a sense of inclusion for the G2 group. The ability to elect a board member gives G2 professionals a sense of representation and influence. The board can be the mechanism for answering thorny questions about G2 ownership, such as "If I only own one percent, what voice will I have?"

Governance as a Function of Size

As it says in Ecclesiastes, there is a time and a place for everything. The same can be said of firm governance. Different governance structures are needed and each functions at its best at different times in the history of a firm. Just as it is a mistake for a firm to not evolve beyond a family culture as it grows, it is a burden for small firms to grapple with the formalities of a board of directors and a dedicated CEO. Governance should be built incrementally as the size of the firm—and particularly the size of the ownership group—increases. As the ownership group grows larger, structures become more complex.

Small Firms

Small firms are those with *less than $500 million in assets under management (AUM)*. These firms should establish a governance model focused on the basics:

- Accountability
- Articulating a vision
- Finding leaders

While dedicated professional management is important in large firms, in small firms it is critical to get every owner interested in the management of the firm, if not necessarily involved. When all owners pay attention to management, it emphasizes the significance of that function to the firm, gives it a sense of priority, and creates accountability.

At this size it is also critical to set a vision for the future. This vision should be inspired. Inspiration can come from the founders or be the collective brainchild of all the professionals, but it has to be there. A vision will guide the firm as it makes many important decisions ahead. In the absence of a vision, even as a firm grows it will always struggle to answer crucial questions as they arise: Should we hire additional professionals? Should we pursue a new market? Should we merge?

Finally, this early stage is a good time to identify leaders. Not everyone wants to be a leader. Not everyone *can* be a good leader. Nevertheless, a firm needs leaders. If any of the founders or highly producing partners have doubts about their desire to lead, now is the time to find out. When the organization becomes larger and more complex, having reluctant leaders can be very damaging.

Medium-Size Firms

Medium firms are those with *$500 million to $1 billion in AUM*. These firms should establish a governance model focused on a sustainable management structure, which entails:

- Separating management from ownership
- Clarifying ownership criteria

A small firm should get all owners interested in management, or at least convince them of its importance. A midsized firm, in contrast, should convince most owners to stay out of management. This sounds like a bit of a contradiction, but it is very true. The same principle holds for any representative democracy. People should be interested in the issues but also trust those who are elected to tackle them on their behalf. At this size it is impossible to have all partners involved in management. Attempting to do so can paralyze decision making and implementation.

This is also the time to clarify ownership criteria. Who are the owners? What does it take to become an owner? Setting and communicating clear criteria powers the entire career track and promotes a sense of fairness throughout the firm. It also enables firms to clearly express their values.

Large Firms

Large firms have *more than $1 billion in AUM*. These firms should establish a governance model that focuses on increased leadership complexity:

- Creating a board
- Beginning a cycle of leadership succession

The largest firms likely have ownership groups that number in the double digits. At this point there needs to be a mechanism for working with the CEO and a system of checks and balances on executive powers. Firms at this level should create a board and perhaps an executive committee to represent the owners.

At this size firms should also constantly be asking, "Who will be our next CEO?" The answer does not necessarily have to be the name of a specific person. It could be a mechanism for identifying the right individual and training him or her for future responsibilities. Not having a plan and relying on the current leader to be "CEO for life" is not a productive strategy.[7]

Reviewing Your Governance Model

The way in which most firms are governed often has more to do with the past of the firm than the future. The structure of ownership and decision-making responsibilities in these firms can be reminiscent of old neighborhoods in cities like Rome or Paris. Ancient walls become the façades of family houses, cobblestone streets merge into busy boulevards, glass-and-metal terraces are retrofitted into stone buildings from the past. While the past and present combine to create a view that is beautiful, it is hardly efficient, always congested, and perhaps a bit dysfunctional.

A good wealth management firm will frequently revisit its ownership and governance structures and update them with a view to the future of the firm. Every firm would be well served to imagine at least for one day that it had no history. The question then becomes how the firm would structure ownership and governance if it had to start from scratch. That's essentially what Baron Haussmann did in Paris in the nineteenth century, creating all the wide boulevards and modern infrastructure.

---

[7] I heard this phrase from Tim Kochis, former CEO of Aspiriant and founder of Kochis Fitz. Tim uses the phrase in a longer form: "No one should be CEO for life!"

Architecture analogies aside, decisions made with respect to ownership and governance have a long-lasting and deep impact on the ability of a firm to pursue its vision successfully. The test for any governance structure should include the following questions:

- Do we have a compelling vision? If so, are our owners, leaders, and managers aligned behind that vision? If no vision is present, is it clear who will be responsible for articulating it?
- Does our governance structure support our vision?
- Have we clearly identified who is responsible for making decisions at every level, from high-level governance to daily management tasks?
- Are the key people in our firm (i.e., key contributors to growth, client management, and intellectual capital) deeply involved in the future of the firm?
- Is the ownership of our firm sustainable in the long run? Does our ownership structure provide the necessary stability to allow for professionals to commit their careers and for clients to commit their plans to us?
- Can our firm pursue the strategic initiatives necessary to grow? (Usually this means that the firm is open to exploring lateral additions of experienced professionals, mergers with like-minded firms, acquisitions if those are strategically valuable, and being acquired if that's in the best interest of clients and owners.)
- Does our firm have the right capital structure to invest and be resilient in down markets?
- Does our firm have the right kind of executive decision making? Does our executive structure allow for effective day-to-day management without the delay of partnership deliberations or the friction between managers and owners that often plagues larger firms?
- Is it clear in the culture of our firm what it means to be an owner? Does that definition allow for an attractive career track in a competitive industry?

These are very broad, somewhat abstract questions that can consume days and even weeks of discussion. While such discussion can be very valuable, it is often not practical. Perhaps all of the right points are made, but they do not result in decisions. A firm that is reexamining its governance structure should be very intentional about the process behind such an examination.

I have a process I would like to propose. Before we examine this process, however, we first need to decide who should be involved. Having the right people at the table is the only way to achieve a constructive outcome. If G2 professionals are not involved in a discussion about the future, something has gone wrong. On the other hand, a process that is too inclusive can become unwieldy and confusing.

As a rule, a meeting should not be larger than 10 people if it is to allow for the exchange of ideas and meaningful debate. Larger meetings can be had when there are clear presenters and a passive audience, but a meeting focused on interaction becomes impractical with more than 10 participants.

Selecting the right participants is also very important. While every organization will have its own combination of people, positions, history, and talent, as a rule of thumb an examination of governance and leadership should include the following participants:

- Everyone who has more than 5 percent ownership in the firm, unless they have very explicitly stated that they are passive owners
- The CEO, president, and COO of the firm, regardless of their ownership stakes
- The intellectual leader of the firm (i.e., the person who is the brains behind developing the knowledge base)
- The top business developer in the firm, regardless of ownership or position

These are only ideas—not specific requirements—and many of the positions mentioned above will overlap. The main point is that you need to include the key people at the firm: professionals who are the most invested in the firm in terms of capital and reputation and have the most to say about its future.

Begin the process by interviewing all of the high-performing people at your firm. *High-performing* can be tough to define. Sometimes these individuals are your partners/owners. Sometimes they are leaders whom everyone recognizes. Often they are your existing executives. The organization relies on them in one way or another, and their perspectives should be captured and examined carefully.

Each high-performing professional in your organization holds a unique view of the firm's current performance and future opportunities. These individual interpretations of vision and strategy—what works and what doesn't—are very valuable to collect at this stage. Asking questions also prepares everyone for the future discussion on governance:

- What is the vision for our firm in the future? Is that vision clear and compelling to you?
- Where do you see your own career taking you in the next 5, 10, or 20 years?

- What does ownership mean to you? Who should be an owner in the firm?
- How could our firm be managed to pursue strategy more effectively? Are decisions being made in the right way?
- Are there executive responsibilities that are perhaps unclear or need to be redefined?
- Are significant ownership changes pending? If so, how should they be handled?
- Are you personally interested in acquiring more ownership? What are your thoughts on the capital structure?
- What does control of the firm mean to you? Who should have control?
- Do you anticipate any mergers or acquisitions in the immediate future? If so, how important are those to the future of the firm?

Individual perspectives should be gathered during one-on-one interviews, as these allow the firm to focus on each person's view and potentially explore sensitive issues that would be difficult to broach in a group meeting. Individual perspectives matter a lot at this stage in the process. To a degree, reexamining the governance structure of a firm is a question of who will be part of its long-term future and who will be part of its past.

In many cases, starting a discussion about the future governance of the firm may drive some owners (both founders and those who joined later) to clarify their personal plans and perhaps choose retirement. I have spoken with many G1 partners who recognize during the process that retirement "is the right thing to do for the firm, it is just not what I want to do." When individual plans, ambitions, and concerns are disclosed and put on the table, it becomes much easier to discuss the right structures to achieve the firm's goals. If key people are either unable or unwilling to disclose their agendas, it can be impossible to make progress.

Achieving Results

Once individual perspectives have been catalogued and understood, each element of governance discussed in this text can serve as a subject for a meeting or decision point: fiduciary attitude, accountability, vision and strategy, shareholder entry and exit, management and executive powers, and the role of the board and executive committee in momentous events. The result of each discussion should be a decision on how the firm will tackle the issue and what corresponding changes to internal structures and legal documents are needed.

The governance structure of a successful firm should promote stability while allowing G2 professionals to invest their careers in the firm with all the creative energy and passion they can muster. It should promote a fiduciary culture of doing what's best for the firm, delineate responsibilities, and establish accountability. It should allow the firm to pursue its vision and also contain checks and balances that protect the firm from veering off course, due to either the actions of management or the force of circumstance. Finally, it should allow new owners to join the firm, contribute, and someday leave. Don't forget that behind G2, G3 professionals are waiting patiently in the wings, eager to be involved.

CHAPTER 14

Succession

A leadership development plan is moot without an understanding of the future of the organization to which professionals are committing their careers. It is unrealistic for a firm to ask for the talent, commitment, effort, and heart of G2 professionals without providing a credible plan for the exit of the founders, especially if that exit is visible and necessary (i.e., in the foreseeable future).

A succession plan does not always have to be limited to transactions internal to the organization. A good succession plan should be flexible and open to the possibility that not every future owner will come from within the firm. In many cases, the succession plan may involve a combination of internal and external transactions. A good plan, however, defines the values and goals of the organization to be preserved and realistically addresses the steps the firm can take to protect those values.

For example, the statement "We will never sell the firm to anyone who does not work at the firm" may be premature and unrealistic. As many founders have found out, G2 professionals are not always interested in buying all of the firm. "We will ensure that future owners share in the same values that we live by as an organization and will not consider organizations or people who have not proven that they live by the same values" is better stated.

Internal succession is always a critical process, even if the ultimate exit of the founders is facilitated through an external transaction. After all, succession is not only an equity transaction. It is also a process of transitioning responsibilities for clients, management, and leadership. A firm needs to transition those responsibilities regardless of who the new owners are, and this is where internal succession is essential.

Different Aspects of Succession

Let us review what founders do in a firm with the purpose of understanding the pieces that have to be replaced with their departure. As used here, the label *founders* denotes the most experienced professionals in a firm who may be departing in the next 10 years. Sometimes such professionals are not technically founders, but the significance of their contributions to the firm necessitates the same thought process. Founders play various roles in a firm:

- **Professionals:** Founders are professionals who work with many of the key clients and provide much of the knowledge and experience on which the firm relies. A good succession process seeks to transition client relationships and ensure that G2 professionals have earned the confidence of clients. The succession process also ensures that the next generation preserves the founders' body of knowledge and continues to enhance it. That includes wealth management expertise and very often investment expertise.
- **Growth generators:** Founders are often the growth engines of a firm. Without the reputation and contacts of the founders, the firm may have a hard time growing, and that can render any succession plan ineffective.
- **Managers:** Founders often serve as CEOs, CIOs, COOs, and other key positions with high management responsibilities. A succession plan must address who the key managers will be in the future and how they will take over the responsibilities of running the firm.
- **Leader:** Founders are often leaders. They answer difficult questions, convince people to support their vision, and inspire action. As we discussed, leadership is not the same as management. A good succession plan considers who the leaders of the firm will be in the future.

While the equity ownership of the founders attracts the most attention, other components of succession can be even more important. Without a successful transition of client, growth, and management responsibilities, the equity transaction is doomed to fail. Not all founder responsibilities transition in the same way. It is entirely possible—likely, in fact—for client and growth responsibilities to transition to a different set of people than those who become owners of equity. It is also likely that a founder is succeeded by a group of G2 professionals rather than a single individual. Some members of this succession group can be involved in management and others not. This is where the governance structure of the firm becomes essential.

Internal Succession of Ownership

An internal transition of equity deserves a chance, but it may not be viable for a variety of reasons. For example, if the founders never hired younger professionals, the next generation of partners will not exist within the firm. Perhaps the firm has G2 professionals, but they are too underdeveloped in their skills to be ready for ownership. Another possibility is that the G2 group is unwilling to take on the significant financial and business risk necessary to buy out the founders. The price of a big, successful firm might be too much for younger partners to buy into. The necessary capital may not be available to younger advisors.

Still, where there's a will, there's a way. Many of the difficult decisions in internal succession come down to the commitment of the two sides involved. If the founders truly desire to create continuity in the firm—what Tim Kochis describes as a "permanent firm"[1]—and they are met by an equally committed group of G2 professionals who are willing to act as entrepreneurs and leaders and take on personal risk, any financial obstacle can be overcome.

Both pieces have to be in place. G2 professionals cannot expect to become successors without taking any personal risk. That is unrealistic and self-indulgent. Likewise, if founders want to see the firm remain in the hands of advisors who grew up at the firm, they have to be willing to make some compromises with timing, price, and risk. When those two prerequisites are there, many succession options become available. Let's now discuss what G2 professionals have to do to ensure a successful succession.

Finding the Motivation

I often hear G2 professionals asking founders, "How do we know the firm will be profitable in the future? How do we know clients will stay when you leave? Why should we believe that the firm will grow?" While these are all good questions to ask—fantastic questions, in fact—they have a certain passive connotation. These are the kinds of questions that passive investors ask.

The path for G2 professionals to become successors begins with ideas: "How can we grow faster? How can we make the firm more profitable? How can we retain key clients?" These ideas should percolate through the succession

---

[1] Timothy Kochis, *Success and Succession* (Hoboken, NJ: Wiley, 2015).

conversation. Without this attitude or conviction, G2 professionals risk being seen as overly conservative and perhaps unable or unwilling to be successors.

Sometimes ownership requires taking a leap of faith. Perhaps a leap of faith is exactly what the second generation needs. It is not always easy to adopt an "I can do it!" mentality when you don't feel empowered or in control. I can relate, as I have been both a G2 professional and a founder in my career. Focus on your ideas for improving the firm and make those ideas known. A positive attitude can make the leap less intimidating.

Founders of advisory firms often overanalyze the issue. Rather than reflecting on how they became entrepreneurs and learned to take on risk and responsibility, they turn to studies on the social characteristics of Millennials or Gen-Xers that present inaccurate stereotypes. Instead, firms should employ strategies that motivate G2 professionals to take on a successor mentality. We will discuss three such strategies:

1. Encourage the second generation to work together as a team.
2. Allow leaders to emerge within the second generation who can lead the new group, letting group dynamics play their course.
3. Remove the *training wheels* and expose the second generation to risk and risky decisions with unclear results and meaningful impact.

Bringing G2 Professionals Together

I've seen a lot of succession plans in which all the components are in place— the price is right, financing is available, and the terms are reasonable—but there's still one problem: The second generation is surprisingly unwilling to acquire the equity. This is often not a problem of risk taking, but rather a problem of mutual trust. You may be willing to take a risk, but if you doubt that your other 10 partners are capable of making it work, you will likely not want to be jointly and inseparably responsible for a $15 million loan. For internal succession to be viable, the G2 group needs to have cohesion and respect each other.

In many firms, G2 professionals are not given the opportunity to learn to work together as an independent team. Their relationships with one another tend to always be managed through the founders. My kids are a bit like that. My son is eight years older than my daughter, so while they are both G2 in the family context, their age difference tends to keep them apart. The only time they do anything together is when my wife and I are with them. If we are not in the house, they stay in their respective rooms and may not talk to each other for hours. The G2 group will be like that, too, if they are never encouraged to directly work together without depending on the founders.

The problem firms have is that G2 professionals do not know how to deal with each other without the presence of the founders. They don't know how to make decisions together. They don't know how to disagree or even fight. They don't know who their leaders are. They don't trust each other enough to take a great risk together.

To help G2 professionals develop relationships with each other, they should have the chance to work on committees and teams where the founders do not play a role. There are many such opportunities available, and the experience of working independently is invaluable to professional growth. These activities should not be considered the *kids' table* of initiatives, but rather important and impactful projects where the G2 group can demonstrate their ability to get organized and achieve results. In the worst-case scenario, they will learn how to deal with not achieving the expected results—also a valuable lesson. Camaraderie is more likely to develop when something is at stake. That's why groups that go through exciting episodes in life tend to stay connected for a long time. Consider sports teams, adventure travelers, start-up teams, and similar groups. Their connections endure because of the circumstances in which they were built.

Encouraging Leaders to Emerge

Advisory firms frequently act like a family and adopt family-like values in dealing with people. In an ideal family, all children are treated the same. Giving one child more opportunities, attention, or training is an absolute no-no of parenting. Unfortunately, family structures are not results oriented, and promoting them may come at the expense of developing much-needed leadership qualities.

While all of the children in a family should be treated equally, doing the same in a business setting is a mistake. Businesses need leaders to emerge. Leaders are willing to take the risk of making a decision when the cost is high and the information is imperfect. Leaders inspire, encourage, and hold others responsible. Leaders are willing to show the way when the map fails.

Such people are hard to find. Founders may even be chasing them away by enforcing an undesirable and unsustainable equality among the G2 group. Fear of friction or conflict frequently drives firms to step in and try to mediate or engineer every contact between their G2 professionals. The result is a situation where younger advisors can't function without the founders' supervision.

Advisory firms should instead look early for employees who have leadership potential and encourage them to take on challenges that will further develop those skills. This does not just mean reading books and attending seminars, but also championing projects, leading committees, and making decisions on behalf of the firm. Let them take risks. Let them succeed. Let them fail. Most importantly, let them lead their peers and take responsibility for the results.

In some firms, leaders emerge naturally and are very authoritative. In others, the group takes turns assuming the leadership position depending on which member of the group is most comfortable dealing with a particular situation. Whatever the model may be, leadership is needed for decisions to be made. Without leadership, the successor group can become frozen and indecisive. While they may be willing to take on risk as a group, they won't know how to come to a decision. They may have to call in a senior figure to make a decision for them. To avoid this, founders should encourage leaders to emerge. The next generation will figure out how to organize themselves if they are allowed to experience the natural evolution of building an effective team.

Letting G2 Take Risks

You can't learn how to ride a bike without getting on one. Similarly, you can't learn to take risks without taking risks. Ironically, in an industry where advisors build careers out of making investment decisions for their clients, many employee-advisors never make the decision to invest money in their own companies and business plans.

Partner introduction models are often heavily subsidized and do not ask advisors to give up much, if anything. Incentive compensation plans are deliberately managed to only produce positive results. Even careers are carefully managed to ensure that no one is left unprompted or waiting too long. The result is a generation of owners who have never really taken a risk with their careers or their money. If they have never had to risk losing a bonus, how will they ever be able to stomach borrowing $20 million?

Time and again, firms miss opportunities to expose their younger advisors to risks and thereby teach them how to make decisions when the losses are real. In these firms, G2 professionals are like boxers who have only ever trained with a heavy bag and have never been in a real fight. If someone is not punching back, you will never know what it is like to be in the ring.

Internal succession is absolutely necessary in order to transition client, management, and leadership responsibilities, even if the succession of equity is opened up to external transactions. For internal succession to have a chance,

G2 professionals have to come together as a team, identify their leaders, and learn how to take some risk. Only then will they be ready for all the equity transactions and associated risk that may be required by a succession plan.

The Big Transaction

The most straightforward strategy for founders to sell internally is to simply sell their equity to the next generation in one big transaction. This purchase may be financed by either the founder or a third-party lender. The sheer amount of financing involved may make such a transaction difficult to execute. Raising $10 or $20 million and taking on the risk of making loan payments is quite a challenge for G2 professionals. Likewise, selling the firm and then waiting up to 10 years for the payments to arrive is a lot to ask of founders, especially when they are entering retirement. While loans and private equity are available, they still require G2 professionals to stretch beyond their comfort zones.

The key in such a transaction is the relationship between the price and the cash profits of the firm. If the after-tax profits of the firm are higher than the payments on the succession mortgage (the loan to buy out the founders), then the transaction will be very smooth. G2 professionals will generally be on board because all they have to do is maintain the revenue of the firm. With 10-year loans becoming available at larger amounts, this possibility is becoming more common.

Unfortunately, taxes take a good bite out of the profits of the firm. While interest on the loans is possibly tax deductible, chances are that the first two or three years will require G2 professionals to give up some of their compensation. Even without the deficit, G2 owners should anticipate only minimal growth in personal income while they are completing the big transaction. This is very difficult to sustain for many G2 members since the transaction tends to catch them in their late thirties and forties. At this stage in their lives, they are facing high demands on their income and do not yet have reserves on which to rely.

The only solution to this problem is growth. A firm that is growing at 15 percent per year will quickly close the deficit and create enough profit growth to allow G2 owners to experience some growth in income. In the absence of growth, G2 professionals must be willing to stay at the same level of compensation for a while. This financial model can be very vulnerable.

Another issue with big transactions is the discrepancy between the "external price" and the "internal price." The valuation external buyers such as banks or serial acquirers can offer is usually higher than what internal successors can pay. Founders rarely insist that G2 professionals match the external price, and most are content with accepting a lower price as long as they don't feel that the internal offer is unfair. Still, fairness is difficult to define here. At times, founders may feel that they are being taken advantage of. While a big transaction is still a viable strategy, a better approach requires founders to divest their equity faster and more often.

A Large Number of Small Transactions

Most large firms make a lot of small equity sales to introduce key people to the ownership group. While small in terms of percentage, these sales can approach the millions in terms of value. New partners buy between 1 and 10 percent each. The larger the firm, the smaller the percentage. These small purchases motivate new partners and give them skin in the game. A strategy that employs a large number of small equity transactions can be instrumental to a succession plan. While the small size of such transactions may not be nearly enough for the eventual succession of the founders, it is a solid and necessary start:

- Over time, sales of 3–4 percent to a growing group of partners can transfer a significant amount of equity, eventually giving the junior partners 20–40 percent of a firm.
- An initial small transaction can pave the way for a future larger deal by giving G2 professionals the experience and confidence to make such purchases.
- Every 1 percent bought and fully paid for can later finance the purchase of another 2 percent in equity through the cash flow it creates. Early purchases can bridge the deficit between loan payments and the after-tax cash flow. For example, if you were to buy a 20 percent equity tranche with 0 percent existing equity, you would likely have a cash flow deficit in the first three to four years, depending on growth. However, if you already owned 5 percent at the time of the 20 percent purchase, the cash flow from the 5 percent would close the deficit created by the 20 percent.

Passive Ownership

If equity cannot be transferred, founders can remain passive owners of the firm, holding onto some shares even as they step away from daily operations.

For example, let's say I started Bulgarian Managed Wealth (BMW) and have been the CEO since its inception. I have five partners who are very capable of running and growing the business without me. They have a combined stake of 30 percent, while I have the remaining 70 percent of the equity. It might be logical for me to step down as the CEO and retire from the firm while keeping some or all of my 70 percent. This is an intriguing idea and very tempting to many founders. Passive ownership has several key advantages that deserve consideration:

- There is no need for a massive buyout by G2; thus it is not necessary for them to raise capital and take on the risk or burden of payments.
- The founder is able to continue enjoying the cash flow from the business.
- The founder and the second generation will stay on the same page, since both are focused on continued cash flow and profitability.
- Equity can be passed on to the founder's children and family without disrupting the business.

While the idea has potential and is worthy of consideration, it is not without its significant flaws. Returning to our example, if I were to retain 70 percent ownership interest, my successors would have to mail out 70 percent of the profits every year. There would come a time when they would start to view the situation as unfair. There will always be a clash of interests between working owners who are trying to manage a firm and invest in its growth and passive owners who are sitting back and collecting checks.

While it may be possible to distribute most of the profits of a public company to an abstract and large group of shareholders, the same process becomes very personal and potentially resentful when we are dealing with a small group of owners. That said, I believe that passive ownership can have its place in a succession plan as long as a couple of prerequisites are fulfilled that mitigate conflict and resentment:

- Passive ownership should never be majority ownership. If more than half the profits leave the building, it is difficult for working owners to see themselves as having control and benefiting from the work they do. Minority passive ownership may not cause the same reaction. A 20 percent or 30 percent passive interest could be just fine. There are several examples throughout the industry of firms with a minority passive owner that have not had any issues arise. On the other hand, there are many cases of firms with a majority passive owner where the friction is high and the tension between the two groups hinders growth.

- Passive ownership requires a very strong corporate governance structure. For passive owners to feel that their interests are protected, there should be a governance process that includes a board of directors to represent shareholders and provide passive owners with the necessary levers to exercise their rights. Further, the firm should have a structured management process and a good deal of fiscal discipline. Such good housekeeping will help both passive and working owners.
- Over time, passive interest should decline. This is not an absolute requirement, but as a firm adds more owners and grows, it will need to use equity. When equity is needed, it is perhaps best to continue buying out passive owners and move closer toward a complete exit.

The Intermittent Transaction

An underutilized but powerful instrument in internal succession is the *intermittent transaction*, or a sizeable transfer of equity that can be executed while founders have not yet exited. Staying with our BMW example, imagine that I were to sell 30 percent of the firm's equity to my partners while I still worked as CEO at the firm. This would reduce my ownership stake from 70 percent to 40 percent and facilitate my eventual complete exit. The firm would help the G2 group secure (i.e., guarantee) the necessary loan to buy out this chunk of equity, and the plan could stipulate that all payments be completed before I leave.

This intermittent transaction significantly reduces my equity and, more importantly, significantly increases the equity of the G2 group. The risk is low since I am still at the firm and there is no danger of clients experiencing a disruption caused by a change or deterioration of firm management. When completed, the transaction will give G2 owners a significant existing stake in the profits and, therefore, significant access to the dividends generated by the firm. They will enjoy the full benefit of the 60 percent of profits already in their hands while they service a loan for my remaining 40 percent.

One issue frequently encountered with intermittent transactions is that the G2 group is not yet cohesive or well organized, and thus not ready to take on such a sizeable risk. Imagine BMW is worth $10 million. If we would like to execute an intermittent transaction for 30 percent of the equity, the G2 group needs to collectively borrow and pay off $3 million. This may require them to forgo increases in income and personally guarantee large loans, putting their houses and everything else on the line. The risk can seem overwhelming.

There are also some technical issues with such partial redemptions. Many lenders who provide capital for succession use Small Business Administration (SBA) loans, and SBA rules prohibit partial redemptions. There may also be tax issues related to a partial redemption being considered for capital gains treatment rather than as a dividend distribution in the context of a subchapter S corporation. As always, consult your CPA to ensure that you have fully thought through the tax consequences.

Finally, founders are often not very eager to sell a substantial amount of shares while they are still working at their firms. They may feel that going from a majority to a minority interest is too big a step to take. They may fear that they are leaving too much appreciation on the table, since that 30 percent sold in an intermittent transaction could have grown quite a bit had they retained it. This brings us back to making a commitment to create a firm with longevity. When founders make that commitment, these issues either do not exist or are rendered insignificant.

Equity-based Compensation

Another possibility is using equity as compensation, thereby systematically reducing the ownership percentage of the founders. This possibility is rarely used in advisory firms, but many of the older investment management firms have a history of such compensation plans.

For example, suppose that BMW paid 1 percent of its shares each year to team members according to their performance and responsibilities. By tying shares to performance, this stock compensation process channels equity into the hands of those who are most deserving. It also has the potential to bring equity to key people who perhaps would not otherwise have the ability to purchase it through other programs.

Stock compensation programs are usually used by firms that believe in very broad ownership. Such firms want to see all employees who have been with the firm for a long time and contributed to a certain level become owners. There is something very democratic and inclusive in this approach. It can send a powerful message that all employees are valued, not just a select group of elites.

Indeed, stock compensation programs can end up being too democratic, leading to a very broad ownership base instead of concentrating ownership in the hands of the top contributors. If the ownership is too widely distributed, it can create corporate governance problems. How do you handle the management team's fiduciary responsibilities with a very large group of owners? And what happens when an employee leaves?

Stock grants also tend to undermine the value of other shares, since employees would much rather *earn* shares than buy them. Even when granted as part of a compensation program, shares have value and are therefore considered taxable income that the recipient has to pay. Because of these issues, stock compensation is not often used by advisory firms, but it is still a viable option.

Profits Interest Options

Another underused instrument in internal succession is the *profits interest* approach. A profits interest formula sets a base amount of value and profits and then shares the growth and appreciation with the new owners. Such agreements are well suited to professionals who will quickly become major contributors to growth.

Returning to our example, suppose BMW has $1 million in profits, and I am the only owner. Brandon joins as a partner, and we create an agreement whereby Brandon owns 50 percent of all profits above $1 million. After five years, BMW has $2 million in profits. Now Brandon owns 50 percent of the additional $1 million ($500,000 of the $2 million), or 25 percent of the equity of the firm. This approach requires a bit of calculation, but it is not overly complicated. Notice a few characteristics of this approach:

- Brandon does not have to write a check! He does not need to pay anything upon signing the agreement, since we set the base at the actual profits made last year.
- If the firm does not grow, Brandon does not own anything.
- The more Brandon contributes, the more his equity grows.
- Brandon has real equity. It is subject to the same taxation and capital gains taxes if structured well.
- As founder, I can still look at the firm and feel that I own 100 percent of everything I originally created.

The drawback of this approach is that it can be slow—very slow. Imagine that Brandon had 10 percent of the appreciation instead of 50 percent. If the firm doubled in profits, he would be the owner of 10 percent of $1,000,000, or $100,000. This is only 5 percent of the total profits, which is a small amount relative to the growth that was experienced. Another unpleasant feature of this formula is that in a recession, Brandon will not only see the firm's profits decline, but also his ownership percentage. Taking a hit on both sides can be a very painful experience.

I have used a profits interest agreement more than once and have always found it to be a good mechanism to reward high contributors who cannot write a check. That said, this kind of equity incentive is more commonly found in hedge funds than advisory firms. It is also viable for LLCs, but may be difficult to implement for S corporations due to tax rules. As always, check with your CPA.

Nonvoting Shares

Nonvoting shares are surprisingly popular. Many firms use them because they preserve control with the founders while allowing G2 professionals to share in the appreciation of equity and the profits of the firm. Since G2 professionals rarely buy a controlling share, their nonvoting status should perhaps not matter.

Unfortunately, nonvoting status does tend to matter in practice. Some of the worst blowups of firm governance I have ever witnessed were associated with nonvoting shares. Nonvoting shares send the wrong signal. They are like the learner's permit of ownership: You can drive, but you need your mom in the car with you. If G2 professionals are really going to be partners, it is better to allow them to experience the full scope of ownership.

Synthetic Equity

There are also many synthetic equity instruments available, such as options, phantom stock, stock appreciation rights, and warrants (which are very similar to options). While synthetic equity has its uses, those are fairly limited. Usually, it is used in situations where founders are not ready to give up any ownership to G2 professionals, or in cases where G2 professionals simply do not want to be owners. This could be a reflection of either perceived risk or personal preferences.

Synthetic equity instruments work well if a firm strongly believes that it will be sold in the near-to-intermediate future and wants to retain its professionals. It is a way to share the appreciation and value of the firm without complicating the ownership agreement and corporate governance. Unfortunately, most synthetic instruments are subject to ordinary income tax rates.

Mergers Facilitating Succession

In recent years, many firms seeking to solve their succession challenges have chosen to merge with larger firms that have both the balance sheets to finance the exit of the founders and the professionals to step in and take over client relationship, management, and growth responsibilities. Another registered investment advisor (RIA) with a deep bench of professionals can be seen as a step between the internal-only and the external succession solutions.

Another RIA will likely have a similar culture and client philosophy and can perhaps help internal G2 professionals succeed. This is particularly true for firms where the G2 group is capable but not large enough to do it all on their own. A larger firm can help not only with financing, but also through recruiting people and helping train and develop them.

Creating a Lasting Firm

To paraphrase something John Adams said in the wake of the American Revolution, we must be soldiers, so that our sons can be farmers, so that their children can be poets.[2] Sound advice, but perhaps a healthy advisory firm needs to have its soldiers, farmers, and poets in the same generation, working together and helping each other out.

A successful firm requires professionals to exhibit all of these skills in order to survive. To create a lasting firm you need to defend it from competition, and be patient and conservative as you cultivate growth and inspire people to follow a vision. Finally, and most importantly, you need to leave and pass the firm on to the next generation. There are many methods of ownership transition available to you. If you have the will, you'll find a way.

---

[2]John Adams to Abigail Adams, May 12, 1780. Accessed May 2, 2017, from https://founders .archives.gov/documents/Adams/04-03-02-0258.

CHAPTER 15

Keeping Up with the Industry

We have spent an entire book looking at advisory firms from the inside. There is a reason for this emphasis on the internal perspective: Most development, training, and responsibilities are internally driven. However, we can't forget that the advisory industry is quickly changing and ever-evolving. Firms are always in search of better market positioning by differentiating themselves and improving their client services vis-à-vis the competition. You can't develop as a professional by ignoring what the rest of the industry is doing.

Founders spend a lot of time in the company of other founders. Custodian meetings and industry associations bring them together frequently while study groups and even informal meetings and calls strengthen that connection. Both founders and their firms have benefited tremendously from the shared knowledge, networking, and support provided by industry collaboration. G2 can use the same support system. By getting active in study groups and industry meetings, G2 professionals can accelerate their development, improve their technical knowledge, learn best practices, and create lifelong industry connections.

If you have spent any time at industry forums as a G2 professional, you probably already realize that you are part of a growing group of people who feel a lot of camaraderie for each other. Every year The Ensemble Practice starts a new class of our G2 training program, and we are always amazed to see the energy and peer support the 50 members of each new class bring. G2 members are eager to share experiences, meet each other, learn from each other, and support each other. That sense of community and sharing is very powerful encouragement.

Being a Student of the Industry

To be a successful professional you must be a keen student of the industry. This includes not only constantly updating your knowledge of planning and investments, but also developing your understanding of the industry itself. Which firms lead it? Which firms do you compete against? How can you stay on top of the latest business management practices?

There are many publications available that you can follow to stay current on industry news and keep your firm up-to-date with industry trends. It almost does not matter which publications you follow as long as you follow some. They all publish industry news daily. Most of them also publish lengthy articles on developments in the industry. If you haven't already, make it a point to read an industry magazine at least once a month. This is a great habit to develop.

There are also many industry organizations that deserve your time and attention. NAPFA (National Association of Personal Financial Advisors) and FPA (Financial Planning Association) are great places to start. They both offer conferences that are rich in content and opportunities for making contacts. Custodian and broker-dealer conferences are also excellent venues to meet other G2 members and hear from industry experts. Study groups provide yet another opportunity to meet other professionals. These smaller meetings offer a more intimate setting, enabling you and your peers to engage in deeper dialogue and learn more about each other. Many study groups are forming G2 sections that are specifically designed to connect G2 members.

Wherever you choose to go, get out of the office at least once or twice a year and spend some time with your industry peers. I often see professionals forfeiting such opportunities because of busy schedules and multiple responsibilities. There may also be a bit of professional pride at play: "We know all we need to know and we already do it better than those other firms." Even if that's true, gaining industry perspective is invaluable, and the connections you make will benefit you tremendously.

Developing Your Industry Connections

Developing industry connections is a vital skill to learn if you plan to have a successful career. While industry connections serve many purposes, they are most importantly a source of invaluable information. Professionals in your same position at different firms are perhaps the most important connections to cultivate. They will be able to understand your perspective while providing more objectivity on your situation. Maybe they have also seen or experienced things you should be aware of or learn about. You can use these industry connections in a number of situations:

- You have a professional question that you have been struggling to answer.
- You seek information that you don't have but other firms might.
- You need to evaluate a vendor and want to gather some unbiased information by speaking with some of their customers.
- You need an introduction to an industry resource or firm.
- You need a good attorney or other service provider.
- Your firm is recruiting and needs referrals to find talented people.
- You are struggling with something and need the advice of someone in your same situation.
- You are at an industry conference and don't want to go running alone.

Industry connections can also be a great source of emotional support. Whenever I feel that I am not doing so well, having a conversation with one of my industry friends is always immensely encouraging. This is also the most meaningful kind of encouragement, because it comes from people who do what you do. I have noticed the same thing at the boxing gym. When you get a bit beat up in a sparring match, the encouragement from your friend who has never boxed in his life means very little. On the other hand, getting encouragement from the person who just kicked your behind means a ton!

Benchmarking Your Client Services

I often say that if the advisory industry were like the restaurant industry, advisors would be great chefs who simply needed to learn how to run their tables and staffs better. While that generally holds true, let's expand the analogy. Just as great chefs must continually update their recipes, great advisors must continually update their client service offerings. The advisory industry changes very rapidly, and the body of technical knowledge and service methods is constantly evolving. Services that were once differentiators are quickly becoming table stakes for most client relationships.

The word *coopetition*—cooperation between competitors—was used for a while in the late 1990s before disappearing from our vocabularies, but it remains an accurate way of describing the behavior of advisory firms. While all firms compete for more or less the same clients, they also have a common interest in upholding the high standards and reputation of the industry so that the investing public will continue to value working with advisors. There is also camaraderie between business owners and a willingness to exchange techniques, even if there is a small chance that those techniques will be used against them in the marketplace.

I frequently spar with the same boxing partner, and we have developed an interesting relationship. While we hit each other almost weekly, we also feel a sense of camaraderie from learning together. We have gotten to know each other well. If I know a technique that can help Jerry, I can't keep it from him. It just doesn't feel right. Even though I might eat a punch or two for doing that, it also pushes me harder to learn something new.

The relationship I have with Jerry in the boxing ring also applies to how advisors operate in our industry. It just feels right to help out those you may end up competing against. In return, they also give you knowledge you need. This exchange pushes you both to keep changing and innovating. The advisory industry is remarkable in its camaraderie, and I hope it retains that even as firms grow larger and start competing more often.

Learning Best Practices

There is a theory in chess that to be a good player you must completely understand 300 positions that frequently occur on the chessboard. The same could be said about being a good advisor. There are a number of critical situations that occur frequently. A situation in this context may describe a common question that clients ask, a technical problem that frequently occurs in practice, an employee issue that requires attention, or a management technique that helps accountability. Good professionals will continuously develop their situational databases, adding solutions and techniques that may be handy in the future.

This situational database is where you will find your best practices, not in some white paper or PowerPoint presentation. The database serves as your mental reference library of things to do when something happens. Regularly updating your database is critically important in order to effectively service clients and manage the firm. These updates can happen during formal exchanges such as study groups and industry forums, or they can be more casual (but no less meaningful).

For example, a conversation with a colleague about a difficult issue you are experiencing is a great way to learn about a solution used by another firm. The same can be true of an article you read or a panel discussion you hear.

Little pieces of knowledge quickly accumulate into a formidable library. That's one of the best things about getting out of the office and spending time training with your industry peers.

Participating in External Training

Tricia Turton, my business partner at the boxing gym, is a boxer with amazing credentials. She has fought twice for world professional titles, spent decades coaching boxers, coached other coaches, and worked the corner for professional boxers. She is the most accomplished coach I know, and still she never stops acquiring more training and knowledge. She comes back from every tournament with something new to integrate into her vast knowledge base. To this day she continues to take classes on topics ranging from movement to therapy.

The desire to know more and to apply more in your work should never cease to drive you. A lot of that learning can—and should—happen outside the firm. External programs provide you with perspective, expose you to new ideas, and, once again, give you the chance to meet your peers. There are many high-quality programs inside the industry, and many that are not industry specific. Both are valuable in their own way.

A lot of business theory has been developed to apply to technology, retail, and manufacturing businesses. While the size of the companies involved and the nature of their workforces make some of the findings less applicable to our industry, there are still many developments and best practices that we can adopt from other businesses, particularly other service businesses. I will not attempt to list all of the great training programs available, since by the time you read there may be many more, but I will summarize what I consider to be the criteria for a good external training program:

- The program description speaks to a topic of interest to you that also has practical importance to your firm.
- The program is delivered by a reputable firm or expert who has worked with your industry contacts and receives good reviews.
- You can sample the work of the experts through their articles, books, or blogs, and their insights are on point.
- The program features diverse points of view through the use of multiple speakers, firms, or panels.
- The program does not offer a magic-pill solution: "Become a million-dollar producer!" or "Learn the habits of the most successful advisors!" Instead,

the topic is very specific and functional: "Developing new business using a niche strategy" or "Listening to and acting on client feedback."

- The program gives you a chance to meet and interact with good contacts. These can be experts or industry peers.
- The program has some continuity. A single visit to the gym is not going to change your fitness, nor will one presentation turn you into an expert. In particular, topics that focus on building a skill are best explored in continuous programs.

Treat these training programs like a potluck picnic: Bring a dish and sample others. In other words, take what interests you from the program, but don't forget to contribute something as well.

Contributing to the Industry

Our industry has many resources available that benefit all firms. We have publications that keep us informed. We have professional associations that train us and disseminate information. We have meetings that bring us together. We have a variety of local study groups that help us improve. All of these resources need the next generation to contribute their energy, ideas, and time.

Your job as a G2 professional is not done when you close the office door. Industry groups and resources need to find their future leaders, too. The founders built many of the groups and resources we see today, and they need you to take over. Our industry would not be nearly as successful without those professionals who volunteer their leadership to associations and other groups. Contribute to the industry. You will help all firms in our community by doing so and cultivate a richer and better career for yourself at the same time.

CHAPTER 16

Conclusion

This is an optimistic book. I wrote it with the sincere belief that the financial services industry already has a fantastic group of professionals who are eager to take on more responsibility and lead their firms into the future. As G2 and G3 make their way further down the career track, they must support one another to ensure the firm continues to grow.

Advisory firms and their founders only need to look around to find the team they have been waiting for. Many of those professionals are already at the firm, and those who are not can be attracted to join. All that the next generation needs is inspiration, training, and opportunity. They will do the rest.

From G2 to G3

G2 is perhaps better described as a *group* than a *generation*. Some G2 professionals are in their twenties and belong to the Millennial generation, while others are in their forties or fifties and belong to Generation X. Their identity within the firm is not driven by the year they were born but rather the role that they play. G2 is a group of professionals who are defined by their responsibility to act as a bridge between the founder-centric past of the firm and its organization-centric future.

The reality in most firms—especially large firms—is that beyond the founders, the generations start to blur as people join and exit the firm in a continuous process on their way through the different stages of the career track. Instead of a distinct generational event, succession becomes an ongoing process in a firm, and it is never as dramatic as the initial retirement of the founders.

Ideally, no professional is so critical to the future of the firm that her exit creates an emergency. After G2 comes G3, and perhaps G4, but better to

225

abandon the concept of generations altogether and instead see professionals in the firm as members of an ever-evolving team that continues to add talent and experience as needed. In such a firm, there will always be professionals who are more experienced and those who are less experienced, and their identities will be defined by the stage they have reached on the career track, not the year in which they joined the firm.

Unfortunately, G2 is in danger of being written off, as some firms turn all of their attention to G3 and beyond. I hear such thoughts expressed frequently. "G2s are never going to replace the founders. They were hired to be service people. To find business developers, leaders, and entrepreneurs, we need to go to G3!" Statements like this make me jump out of my chair. It is such a gross generalization and misrepresentation of the skills and abilities of G2 professionals.

G2 is often treated as a failed experiment. Many founders regard them as the X-Men of professional services; they seemed like a good idea at the time, but the results are undesirable. Founders have become frustrated by the difficulty of growing G2 professionals into potential successors. While the temptation to wipe the board clean and start all over again is strong, the logic is flawed. All G2 professionals need is a chance and some training, and they will soon be taking over. They may even take the firm further than it has ever been. In fact, G2 will be much better at growing G3 than the founders could ever hope to be.

Much of this book has focused on the rise to prominence of G2 and how G2 professionals can assume higher levels of responsibility, become leaders, contribute more, and eventually take control. This rise is not driven by succession—it is driven by growth. It is also simply part of the nature of the industry that G2 will eventually replace the founders. Indeed, the day is not far off when G2 professionals will be the new CEOs, COOs, and CIOs of their firms.

The Role Reversal

G2 professionals will soon find themselves in the shoes of the founders. The years go by surprisingly quickly, and G2 professionals may suddenly discover that they are the older people in the room and have a long list of responsibilities on the table in front of them. Even before the founders retire, chances are good that as a G2 professional you are already managing a team and starting to hear some of the same questions you used to ask: "What is my career going to be like? Can I be partner someday? Do I need to develop new business? How will I ever buy into a successful but expensive firm like this?"

It is your turn to formulate the answers to these questions and communicate them to the group coming up behind you. It is your turn to struggle with some of the difficult and unclear decisions that have to be made. The first step, as always, is to accept your responsibility. Being a manager, mentor, and leader to G3 is both a privilege and a burden. Being responsible for G3 may feel like a question for which you do not yet have an answer. Think of it like being an older brother or sister. You still feel like a kid, and now all of a sudden you have to babysit your younger siblings and tell them to stop watching cartoons and go to bed. Perhaps you haven't grown out of watching cartoons yourself.

You may sense that G3 is trying to leapfrog over you and get the attention of the founders. It is a natural inclination to try to speak to the CEO or founders rather than those professionals who are immediately ahead of you on the career track, despite the fact that those are the professionals who can offer you the best perspective and observations on your career. If that should happen, don't let it upset you. Just let it be.

There is no reason to feel competitive with G3 because you are not. You are already established and experienced and you have much more to share and offer. Gently but firmly establish yourself as a leader to G3 and let your knowledge and experience shine. As a G2 professional, you can help G3 more than anyone else in the firm.

Making It Easier

When managing and leading G3s, you should strive to make their careers smoother and easier than yours has been. Help them avoid your mistakes. Help them survive the struggles you had to endure. If there were obstacles in your career, try to remove them for G3s. Help them progress faster in their careers.

Sometimes there is a temptation to ask the next generation to go through the same trials you did. Why should it be easier for them? Indeed, that's the same logic that many founders apply to G2: "It was hard for us when we started the firm, so it should be hard for you." As a member of G2, you should remember how much you hated these statements.

Of course, sometimes knowledge can only be gained the hard way, through experience. That said, one of the defining characteristics of our species is that we pass down our knowledge from one generation to the next without having to repeat every experience. We don't need to personally try every mushroom in the forest to identify the poisonous ones—we have very nice books for that. Every experience you had that you hated, every piece of information that you learned too late, is an opportunity for you to make an improvement for G3—and for the firm overall.

Making It Harder

While you should not make G3s suffer through meaningless trials, neither should you lower the bar for them. This mostly applies to the criteria for advancement and promotion. The compassion of G2 for G3 often results in a career track that is diluted and produces professionals who are lacking basic skills, particularly the ability to develop new business or take the lead.

In an ideal firm, every generation should be better prepared to be leaders than the last. Each successive generation should be more knowledgeable and more capable. Since training programs in the firm become more established and better designed with time, every next group of professionals should learn more and learn faster. If nothing else, the growth of the firm should allow it to access a better talent pool and recruit professionals of ever-higher quality.

Building the Firm

As a member of G2, you hopefully already realize that the day will come when younger professionals will be thinking about your succession plan and retirement. You may have acquired, or are in the process of acquiring, quite a bit of the stock from the founders. If you want to exit the firm someday and receive your return on investment, you need to start thinking early about who your successors will be and what will prepare them to buy you out at the valuation you want.

This entire conversation—this entire book—will quickly flip on you. Suddenly you will discover that you need to coach every skill we have been discussing. You will need capable lead advisors to become your partners, otherwise you won't be able to grow the firm. You will need capable business developers to bring in new clients, otherwise the firm will eventually erode to nothing. You will need good managers and good leaders, otherwise there will be no one to take the reins from you.

The responsibility to grow and prepare G3 belongs to G2. While founders may sometimes try to play a role, as a G2 professional you should help them recognize that it is your turn to be a coach and mentor. You will be working with G3s for much longer than the founders will, and you will have a lot to say and contribute to their development. Don't let the founders leapfrog over you in this process.

It is shocking how quickly the tide turns. At this point in my career I have been working in the advisory industry for 18 years. For the first eight years, the partners were an abstract group of people to me. I wanted to join them, but I also looked up to them. This was the group that was supposed to lead the firm, and I was supposed to grow my career. When I became one of the partners, suddenly the idea that "they should be doing this" morphed into "I need to be doing this." Managing others became one of my primary responsibilities. I started having to answer difficult questions I did not even want to ask.

Then the day came when I became a founder and had to start thinking about how to involve my younger colleagues in the growth and development of the firm. That day came way too fast. I still feel like a part of G2. And if I see myself as G2, I suppose it is now my turn to develop G3. So let's do it together.

A Note of Optimism

I struggled for a while with the decision to write this book. I wondered if the leadership of the firms in the advisory industry would believe that they can develop the next generation. "A recruiting dollar is a dollar better spent than a training dollar" and similar statements discouraged me. I also wondered if G2s would believe that they can acquire the skills they need, and whether they would in fact be excited about being in charge. I wondered if they would believe that the founders would give them enough control and opportunity.

Then I met two classes in the G2 Leadership Institute development program that my firm The Ensemble Practice organizes. They were so talented, energetic, ambitious, and accomplished that I could not wait to sit down and write. If I ever wavered in my conviction that stereotypes are not true, this group quickly dispelled all that fog. They were entrepreneurial. They wanted to be leaders. They wanted to be owners. They wanted to take risks. They wanted to grow. They may not be ready yet, but it won't be much longer until they are. Working with the 100 individuals in this program left me with no doubt that G2s will be successful and achieve a lot. They already have.

I refuse to believe that G2 professionals are not entrepreneurial enough. They have ideas and want to take the risk necessary for those ideas to come to fruition. To show their entrepreneurial spirit, though, they need to be given more responsibility and more control. They need encouragement and mentoring to attempt endeavors that may seem difficult or uncomfortable. Entrepreneurs are not born that way. They learn to be innovative and to create through the combination of experience, resources, and opportunity.

G2 professionals are more than capable of growing the advisory business. What is more, they are capable of reaching the younger clients that every firm craves. While they may not have done much business development in the past, that is once again a function of training and opportunity. They have the talent and the desire. They just need to find their own way to reach prospective clients. Their way may be different than the way of the founders, but it will be just as effective.

The next generation needs clearer signals from their firms: What should they be doing? How should they behave? What can they expect from the future? What do they need to prepare for? Time and again, firms send mixed signals. We want you to develop new business, but please focus on servicing existing clients. We want you to have a balanced life, but we expect to see you at the office until 8:00 at night. We want you to be a leader, but don't disagree with us or challenge us. We want you to be an entrepreneur, but only in a way that we approve and only when we say so.

That is not to say that the responsibility of developing G2 falls to the firm. That is not the case. The burden of development rests squarely on the shoulders of G2 professionals themselves. They must speak up about their needs, ambitions, and desired experience. They must identify gaps in their knowledge and skillsets and then find ways to fill those gaps. They must find mentors and build relationships with them. If G2 professionals disagree with founders and what they have built, they must find a better way to do things. They must also train and develop G3 and the generations beyond. There is much that G2 must do!

Ultimately, the segmentation of professionals into generational groups—G2 and founders, G2 and G3, Millennials and Boomers—is an overgeneralization. In reality, we are all professionals who belong to an organization. We are only successful when our organization is successful, and thus founders and G2 have to find a way to work together. Neither group can achieve its respective goals on its own.

The term *G2* nicely encapsulates a very diverse group of professionals. To summarize the working definition used throughout this book, G2 is a group of prominent non-founders who are very important to their firms. In many firms, G2s are quite inexperienced. They are still early in their careers and learning how to be good professionals. They will eventually learn how to be good managers and leaders. However, G2 also includes many professionals who are already in leadership positions. Numerous firms in the industry are led by individuals who are not founders. These leaders grew up inside their firms and are now taking them to the next level of growth and performance.

A good example of a post-founder firm is Cornerstone Advisors in Bellevue, Washington, where CEO Ken Hart and a team of executives and owners are building one of the premier multifamily office organizations. Another good example is JMG Financial Group in Chicago, where CEO Anthony Cecchini leads a large and successful group of highly qualified professionals. Anthony and his partners acquired the firm from the founders in an internal succession plan. Ken and his partners did something very similar. Such stories are becoming more and more common. G2 professionals are not just rising in prominence. Many of them are already in charge.

As I was writing this book, I kept asking myself, "What are the characteristics of a highly performing partner in an advisory firm?" I wanted to provide a guide to those professionals who aspire to become partners at their firms while perhaps also speaking to professionals who are already owners but looking to improve their skillsets. To me, being a partner is not simply an indication that the firm is operated as a partnership. Rather, the title *partner* is a statement that the professional is engaged in both client work and firm ownership and governance.

Every partner should contribute in four critical areas of the practice: client service, growth, team building and management, and leadership and governance. Some partners do not spend a lot of time on management while others end up specializing as managers. Some partners rarely develop new business while others concentrate on creating growth. Partners do not need to be experts in all things. However, a good partner will have knowledge in each of these critical areas and be able to contribute to every aspect of the practice. This creates a well-rounded career and a better firm.

An important premise throughout this book is that every skill can be developed. Skills are not innate gifts hardcoded into our DNA. They are the product of study, persistence, and practice. That is why I spent time discussing how G2 professionals can contribute to each critical area at their firms. Much too often, I see careers defined by deficiencies rather than skills. So many professionals occupy roles at their firms based on what they cannot do rather than what they are good at. In particular, many G2 professionals are judged "unable to sell" and haunted by that label throughout their careers. Similarly, a reputation for not being able to manage people or work in a team has limited what many professionals can accomplish. While some professionals will naturally be better business developers and others will naturally be better managers and leaders, every professional can achieve some level of proficiency in these and other critical areas.

Being a professional in an advisory firm is a career, and a career lasts a surprisingly long time. An advisory career represents a lifelong dedication to helping clients and serving alongside a team of other professionals. At the beginning of this career, many young professionals are eager to acquire experience, knowledge, and responsibility immediately. They often grow impatient and get discouraged when progress seems slow. However, when viewed in the context of a career, a span of three or four years is a negligible amount of time. Give your career the time it needs to become a success story.

Let me give you an example of one such success story. I met Will Beamer in 2005 as he was just starting out as an advisor, having left previous careers in the navy and business consulting. At the time, Dowling & Yahnke in San Diego was a growing independent registered investment advisory (RIA) with five or six professionals. The firm had just promoted its first professional to partner, and Will was looking forward to traveling the same path. Today, 12 years later, Will is president of the firm and manages a team of close to 30 professionals, including many younger professionals who are likely future partners of the firm.

Our industry is changing rapidly. Advisory firms today are no longer small, unsophisticated service firms. Rather, they are large and complex enterprises owned and managed by a cadre of founders and professionals who joined the firms in their later stages of development. This growth and success is in large part due to the contributions of G2 professionals.

The desire of G2 to better manage and systematize what advisory firms do introduced a new approach to our industry. G2 professionals created and put in place many of the systems and processes that enabled the tremendous growth we have seen. They are also responsible for focusing industry efforts on increasing the longevity of firms, ensuring that they will be able to work with clients for many generations to come. The emergence of G2 professionals in our industry is not news. They have been here for a while.

G2 professionals are not merely replacements for the founders. Reducing their role to the successors is to seriously miscalculate their significance. I began this book with a story about painting a picture. You may recall Becky Krieger in Chapter 1 declaring that G2 professionals are not curators, but artists in their own right. G2s are not here to simply preserve what the founders have created. They want to paint their own masterpieces. Today, Becky leads Client Services and New Business Development for Accredited Investors and is rapidly building an outstanding reputation throughout the Minneapolis community and the advisory industry at large. Becky embodies everything that G2 represents. G2 is the growth and the change in our industry.

I started my career 18 years ago in a cubicle as an entry-level consultant with Moss Adams. For quite some time, I was always the youngest person in the room. Most industry meetings were populated by founders, and I would often be the only person in attendance under the age of 40. But those days are in the past in more than one way. Today, I am no longer under 40, but most importantly there are many professionals under that age in the room. Advisory firms have added an amazing cadre of young professionals.

Today, as I look across the organizations we work with at The Ensemble Practice, I am excited to see so many young professionals who are emerging as leaders at their advisory firms. I am no longer in their shoes, having gone from G2 to founder, but I have not forgotten what it feels like to break in the leather. G2 professionals are not just the future of the industry. They are the present. They are professionals, managers, owners, and emerging leaders. As an industry, we need more of them. I hope this book helps us create them.

Bibliography

Blanchard, Ken and Sheldon Bowles. *Raving Fans: A Revolutionary Approach to Customer Service* (New York: William Morrow, 1993).

Cialdini, Robert B. *Influence: The Psychology of Persuasion*, revised edition (New York: Harper-Collins, 1993).

Cerulli Associates. *Advisor Metrics: Understanding and Addressing a More Sophisticated Population* (Boston: Cerulli Associates, 2013).

Collins, Jim and Jerry I. Porras. *Built to Last: Successful Habits of Visionary Companies* (New York: HarperCollins, 1994).

InvestmentNews Research. *Adviser Compensation and Staffing Study* (New York: Investment-News, 2015).

InvestmentNews Research. *Financial Performance Study* (New York: InvestmentNews, 2016).

Johnson, Kim. "Business Journal Names 2016 Best Places to Work Honorees." *Minneapolis/St. Paul Business Journal.* June 24, 2016. www.bizjournals.com/twincities/news/2016/06/24/business-journal-2016-best-places-to-work-winners.html.

Maister, David H. *Managing the Professional Service Firm* (New York: Free Press, 1993).

Neilson, Gary L. and Julie Wulf. "How Many Direct Reports?" *Harvard Business Review*, April 2012. hbr.org/2012/04/how-many-direct-reports.

Oran, Olivia. "Goldman Names 84 New Members to Partner Class, Six More Than Prior Group." Reuters.com, November 9, 2016. www.reuters.com/article/us-goldman-sachs-partners-idUSKBN134376.

Ramón y Cajal, Santiago and Raoul M. May. *Degeneration and Regeneration of the Nervous System*, translated and edited by Raoul M. May (London: Oxford University Press, 1928).

State Street Global Advisors and Knowledge@Wharton. *Bridging the Trust Divide: The Financial Advisor–Client Relationship* (Philadelphia: The Wharton School of the University of Pennsylvania, 2007). knowledge.wharton.upenn.edu/special-report/bridging-the-trust-divide-the-financial-advisor-client-relationship-2/.

Vanderkam, Laura. "Why Managers Should Spend Exactly 6 Hours a Week with Each Employee." FastCompany.com. July 14, 2014. www.fastcompany.com/3032972/why-managers-should-spend-exactly-6-hours-a-week-with-each-employee.

Wershing, Stephen. *Stop Asking for Referrals: A Revolutionary New Strategy for Building a Financial Service Business That Sells Itself* (New York: McGraw-Hill Companies, 2013).

About the Author

Philip Palaveev is the founder and CEO of The Ensemble Practice, the leading business management consulting firm for the financial services industry. Palaveev specializes in helping financial advisory enterprises grow their businesses by tackling complex decisions concerning strategy, equity and partnership structures, career paths, succession, and compensation.

Palaveev also served as president/owner of Fusion Advisor Network until its acquisition by Kestra Financial. As a partner in Moss Adams LLP, Philip helped propel the firm to prominence in the financial advisory industry.

Palaveev is the author of the book, *The Ensemble Practice*, which is widely considered to be the roadmap to building a successful multi-professional firm.

Philip lives with his wife, two children, a dog, a cat, and a fish in Seattle, Washington. He dabbles in boxing and is a co-owner of Arcaro Boxing Gym. He is also an occasional marathon runner and a relentless traveler who dreams of writing an article in Spanish or Italian someday.

Index

Printed and bound by CPI Group (UK) Ltd, Croydon, CR0 4YY

04/06/2023

03224091-0002